Implementing Palo Alto Networks Prisma® Access

Learn real-world network protection

Tom Piens Aka 'Reaper'

Implementing Palo Alto Networks Prisma® Access

Group Product Manager: Pavan Ramchandani

Publishing Product Manager: Neha Sharma

Book Project Managers: Srinidhi Ram and Neil D'mello

Senior Editor: Sujata Tripathi

Technical Editor: Irfa Ansari

Copy Editor: Safis Editing

Proofreader: Sujata Tripathi

Indexer: Rekha Nair

Production Designer: Prashant Ghare

DevRel Marketing Coordinator: Marylou De Mello

First published: May 2024

Production reference: 1190424

Published by Packt Publishing Ltd.

Grosvenor House

11 St Paul's Square

Birmingham

B3 1RB, UK

ISBN 978-1-83508-100-6

www.packtpub.com

Dedicated to my wife and son, who lovingly ensured that this book took much longer to finish than it otherwise would have.

Foreword

As a security professional at Palo Alto Networks, I have had the privilege of witnessing the transformative power of Prisma Access firsthand. While my journey didn't involve formally writing this book, my contributions to research, testing, and real-world implementations have helped shape its content.

This book marks a collaborative effort, drawing upon the combined expertise of myself and my esteemed ex-colleague, Tom Piens. Our years of experience have brought my insights and countless hours of testing to life on these pages.

Within these pages, you'll find a comprehensive guide to navigating the evolving security landscape with Prisma Access. From foundational concepts to practical applications, the book caters to both seasoned professionals and those new to the SASE revolution.

However, I would be remiss not to acknowledge my limitations as a contributor. While I haven't personally crafted the words, I stand firmly behind the knowledge and experience embedded within them. I hope that this book empowers you, like me, to harness the power of Prisma Access and confidently navigate the future of network security.

Delve into the world of Prisma Access, uncover its potential, and become an expert in securing your organization's future.

Remember, the knowledge shared here is a culmination of countless voices, including my own, all seeking to make the SASE journey smoother for everyone.

– *Rutger Truyers, SASE Expert*

Contributors

About the author

Tom Piens Aka 'Reaper' is a seasoned expert in network security and cybersecurity, boasting over two decades of dedicated experience in the field. His journey has been marked by a 14-year focus on Palo Alto Networks products, during which he made significant contributions over a 12-year tenure at the company itself. Tom distinguished himself as the first international support engineer at Palo Alto Networks, later transitioning to a pivotal role in the LIVE community department. There, he played a crucial role in rebuilding the knowledge base, moderating the forum going by his alias "Reaper," and authoring numerous insightful articles.

For the last three years, Tom has embarked on an entrepreneurial venture, founding PANgurus BV. Under his leadership, the company has specialized in Prisma Access solutions and has been instrumental in enhancing customers' firewall configurations through meticulous audits and the implementation of best practices. Tom's commitment to excellence in cybersecurity and network security, coupled with his hands-on approach to solving complex challenges, positions him as a leading authority in the industry.

About the reviewers

Dimitri Zuodar graduated in 2000 as an industrial engineer and embarked on a career in data communications. By the end of 2002, his commitment toward specializing in routing and switching resulted in his becoming CCIE certified (#10782). This strong technical foundation, combined with his personal development in architecture, project management, and pre-sales roles, resulted in the decision to become an independent consultant in early 2010. Over the past 14+ years, Dimitri has been hired as a trusted technical consultant by his customers in several industries. His *always-learning* mentality has since resulted in achieving multiple certifications in public cloud, multi-cloud networking, and OT cybersecurity (IEC 62443 Cybersecurity Expert).

Kim Wens has accumulated over 20 years of experience in the field of network security and has spent the last 13 years working for Palo Alto Networks. In 2011, Kim joined Palo Alto Networks as a TAC engineer, and for the past 8 years, he has been engaged in Palo Alto Networks' LIVE community providing solutions for customers, adding content, and moderating the forum. The CISSP certification he holds is a testament to his mastery of information security concepts and practices and underscores his commitment to excellence and proficiency in safeguarding critical information assets.

Table of Contents

Part 2: Configure Mobile User and Remote Network Security Processing Nodes

6

Configuring Mobile User SPNs   117

7

Securing Web Gateway   183

8

Setting Up Your Security Policy   205

Part 3: Advanced Configuration and Best Practices

9

Preface

In this book, you will learn about Prisma Access, the **Palo Alto Networks Secure Access Service Edge** (**SASE**) security and connectivity platform. You will learn how combining cloud technology, IPSec, and SSL/TLS connectivity with a cutting-edge security operating system can create a new and exciting way to provide fast and secure connectivity to the internet and private applications while ensuring the best user experience and maintaining full control over endpoints, wherever they are.

Who this book is for

This book is intended to be a guide for administrators who are going to set up or are in the process of setting up Prisma Access that outlines all the components and how to deploy them successfully.

What this book covers

Chapter 1, *Designing and Planning Prisma Access*, explains how to prepare before deploying Prisma Access, which components to consider, and considerations that need to be made before deploying.

Chapter 2, *Activating Prisma Access*, reviews the process of activating the Prisma Access tenant and activating Cortex Data Lake.

Chapter 3, *Setting up Service Infrastructure*, covers the steps needed to activate the service infrastructure, the backbone of Prisma Access

Chapter 4, *Deploying Service Connections*, discusses service connections and how to configure them.

Chapter 5, *Configuring Remote Network SPNs*, covers the Remote Network Security Processing Nodes, what they are used for, and how to configure them.

Chapter 6, *Configuring Mobile User SPNs*, explains Mobile User Security Processing Nodes, how to deploy them in different locations, and how to set up GlobalProtect.

Chapter 7, *Securing Web Gateway*, discusses the explicit proxy configuration as an alternative to MU-SPN.

Chapter 8, *Setting up Your Security Policy*, explains how to set up security rules for all our Security Processing Nodes.

Chapter 9, *User Identification and Cloud Identity Engine*, discusses user identification and how group mapping via Cloud Identity Engine can be done.

Chapter 10, Advanced Configurations and Insights, covers Insights, Cortex Data Lake, and Autonomous Digital Experience Management.

Chapter 11, ZTNA Connector, discusses ZTNA connector, an alternative to SC-CAN that makes private applications available to users.

To get the most out of this book

This book will assume a basic working knowledge of using Panorama for remote management of Palo Alto firewalls and will focus on the new Strata Cloud Management platform without skipping the most important aspects of deploying Prisma Access in a Panorama-managed environment.

Software/hardware covered in the book	Operating system requirements
Prisma Access	Windows, macOS, or Linux

Conventions used

There are a number of text conventions used throughout this book.

`Code in text`: Indicates code words in text, database table names, folder names, filenames, file extensions, pathnames, dummy URLs, user input, and Twitter handles. Here is an example: "The first `if` statement contains all the things that should not be sent to the proxy, indicated by `return "DIRECT"` at the end. "

A block of code is set as follows:

```
function FindProxyForURL(url, host) {
    /* Bypass localhost and Private IPs */
    var resolved_ip = dnsResolve(host);
    if (isPlainHostName(host) ||
    shExpMatch(host, "*.local") ||
    isInNet(resolved_ip, "10.0.0.0", "255.0.0.0") ||
    isInNet(resolved_ip, "172.16.0.0", "255.240.0.0" ||
    isInNet(resolved_ip, "192.168.0.0", "255.255.0.0")  ||
    isInNet(resolved_ip, "127.0.0.0", "255.255.255.0"))
    return "DIRECT";
    /* Bypass FTP */
    if (url.substring(0,4) == "ftp:")
        return "DIRECT";
    /* Bypass SAML, e.g. Okta */
    if (shExpMatch(host, "*.okta.com") || shExpMatch(host,
"*.oktacdn.com"))
        return "DIRECT";
    /* Bypass ACS */
```

```
    if (shExpMatch(host, "*.acs.prismaaccess.com"))
        return "DIRECT";
    /* Forward to Prisma Access */
    return "PROXY pangurus.proxy.prismaaccess.com:8080";
}
```

Bold: Indicates a new term, an important word, or words that you see onscreen. For instance, words in menus or dialog boxes appear in **bold**. Here is an example: "Our first step is to enable the explicit proxy in **Workflows | Prisma Access Setup | Mobile Users**. Click the **Enable** button next to **Explicit Proxy**."

> **Tips or important notes**
> Appear like this.

Get in touch

Feedback from our readers is always welcome.

General feedback: If you have questions about any aspect of this book, email us at customercare@packtpub.com and mention the book title in the subject of your message.

Errata: Although we have taken every care to ensure the accuracy of our content, mistakes do happen. If you have found a mistake in this book, we would be grateful if you would report this to us. Please visit www.packtpub.com/support/errata and fill in the form.

Piracy: If you come across any illegal copies of our works in any form on the internet, we would be grateful if you would provide us with the location address or website name. Please contact us at copyright@packt.com with a link to the material.

If you are interested in becoming an author: If there is a topic that you have expertise in and you are interested in either writing or contributing to a book, please visit authors.packtpub.com.

Share Your Thoughts

Once you've read *Implementing Palo Alto Networks Prisma® Access*, we'd love to hear your thoughts! Scan the QR code below to go straight to the Amazon review page for this book and share your feedback.

https://packt.link/r/1835081002

Your review is important to us and the tech community and will help us make sure we're delivering excellent quality content.

Download a free PDF copy of this book

Thanks for purchasing this book!

Do you like to read on the go but are unable to carry your print books everywhere?

Is your eBook purchase not compatible with the device of your choice?

Don't worry, now with every Packt book you get a DRM-free PDF version of that book at no cost.

Read anywhere, any place, on any device. Search, copy, and paste code from your favorite technical books directly into your application.

The perks don't stop there, you can get exclusive access to discounts, newsletters, and great free content in your inbox daily

Follow these simple steps to get the benefits:

1. Scan the QR code or visit the link below

https://packt.link/free-ebook/978-1-83508-100-6

2. Submit your proof of purchase

3. That's it! We'll send your free PDF and other benefits to your email directly

Part 1: Activate and Configure Prisma Access

This part covers how to plan for and deploy the base configuration on which all other components in Prisma Access will be built. This part has the following chapters:

- *Chapter 1, Designing and Planning Prisma Access*
- *Chapter 2, Activating Prisma Access*
- *Chapter 3, Setting Up Service Infrastructure*
- *Chapter 4, Deploying Service Connections*

1
Designing and Planning Prisma Access

Prisma Access is Palo Alto Networks' **Secure Access Service Edge** (**SASE**) solution that provides **Firewall-as-a-Service** (**FWaaS**) functions to secure internet and network access for branch offices and mobile users leveraging the full functionality of the well-known **Next Generation Firewall** (**NGFW**) platform. SASE enables a distributed cloud environment with security processing nodes in different countries and locations so that protection can take place close to the branch office or remote user versus the traditional method of tunneling all traffic back to the main data center or headquarters location. This approach ensures low latency and *in-country* internet breakout.

In this chapter, you will be introduced to the basic building blocks of Palo Alto Networks' Prisma Access. We will review which preparations will need to be made and which steps need to be taken before we can deploy a tenant. We are going to learn how each component has similarities and some profound differences from the other components and how this will help us with our design considerations.

In this chapter, we're going to cover the following main topics:

- Planning for routing
- Planning the service infrastructure
- Planning for remote network connections and mobile users
- Planning for service connections

Technical requirements

To complete this chapter, you should have a working knowledge of **Border Gateway Protocol** (**BGP**) and cloud networking.

Routing in Prisma Access

In this section, we'll learn how the basic building blocks of Prisma Access communicate with one another. This knowledge is critical in the later stages when building, planning, and troubleshooting to understand why certain components act differently from others.

Important concepts

Before we get started, we need to learn about the building blocks. We will dive much deeper into the individual components in the next few chapters, but it is important to gain a good understanding of what each component is for so that you can more easily imagine where each piece fits into the puzzle. We'll start with a basic outline and gradually build upon what we've learned. This is what you need to know so that the following sections make sense.

Cloud infrastructure is the base on which everything is built. It is the embodiment of the tenant that is spun up. Any configuration changes you make here apply to everything; it is the cloud where everything else lives. It is the backbone upon which everything else is built.

Service Connection Corporate Access Node (**SC-CAN**) or simply **Service Connection** serves several purposes. The primary task is connectivity toward a data center or public cloud (IaaS) environment, be it virtual or physical, which is achieved by setting up IPSec VPN tunnels. The second role of this type of node is to perform dynamic routing. Lastly, it can serve as a User-ID redistribution node. Service connections do not have access to the internet and do not have any security enforcement. They are treated as a trusted connection between the data center, public cloud IaaS environment, and the infrastructure. A service connection provides unmetered throughput, up to 1 Gbps, and several service connections can be set up to the same data center in a load-sharing configuration. They cannot be set for load balancing.

Remote Network Security Processing Node (**RN-SPN**) is typically used to connect remote offices securely to the internet and internal resources behind – for example – a service connection. RN-SPN has a direct internet connection and functions like a firewall **virtual machine** (**VM**) with security rules from the remote network to the internet or internal resources. The advantage of an RN-SPN is that, because it is a firewall, it can apply deep packet inspection and perform any security check a regular on-premises firewall can. All the same features – that is, Advanced Threat Prevention, DNS Security, Advanced URL filtering, Advanced WildFire, AntiVirus, AntiMalware, AntiPhishing, File Blocking, DLP, IoT security, TLS decryption, Remote Browser Isolation, and Authentication – are available on each gateway (the availability of each feature depends on your license model; we will cover this in the next chapter). An important consideration regarding RN-SPN is that these are metered connections that require a certain bandwidth to be assigned to a node in a region and any peer connecting to them will need to share that bandwidth. However, some load balancing options, such as **Equal Cost Multi-Path** (**ECMP**), are available. The bandwidth for RN-SPN is purchased as a pool of bandwidth (for example, 5,000 MB) that can be distributed to different compute locations, with the minimum amount being 50 MB.

A single node in a compute location can only support up to 1,000 MB, so if you assign more capacity, additional nodes will be spun up and the allotted amount will be divided. For example, if a region is assigned 1,500 MB of capacity, two nodes will be spun up – one with 1,000 Mbps and another with 500 Mbps of throughput. Each node is a firewall VM that can be assigned VPN connections from remote offices.

Mobile User Security Processing Node (**MU-SPN**) functions the same way a traditional GlobalProtect gateway does and is used to terminate user VPN connections. From these connections, users will have secured internet access and access to internal resources. Like the RN-SPN, the MU-SPN is a full **next-generation firewall** (**NGFW**), and security rules can be applied to control what users can access on the internet or from internal resources, and security profiles provide full Layer 7 inspection. Unlike RN-SPNs, MU-SPNs are unmetered. If there are several thousands of users in a single country, it is recommended to reach out to Palo Alto Networks to ensure scaling options are reviewed; similar to how additional RN-SPN nodes are spun up in a compute location for bandwidth purposes, additional MU-SPN can be spun up in a region to accommodate a large number of users. We'll go into more detail about this in *Chapter 6*.

Portal Security Processing Nodes (**PT-SPNs**) are related to MU-SPNs in the same way a regular GlobalProtect portal and gateway form a pair. These portal nodes are used primarily to serve the remote agents with their configuration and as the portal to download the GlobalProtect agent and access clientless applications.

Explicit Proxy Security Processing Nodes (**EP-SPNs**) are an alternative to the MU-SPN, which allows customers to rely on proxied connectivity over a TLS connection to secure internet access instead of relying on an IPSec or SSL VPN tunnel. The advantage over MU-SPN is that legacy proxy setup can be easily displaced and endpoints that do not support a VPN agent can still be safely connected to the internet. However, clients using the EP-SPN will not be able to reach private apps via the infrastructure.

The aforementioned components are primarily hosted on a private tenant in **Google Cloud Platform** (**GCP**), with some backup locations being hosted on **Amazon Web Services** (**AWS**).

Let's move on and see how all these parts tie together.

Cloud infrastructure

The first thing that needs to be set up when a fresh Prisma Access tenant is provisioned is the cloud infrastructure. The cloud infrastructure automatically builds a full VPN mesh between all SC-CANs and RN-SPNs across all compute regions with dynamic routing.

MU-SPNs and portals are connected to their geographically closest SC-CANs; dynamic routing is set so that SC-CANs become route reflectors for their connected MU-SPNs.

Finally, the cloud infrastructure enables MU-SPNs and RN-SPNs to access the internet.

The following figure provides a broad overview of what a deployment might look like, with the cloud representing the infrastructure:

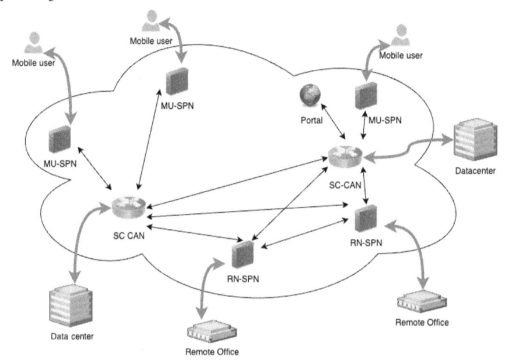

Figure 1.1 – The infrastructure mesh

As we can see, all SC-CANs connect to all SC-CANs and all RN-SPNS, and all RN-SPNs connect to all RN-SPNs and all SC-CANs. Each MU-SPN connects to the geographically closest SC-CAN.

The relationship between remote networks and service connections

Because there is a full VPN mesh between each RN-SPN and SC-CAN, sessions from one node will always use the fastest path available to a destination RN-SPN or SC-CAN. Dynamic routing is configured between all nodes to advertise which routes are available at each node, which also allows for redundancy with the connected remote peers.

As shown in the following figure, even if an internal path is interrupted, the fastest alternative path will be used to get to the desired destination:

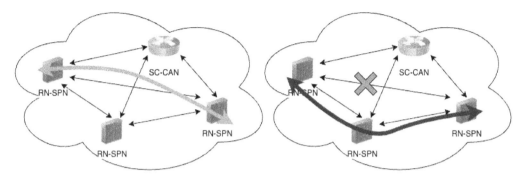

Figure 1.2 – Route redundancy

The full mesh also ensures that geographically distant SC-CANs and RN-SPNs can communicate directly and do not need to rely on complex or long paths to traverse the infrastructure network to the other side of the globe.

The relationship between MU-SPNs and service connections

MU-SPNs, on the other hand, only connect to the nearest SC-CAN and do not build a full mesh with other MU-SPNs, RN-SPNs, or SC-CANs. This means that any connection to or from a remote RN-SPN or SC-CAN will always need to traverse the SC-CAN that the MU-SPN is connected to.

As shown in the following figure, a user on one MU-SPN setting up a session with a user connected to a different MU-SPN that is also connected to a different SC-CAN would need to traverse two SC-CANs before reaching the remote MU-SPN. In short, an IT admin in the US connecting to a user's desktop in Europe will need to pass two SC-CANs:

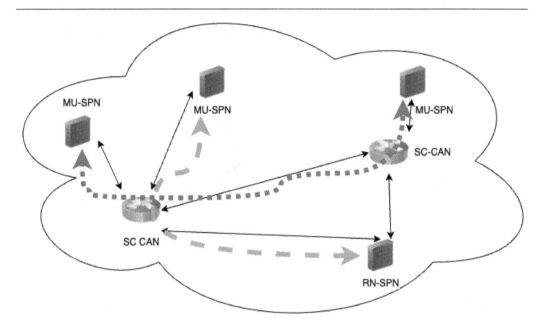

Figure 1.3 – Routing mobile users

The preceding figure also illustrates that any connections between an MU-SPN and an RN-SPN also rely on the existence of an SC-CAN. Since MU-SPNs only connect to an SC-CAN in the infrastructure network, the only way for an RN-SPN to communicate with any given MU-SPN is via an SC-CAN.

If users in a specific region need to be able to set up sessions in a remote office in the region, an SC-CAN should be planned accordingly. An example of this would be employees working from home and needing to print something in their office.

As shown in the following figure, if a user in Europe needs to connect to a remote network in Europe but no service connection is available, the session would need to be routed through the SC-CAN in the US, which may increase latency:

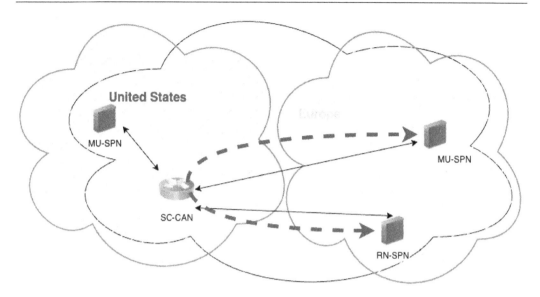

Figure 1.4 – Routing outside of a geographical location

Adding an SC-CAN in Europe will tremendously improve latency on the aforementioned connections. Any SC-CAN deployed for this reason does not require a connection to a data center. Palo Alto Networks will refer to a *dummy service connection* in their customer engagement; an SC-CAN can simply be provisioned in a region for connectivity purposes and not have a VPN set up.

Planning the service infrastructure

As we saw earlier, the service infrastructure is what ties everything together. To ensure all the components can communicate with each other, a subnet is needed; this serves as the backbone of everything. IP addresses will be needed to set up internal VPN tunnels and BGP peers.

Since this subnet serves as your backbone network in the cloud, and the cloud is connected to your data centers, a range needs to be selected that does not overlap with any of the production networks. In most cases, an `x.x.x.x/23` subnet should suffice to provide enough IP addresses to support the entire infrastructure. However, if the deployment calls for several thousands of remote users in several different locations globally or a large number of remote networks in many different countries, a larger subnet may be required.

Planning remote networks

As we touched on earlier, remote networks are deployed based on the bandwidth assigned to a specific compute location. Once bandwidth is assigned, one or more RN-SPN nodes are provisioned for a compute location, and remote networks can be connected to them. The first task when planning the Prisma Access deployment is to estimate how many remote offices there will be and what the bandwidth requirements will look like. Once you know how many sites and how much peak throughput is estimated to be required, you can calculate the amount of bandwidth you will need to purchase.

Consider how much bandwidth will be needed; for anything between 50 Mbps and 1,000 Mbps, a single RN-SPN node is spun up in a compute location, but going over 1,000 Mbps will cause a second node to be spun up and the assigned bandwidth to be divided between the two.

At this time, assigning 1,050 Mbps to a compute location would cause two nodes to be spun up; one node will be capable of reaching 1,000 Mbps and the other node will be capable of 500 Mbps throughput. Prisma Access allows you to oversubscribe up to the maximum capacity of the second node, so traffic will not be limited. Assigning 2,050 would cause three nodes to be spun up, with two nodes with 1,000 Mbps throughput and one node with 500 Mbps capacity, with the same oversubscribing capabilities. This is due to sizing capabilities for individual nodes as they are currently deployed by Palo Alto Networks. In a future release, the distribution will be applied evenly rather than lopsided as it is at this time.

Once your compute location has been provisioned with bandwidth and several RN-SPN nodes have been spun up, you will need to manually select which node is used to connect remote offices. Make sure you spread the load of remote networks evenly or strategically as this is not checked by Prisma Access. You select which RN-SPN is used to terminate the tunnel as no load sharing is available to move a tunnel over to a different RN-SPN (more on load balancing later).

The following figure shows a use case example where 2,500 MB has been assigned to the Belgium compute location. This causes three nodes to be spun up, each receiving two nodes with 1,000 Mbps and 1 node with 500 Mbps from the pool. Multiple remote offices are connected, with three being connected to node1, one being connected to node2, and two more being connected to node2. In this constellation, three smaller offices can share the bandwidth of one node; one remote office has the full bandwidth of one node all to itself and two more offices share the last node.

The following table provides an overview of various examples:

Allocated bandwidth per compute location	Number of RN-SPNs	Egress bandwidth assigned to each RN-SPN
500 Mbps	1	500 Mbps
800 Mbps	1	800 Mbps
1,000 Mbps	1	1 Gbps
1,200 Mbps	2	1 Gbps, 200 Mbps
1,600 Mbps	2	1 Gbps, 600 Mbps
2,000 Mbps	2	1 Gbps, 1 Gbps
2,250 Mbps	3	1 Gbps, 1 Gbps, 250 Mbps

Table 1.1 – Examples of bandwidth allocation to nodes

Following is an example of how bandwidth allocation could look if we assigned 2500MB to a single RN-SPN location:

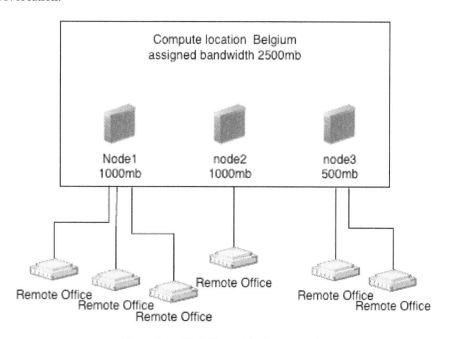

Figure 1.5 – RN-SPN provisioning example

The bandwidth that's allotted to a single RN-SPN node is shared among all of its connected remote networks. If only one remote office is active at any given time, they will have the full use of all the bandwidth available. Additionally, there's a QoS configuration option we'll cover in *Chapter 5*.

As mentioned earlier, each RN-SPN is capped at 1,000 Mbps, so if more bandwidth is required for a remote office, tunnels can be bundled to several RN-SPNs from a single remote office. There are a few things to consider when setting this up:

- Load balancing needs to be set up in the remote network's infrastructure. Any technology, such as ECMP, on the tunnels or using a network load balancer can be used, but the mechanism needs to be set in such a way that sessions, sources, or applications are routed symmetrically across the tunnels. Asymmetric session flows are not supported on the RN-SPNs.

- Each RN-SPN has a unique public IP address, so sessions originating from the remote office will be egressing onto the internet using the IP of the associated RN-SPN. If nodes are used across different countries, this will influence the geolocation of the sessions.

For internet access, this allows you to scale large numbers of RN-SPNs (up to 500 per 1,000 Mbps node in the 5.0 innovation). These can be connected so long as the previous bullet points are taken into account and the on-premises load balancing supports it (for example, some routing devices may have a limitation on the number of ECMP paths that can be selected).

Planning mobile user locations

At the time of writing, there are 116 locations available worldwide to select when deploying mobile user security processing nodes. These locations are spread across multiple major regions: the Americas, Europe, the Middle East, and Asia Pacific. There are also some smaller compute regions, such as the Netherlands, Canada, Ireland, and Hong Kong.

When planning out which countries need to be onboarded, you need to consider that each location that is onboarded will require at least one /24 subnet to serve as an IP pool for the mobile users in that country. For larger countries, multiple /24 subnets may be needed to account for the number of simultaneously connected users. These subnets are assigned to the MU-SPNs at random out of a larger global or regional pool by the service infrastructure. You can choose to use one large global pool or lots of smaller regional pools. If a regional pool is depleted, the global pool will be used to extract additional /24 subnets where needed.

The following figure illustrates that an IP subnet of 10.200.0.0/16 is assigned to the Americas, 10.0.0.0/16 is assigned to EMEA, and a global subnet of 10.100.0.0/16 is set aside as a reserve pool. The US West location in the Americas is assigned two subnets because 350 users are connecting to it. In EMEA, the Netherlands Central location gets one /24 subnet as only 45 users are connecting there, while Belgium received four /24 subnets because 900 users are connecting to this node. The South Korea node receives a /24 subnet from the global pool as no specific subnet was set aside for Asia Pacific:

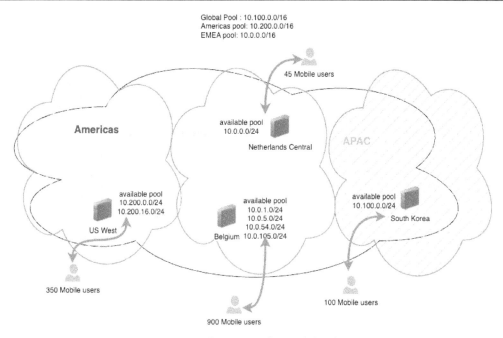

Global Pool : 10.100.0.0/16
Americas pool: 10.200.0.0/16
EMEA pool: 10.0.0.0/16

Figure 1.6 – Illustration of IP pool distribution

The first subnets are assigned somewhat at random when a location or node is activated the first time; additional subnets are assigned whenever there is a need to add IP space. You should not rely on the source IP of a user to identify which country they are originating from as the subnet can be reassigned to a different node.

Summary

In this chapter, we covered the basic building blocks of what makes up Prisma Access and how these are connected. You should now be able to identify that an RN-SPN is used to connect a remote office, an SC-CAN is used to connect a data center, and an MU-SPN is used as an in-country gateway for mobile users.

In the next chapter, we'll go over the activation process and how to deploy the infrastructure and Cortex Data Lake.

2

Activating Prisma Access

Before we can start building our infrastructure, preparing the deployment of the SPNs, and connecting data centers and users, we must first take a few steps to activate Prisma Access and spin up the tenant. In this chapter, we will review everything that is needed to get to a clean *greenfield* Prisma Access.

In this chapter, we're going to cover the following main topics:

- Important considerations before you get started
- The activation process
- Provisioning a Cortex Data Lake tenant

Technical requirements

The topics covered in this chapter mostly cover a step-by-step process to activating Prisma Access. If Panorama is chosen as the management platform, we will assume you already have Panorama up and running. The alternative is the new cloud-based Strata Cloud Manager, which we will cover in a little more detail. It is recommended to have some design experience in a cloud environment as regional compute locations are an important factor to consider while deploying Prisma Access. Prisma Access mostly uses GCP as its cloud backbone, so experience with Google's compute locations and so on is a plus.

Before you start

Before we move on to step 1 of deploying Prisma Access, there are things that need to be considered that will impact every step going forward. The most important decision will be how Prisma Access is going to be managed.

Panorama-managed Prisma Access

When onboarding Prisma Access, the first option you have is that of connecting the infrastructure to a **Panorama centralized management** system. You can connect to an existing Panorama, or a new Panorama can be spun up. In the latter case, a Panorama license needs to be purchased from Palo Alto to be able to set up the system. In the former case, no additional capacity license needs to be added to account for the potentially hundreds of new SPNs that will be added as these are managed by a plugin and don't fall under the managed devices count.

The advantage of using Panorama, especially if you are already using Panorama to manage your other firewalls, is that you don't need to make a change in the way all your systems are managed. A drawback is that Panorama can get a little complex and Prisma Access does not provide exactly the same features in the same location as other firewall systems' templates and device groups. Some settings are controlled in a dedicated plugin for Prisma Access, which we will cover in this book. They require special hardware or a VM spun up on a hypervisor or via a cloud provider, so an additional cost is expected.

Additionally, Panorama is required to run a certain PAN-OS version and has a certain cloud service plugin installed to be able to interface with Prisma Access. Currently, the recommended PAN-OS version for plugin 5.0 is as follows:

- PAN-OS 11.1

- PAN-OS 11.0.0 or a later PAN-OS 11.0 version

- PAN-OS 10.2.3 or a later PAN-OS 10.2 version

- PAN-OS 10.1.7 or a later PAN-OS 10.1 version

To be able to take advantage of 10.2 features (app acceleration, remote browser isolation, and new locations, just to name a few) in Prisma Access, Panorama also needs to be on 10.2.3 or a later release. If Panorama is on 10.1.8 or later, it will be able to control Prisma Access, but the features in 10.2 will not be available until Panorama is upgraded (this is in contrast with regular firewalls managed by Panorama where PAN-OS versions on managed firewalls may never exceed or surpass the Panorama PAN-OS version number).

You can review all the new features on this page and see which version is suitable for your needs: https://docs.paloaltonetworks.com/prisma-access/release-notes/5-0/prisma-access-about/new-features

Do verify whether any new recommendations or requirements have been published on the following Palo Alto TechDocs page: https://docs.paloaltonetworks.com/compatibility-matrix/prisma-access/prisma-access-and-panorama-version-compatibility

Cloud-managed Prisma Access

The second option is **Prisma Access Cloud Management**, which may also be referred to as **Strata Cloud Manager** as Palo Alto is currently taking steps to bring regular firewall chassis and VM management into the cloud as well. The advantage of this management system is that it is fully hosted by Palo Alto Networks and is integrated with several other cloud applications offered by Palo Alto, such as **Insights** and the **Autonomous Digital Experience Manager** (**ADEM**). Best-practice snippets are made available and security rules are automatically checked and marked for best-practice compliance so you can easily ensure a strong security posture.

Activating Prisma Access

When the order has been processed, an activation email will be sent to initiate the process of activating your new tenant that will look similar to the following screenshot:

Figure 2.1 – Activation email

When you click the activation link, you will be taken to the activation web page. You will need to provide your support portal account, and after logging in, you will be presented with the products that can be activated. As shown in the following figure, select all the available options so all licenses are activated. Any item not selected will need to be activated at a later time:

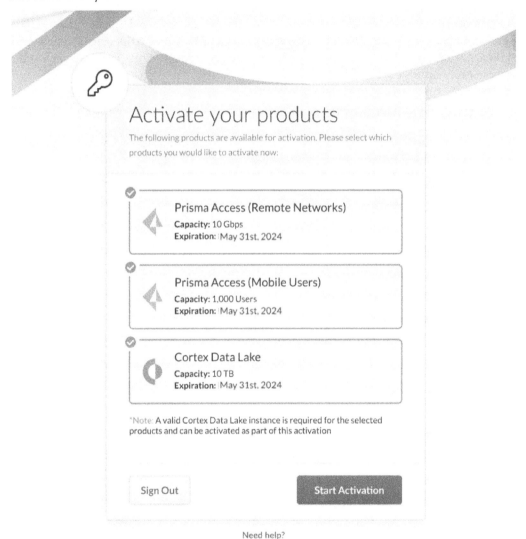

Figure 2.2 – Activating individual products

If your support portal account is associated with multiple support accounts, you will be presented with the option to select which account the new Prisma Access tenant should be associated with, or the option to create a new account:

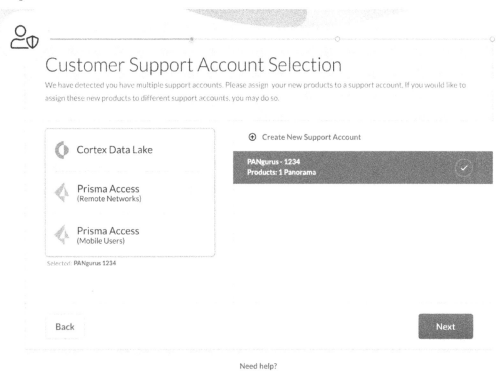

Figure 2.3 – Support account association

After associating the new tenant with a support portal account, the next step will present you with the option to select which management system will be used to manage the new Prisma Access tenant. The available options are to use Prisma Access Cloud Management, associate the new tenant with an existing Panorama management system, or create a new Panorama as part of this deployment.

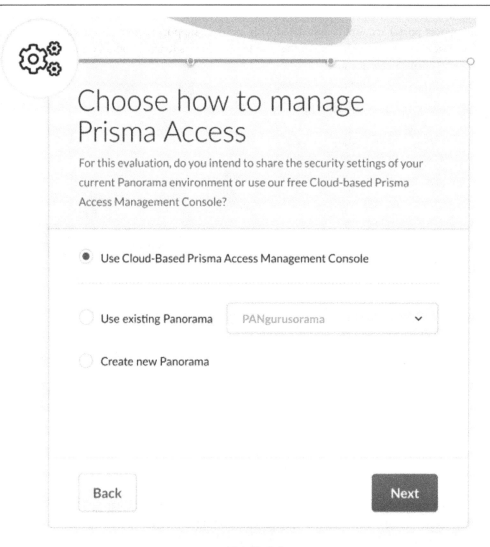

Figure 2.4 – Selecting the management system

Once you have selected the preferred management system, the next screen will show you a summary of the activation process, and a last chance to go back and change those choices. On this screen, you can also select the region where **Cortex Data Lake** (**CDL**) should be deployed. Take a moment to consider which region should apply to you as certain legal regulations might apply. For example, German companies fall under the European GDPR data protection and privacy regulation, which requires EU citizen data to remain within the EU, but also are required by law to retain all data inside of German borders; so, German companies will be required by law to deploy CDL inside of Germany, while other European companies can choose any country as long as it's within the European Union. United States government agencies have a similar requirement to store sensitive data. These are the available regions for CDL:

- AU - Australia
- CA- Canada
- CN - China
- FR - France
- DE - Germany
- IN - India
- IT - Italy
- EU - Netherlands/Europe (default 'europe' location')
- PL - Poland
- SG - Singapore
- ES - Spain
- CH - Switzerland
- UK - United Kingdom
- US - United States
- USA-Gov - United States Government

The location of CDL will also impact where any other cloud services can be deployed, as they should be deployed in the same region to be able to interface with CDL. In the following screenshot, you can see I selected Germany:

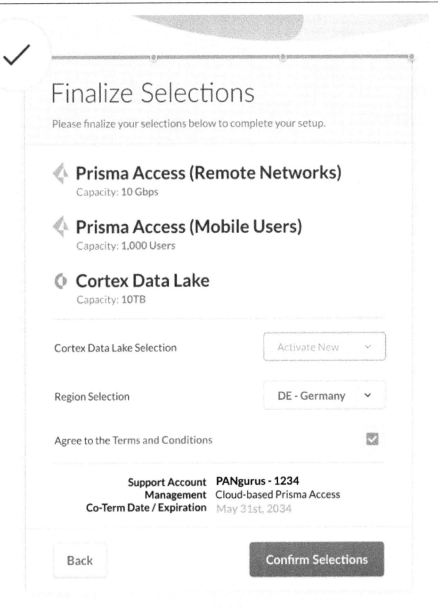

Figure 2.5 – Last step in the activation process

If you selected cloud-based Prisma Access management, this was the last step to gain access to the tenant and the Prisma Access app will now become available on the Palo Alto hub portal at `https://apps.paloaltonetworks.com`.

If Panorama was selected as the management server, you will be redirected to the next page, which contains a **One-Time Password** (**OTP**), as displayed in the following screenshot:

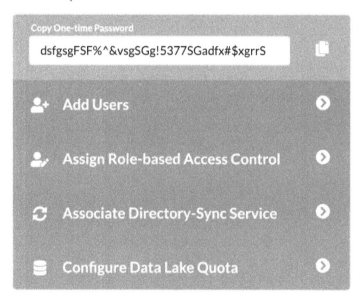

Figure 2.6 – Prisma Access plugin OTP

This last page also offers you additional actions to complete. You can tackle these right now or return to them at a later stage once you've set up the Prisma Access infrastructure. We'll cover these actions in more depth in *Chapters 8* and *10*.

If you haven't done so already, go ahead and download and install the desired version of the Cloud_ services plugin. Verify the PAN-OS version Panorama is currently on is compatible with the plugin you want to install. As a rule of thumb, make sure you have a minimum version of PAN-OS 10.1.8, 10.2.3, or 11.0 running before you install a plugin. You can verify the compatibility matrix on this page: https://docs.paloaltonetworks.com/compatibility-matrix/prisma-access/prisma-access-and-panorama-version-compatibility

Follow these steps to ensure you get the latest available plugins:

1. Click **Check Now** to fetch the latest available plugins from the update server.

2. Click **Install** next to the desired plugin version.

After installing the plugin, you may need to refresh your browser for the **Cloud Services** menu item to appear:

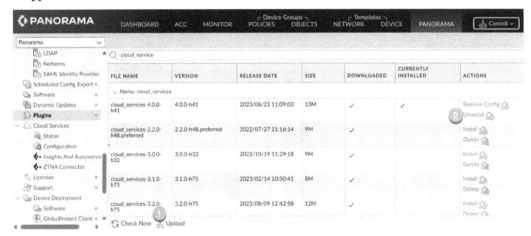

Figure 2.7 – Install plugin on Panorama

If, for any reason, there is an issue with the OTP you received from the activation process (it expired, you accidentally closed the page, etc.), you are still able to generate a fresh OTP by navigating to the Palo Alto support portal at https://support.paloaltonetworks.com under **Products | Cloud Services | Generate OTP**.

As shown in the following screenshot, in the popup, select **Generate OTP for Panorama** for **Device Type** and **Logging Service** for **Select OTP Type**, and select the appropriate serial number for the Panorama that will manage your Prisma Access tenant. Once you click **Generate**, you will receive an OTP that is valid for 10 minutes:

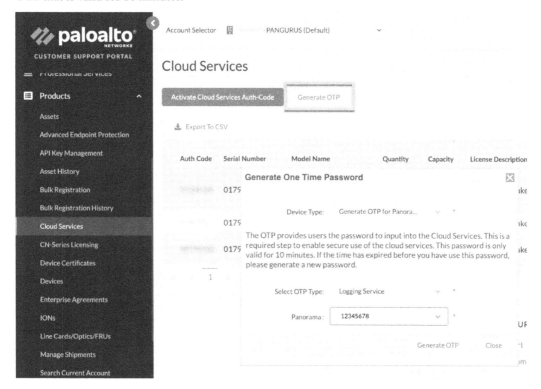

Figure 2.8 – Generate plugin OTP

Once you have copied the OTP you received from the activation process or from the manual process on the support portal, navigate to **Panorama | Cloud services | Configuration** to activate the plugin. You will be prompted that your account needs to be verified. Click the **Verify** button and paste the OTP:

Figure 2.9 – Activate plugin using OTP

Once the OTP is confirmed, you will be able to start configuration on the service infrastructure, which we'll cover in the next chapter.

Summary

In this chapter, we covered the activation process that sets up the Prisma Access tenant and CDL and either provisions Prisma Access Cloud Management or binds Panorama to the newly deployed tenant.

In the next chapter, we will go over the steps needed to configure the service infrastructure, which is the foundation of all the other building blocks.

3

Setting Up Service Infrastructure

In this chapter, we're going to set up the service infrastructure and learn about the different routing modes that can be applied inside Prisma Access. We will cover both a Panorama-managed and a Strata Cloud Manager example. The service infrastructure is the foundation on which all the connectivity nodes are built, so a few important decisions need to be made before moving on to any of the other chapters after this one.

In this chapter, we're going to cover the following main topics:

- Service infrastructure base configuration
- Routing modes
- Preparing the service connection BGP configuration

Technical requirements

This chapter dives into configuring Prisma Access and requires a basic understanding of cloud networking and routing.

Configuring service infrastructure via Strata Cloud Manager

If, during the activation process, you opted to deploy Prisma Access as a cloud-managed service, the first place you should go to access the management interface is `https://apps.paloaltonetworks.com`.

Once you've logged on, your page should look as follows. Once you start adding additional services, such as Cloud Identity Engine, which we'll cover in *Chapter 9*, additional tiles will appear, representing those applications. If there's a little subtext to the tile stating **in progress**, as displayed as **1** in the following figure, the service is still being provisioned and you'll need to wait until the status disappears, as displayed as **2**:

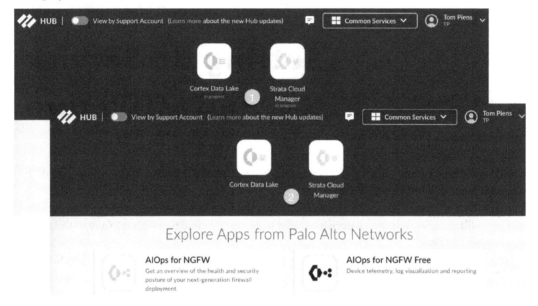

Figure 3.1 – Palo Alto HUB landing page

Once the service is ready, you can click the Prisma Access tile. This will bring you to the **Overview** landing page:

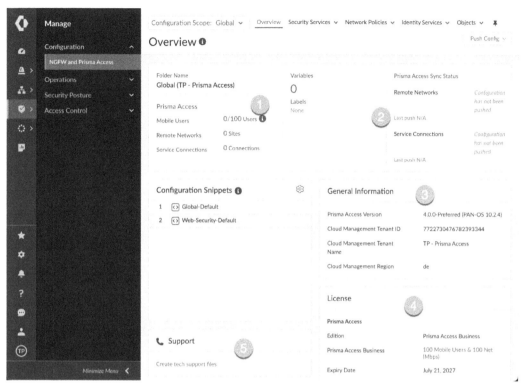

Figure 3.2 – The Overview page

The **Overview** page gives you a glance at a few interesting facts about your Prisma Access deployment:

1. The number of active users (unique users in the past 90 days), number of remote networks, and number of service connections

2. The state of the configuration having been pushed to the components

3. General information on the Tenant, such as ID number, operating system version, and region where the tenant is active

4. Licensing information

5. A tech support file can be generated from here in case a support case is opened that requires one

At the top of the page, as shown in the following screenshot, you will quickly identify some topics that should look very familiar if you've used Panorama before. These are the *firewall* configuration menu items and allow you to control the security rules, content scanning policies, objects, and so on:

Figure 3.3 – Firewall configuration in Strate Cloud Manager

In the preceding screenshot, we have the following:

1. **Configuration Scope**: This area allows you to control the context of configuration. You can set configuration for all components or a specific component individually.

2. **Security Services**: This is where the security policy rules are created, and security profiles can be set up for content inspection.

3. **Network Policies**: These allow you to set up QoS and app override rules.

4. **Identity Service**: This is where additional authentication and user ID integration can be configured.

5. **Objects**: This is where all the objects that can be used in a security rule, such as address objects, custom apps, service ports, and more, can be created.

6. **Push Config**: This is Panorama's counterpart way to send the configuration changes you made to the appropriate components. All changes to the configuration remain inactive until they are pushed to production.

We'll revisit these in more detail in the coming chapters. While we're in this section of the configuration, let's take a quick look at the available options under **Manage**:

1. **Manage** is where operational and security configurations can be set.

2. **NGFW and Prisma Access** is the main section where you can configure all the security settings.

3. **Operations** is where commit jobs can be checked if and when they are completed, and a revision history can be reviewed.

4. **Security Posture** is a set of tools to improve the security policy.

5. **Access Control** lets you change the configuration context and hierarchy in Strata Cloud Manager so that operators and role-based admins are restricted to only the sections they control:

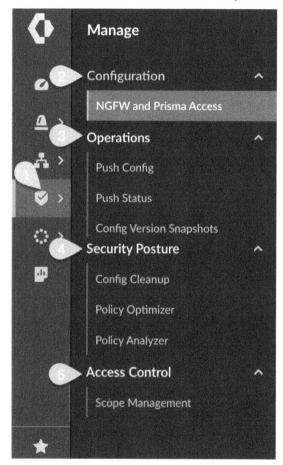

Figure 3.4 – The Manage section

The **Manage** section covers all the topics required to provide security, but our first objective is to set up the service infrastructure. For that, we need to navigate to the **Workflows** section and set up Prisma Access. You can see the available options in the following screenshot:

1. **Workflows** is where you can configure the components that make up Prisma Access.

2. **Prisma Access Setup** provides the basic building blocks for service connections, service infrastructure, mobile users, and remote network SPNs.

3. **ZTNA connector** allows you to set up a connection to private applications.

4. **Software Upgrades** give you an insight into the upgrade schedule for your Prisma Access tenant and allow you to postpone an upcoming upgrade.

5. **Integrations** give you access to your third-party SD-WAN integrations:

Figure 3.5 – The Workflow section

To configure the service infrastructure, navigate to **Workflows** | **Prisma Access Setup** | **Prisma Access**.

You'll see two main sections – **Infrastructure Settings** and **Internal DNS Servers,** as shown in the following screenshot. Some values, such as **Infrastructure Subnet** and **Infrastructure BGP AS**, are prepopulated, while some other values are still empty:

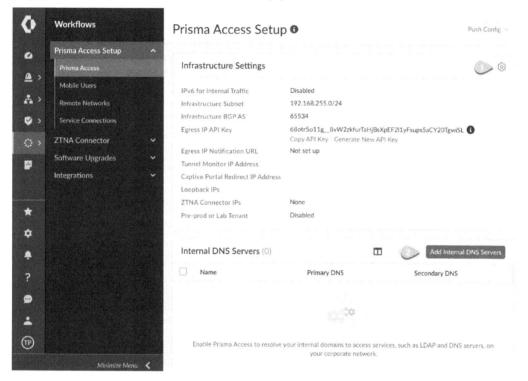

Figure 3.6 – Prisma Access Setup

In the preceding screenshot, you can edit some of the settings to suit your needs:

1. To change **Infrastructure Settings**, click the cogwheel on the right-hand side. You will be taken to a new page that will display all the settings that can be enabled or changed, as shown in *Figure 3.7*:

    *   **Enable IPv6 for internal traffic**: This setting determines if IPv6 can be used between remote users, remote networks, and service connections. With this setting disabled, all IPv6 traffic will occur outside of Prisma Access, which may require an IPv6 sinkhole configuration to be set up to prevent IPv6 traffic from bypassing Prisma Access. We'll cover the IPv6 sinkhole in *Chapter 6*.

    *   **Infrastructure subnet**: This is the subnet that's used by *components* inside the Prisma Access cloud to be able to communicate with one another or provide services. A /24 subnet should be sufficient unless you are facing a very large deployment, in which case you may need a /23. This subnet may not overlap with any subnet that's used within the organization. As a reference, they are used for full mesh connectivity between all the nodes as tunnel IP addresses, and as service addresses such as DNS-proxy or BGP peer IPs.

    *   **Infrastructure BGP AS**: This is the AS that's used for all BGP communication inside and out. Ensure it does not overlap with any AS already in use. Service connections and remote network connections can use BGP to establish dynamic routing and share IP routing information between data centers and branch offices. For the outside world, all Prisma Access components in any location will all have the same BGP AS.

    *   **ZTNA Connectors Application IP Blocks**: This is an IP pool that's used by the ZTNA connectors as internal reference IPs for hosted applications.

    *   **ZTNA Connectors Connector IP Blocks**: This is an IP pool that's used to assign each ZTNA connector an IP on the Prisma Access side.

    *   **Pre-Prod or Lab tenant**: This will only appear if sub-tenants exist for your organization. Setting a tenant to pre-prod will allow upgrades to be deployed to this tenant ahead of a general rollout, but it prohibits production traffic from passing over this tenant.

In the following screenshot, you can see my default infrastructure subnet of 192.168.255.0/25 and an infrastructure BPG AS of 65534. Change these to best suit your organization's IP schema:

Infrastructure Settings

IPv6 for Internal Traffic ⓘ	☐ Enable
Infrastructure Subnet	192.168.255.0/24
Infrastructure BGP AS	65534
Egress IP Notification URL	
ZTNA Connectors Application IP Blocks	**IPs** (0)

☐   IP

  + —

☐ Advertise Application IP blocks to Remote Networks

ZTNA Connectors Connector IP Blocks

IPs (0)

☐   IP

  + —

The existing ZTNA Connectors Connector IP Blocks cannot be modified or deleted.

Pre-prod or Lab Tenant	☐ Enable

* Required Field   Cancel   **Save**

Figure 3.7 – Infrastructure settings

Internal DNS servers let you set DNS rules so that internal domains are resolved by DNS servers of your choice. By default, the infrastructure will resolve **fully qualified domain names** (**FQDNs**) via a public DNS server, but some domains may only be resolved internally, or internal records may need to be retrieved:

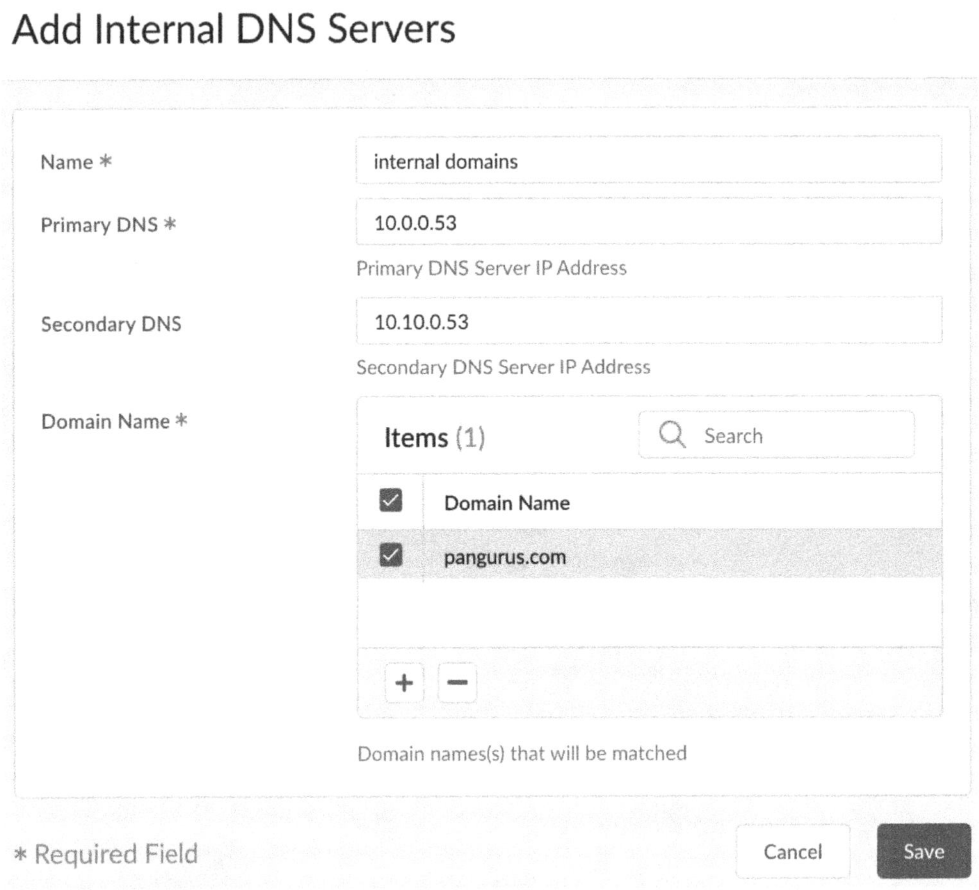

Add Internal DNS Servers

Name *	internal domains
Primary DNS *	10.0.0.53
	Primary DNS Server IP Address
Secondary DNS	10.10.0.53
	Secondary DNS Server IP Address

Domain Name *

Items (1)   🔍 Search

☑	Domain Name
☑	pangurus.com

\+ \−

Domain names(s) that will be matched

* Required Field   Cancel   **Save**

Figure 3.8 – Adding internal DNS servers

Let's take a look at the Panorama counterpart of these configuration settings.

Configuring Panorama's managed service infrastructure

If you manage Prisma Access via Panorama, after installing the plugin, you can start configuring the service infrastructure by navigating to **Panorama | Cloud Services | Configuration**, at which point you'll land on the **Service Setup** page.

As shown in the following screenshot, on the left-hand side, you can change the settings, while on the right-hand side, you have **Service Operations**:

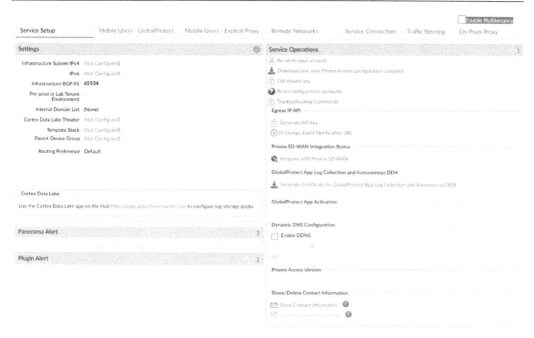

Figure 3.9 – Service Setup

You can change the **Service Setup** settings by clicking the little cogwheel in the middle of the screen.

Settings

On the first page of the service infrastructure settings, you can set the IP subnet that will be used by the infrastructure components. Keep in mind that this subnet should not overlap with any existing subnets in use as overlap could disrupt connectivity or services. This subnet will be used for many different purposes, including loopback addresses, tunnel monitoring, user ID redistribution, Captive Portal, and more.

If IPv6 should be used inside the network, it needs to be enabled here and an IPv6 infrastructure subnet should be added.

The infrastructure BGP AS can be set here. This is the AS that will be used to communicate with all remote BGP peers.

The tenant can be set to **Pre-prod** or **Lab** mode, which enables it to receive updates and upgrades sooner than production tenants. However, this will bar the tenant from running production traffic.

Similar to other template stacks used to manage firewalls, Prisma Access has its own template stack and associated template. You can add additional templates here to associate with the Strata access infrastructure. This can be useful if, for example, all the server profiles have already been configured in a shared template. Unlike other template stacks, the `Service_Conn_Template` template cannot be placed lower than other templates and will always have the highest priority.

`Service_Conn_Device_Group` can be placed in a different parent device group than **Shared** if needed.

In the following screenshot, I added a new IPv4 infrastructure subnet and left everything else as-is:

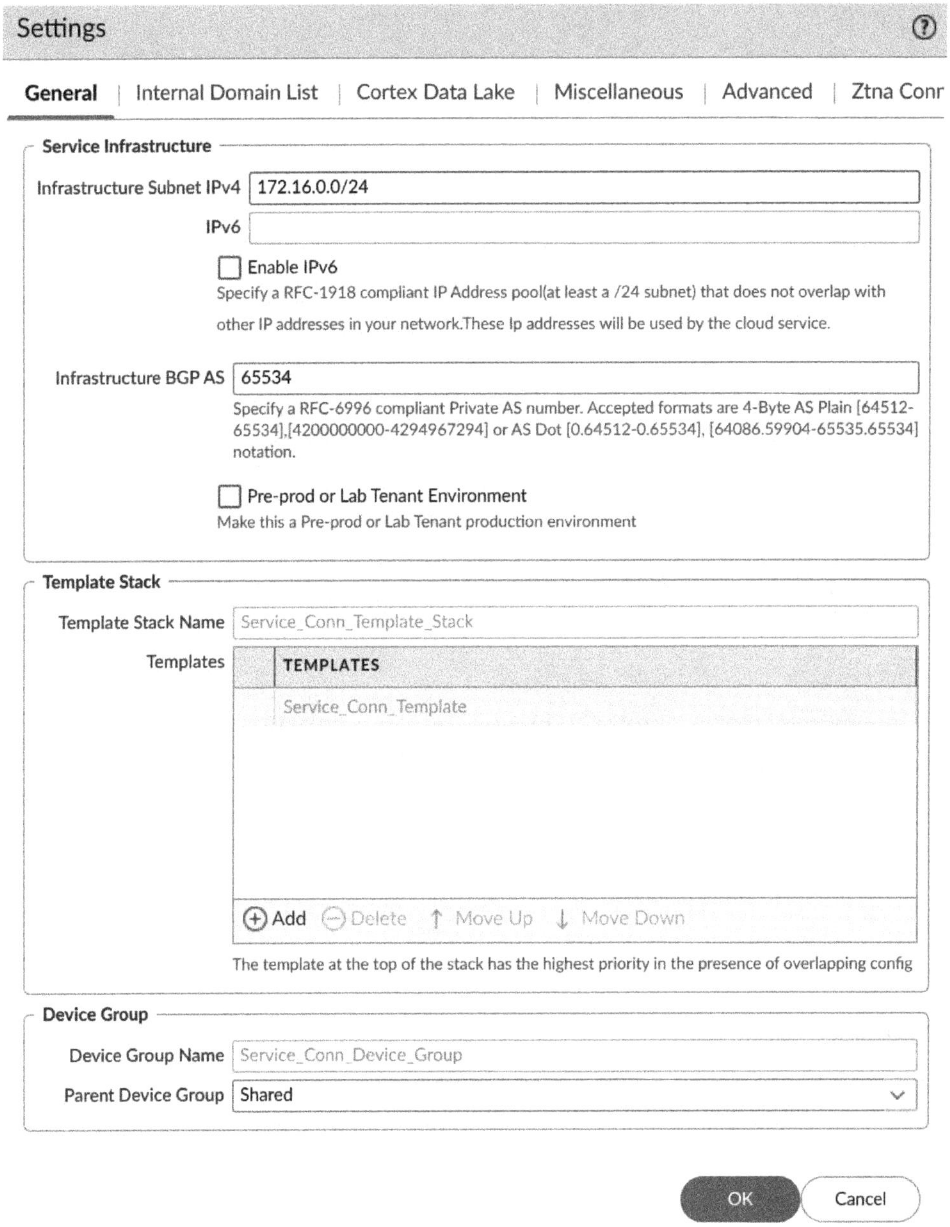

Figure 3.10 – The General tab

On the **Internal Domain List** tab, we can configure internal domains and their internal DNS servers. This will help the infrastructure network resolve internal FQDNs:

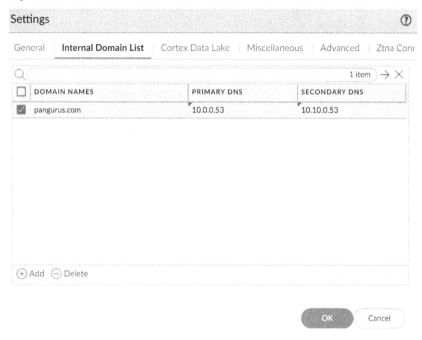

Figure 3.11 – The Internal Domain List tab

From the activation sequence in *Chapter 2*, you may remember the region for Cortex Data Lake that needed to be set. This determined where the **Cortex Data Lake** tenant would be spun up. In the **Cortex Data Lake** tab, we can choose which theater, and associated CDL instance, should be used for this Prisma Access tenant to connect to. If the activation went well, the available regions should be limited to where the CDL was activated. As shown in the following screenshot, I activated CDL in Germany; the option is also Germany:

Figure 3.12 – The Cortex Data Lake tab

The **Miscellaneous** tab lets you set a few options that may be useful, depending on your situation:

- **Append the ending token to the URLs in the URL filtering configuration** will append a forward slash (/) at the end of URLs added to custom URL filtering profiles or **external dynamic lists (EDLs)**. This will ensure URLs are limited to the exact domain and no unintended URLs are allowed.

- **Disable Traffic Logging on Service Connections** can be set if the majority of traffic over the service connections is asymmetric, which could cause excessive logging to CDL. There's no need to enable this setting if there are no asymmetric traffic flows. Asymmetric traffic can happen if load sharing is enabled, and a single data center is serviced by multiple service connections (that is, a bundle of service connections to increase bandwidth to a data center).

By default, these options are disabled:

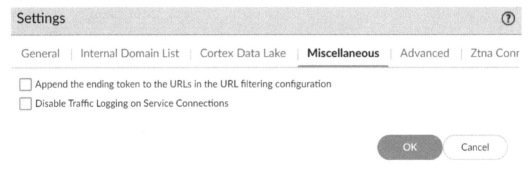

Figure 3.13 – The Miscellaneous tab

In the **Advanced** tab, several routing settings can be changed that will apply to the entire environment:

- **Withdraw Static Routes if Service Connection or Remote Networks IPSec tunnel is down** can be enabled to remove static routes. By default, this setting is disabled, which means that any static routes set to a remote network will remain and traffic destined for that network will not be able to go anywhere until the tunnel is up or restored. Enabling this option will remove the static route from internal BGP distribution, which would then cause any traffic destined for this subnet to seek out the next best route. This could, for example, be a larger subnet learned by BGP over a service connection.

- **Enable automatic IKE peer host routes for Remote Networks and Service Connections** can be enabled so that a host route is added to the RN-SPN for each IKE peer connected to it. This option can be useful if the public IP subnet used by the remote peer is also advertised inside the tunnel (for example, 198.51.100.5 is used by the IKE peer while 198.51.100.0/24 is advertised by the remote BGP peer). In routing, smaller subnet masks have higher priority over larger subnets (for example, /32 will be prioritized over /24 routes), and static routes are prioritized over BGP-learned routes.

- **Outbound routes for the service** can be used to force up to 10 subnets (current limit by Palo Alto) to be routed to the internet. This will override any routes learned from BGP. These routes will be installed on all SC-CANs and SPNs. For example, a customer uses public IPs both on the public and private parts of their network. The sub- or supernet may be learned via BGP, causing all traffic to be routed internally. This option allows you to bypass small sections so that their website remains routed externally via the internet. This allows users to reach it directly. You can also disable **HIP** and **Quarantine List** redistribution if you want to prevent service connections from collecting this information:

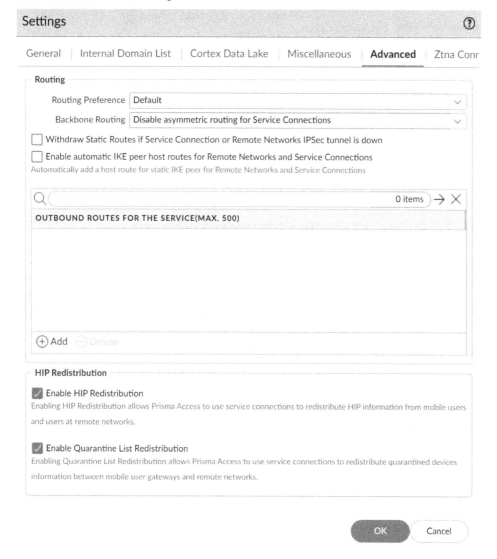

Figure 3.14 – The Advanced Settings tab

Two more settings in this tab will influence how traffic can be routed.

Routing Preference

Routing Preference has two options – **Default** and **Hot potato routing** – as shown in the following figure:

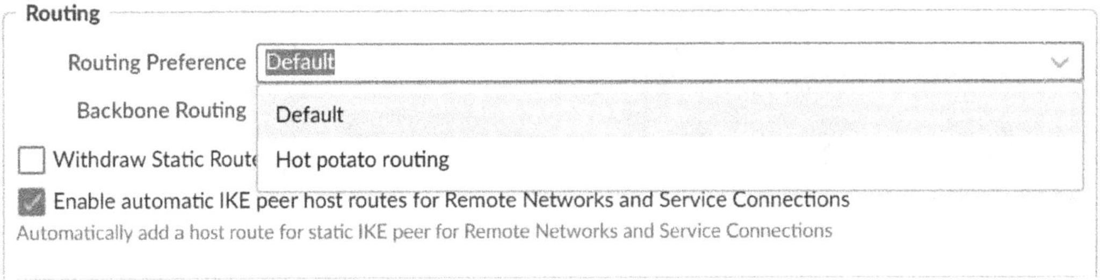

Figure 3.15 – Routing Preference

Default routing will let normal routing controlled by BGP decide which route is preferred. Based on AS path prepends, MED, and metrics, packets will be forwarded to the preferred destination, even if multiple destination routes exist, keeping the packets inside Prisma Access until they've reached the preferred destination.

As an example, a user connected to an MU-SPN in Europe is trying to reach a resource in the US. The EU MU-SPN is connected to an SC-CAN in the Netherlands, which, in turn, has routing set up to the SC-CAN in US-central. An alternative (MPLS, for example) backbone exists so that the US-central subnet is also advertised to the BGP peer in the Netherlands, but with an AS prepend, making it a longer path. Packets will be forwarded from the client to the MU-SPN, the MU-SPN will forward packets to the SC-CAN in the Netherlands, and the Netherlands SC-CAN will forward packets to the US-central SC-CAN where they're transported over IPSec into the data center.

Hot potato routing will egress packets out to the customer's on-premises network as quickly as possible, even if routing distance inside Prisma Access would dictate otherwise.

As illustrated in the following figure, a client tries to reach a web server in **Datacenter 1** on its IP address of 10.0.0.5. The user is connected to an MU-SPN that is connected to SC-CAN 2. Default routing would route the connection from the MU-SPN to SC-CAN 2. Here, a route lookup is performed and it is determined that the shortest route is via SC-CAN 1 as it is directly connected to AS 1000, which contains the subnet for 10.0.0.5. The session is routed to SC-CAN 1 and down the service connection directly to **Datacenter 1**.

With **Hot potato routing**, *offloading* to the nearest data center (which is capable of routing to the final destination) is preferred over routing to another SC-CAN, so the session is transferred to **Datacenter 2** as it also has a route for 10.0.0.0/16, albeit with a longer distance:

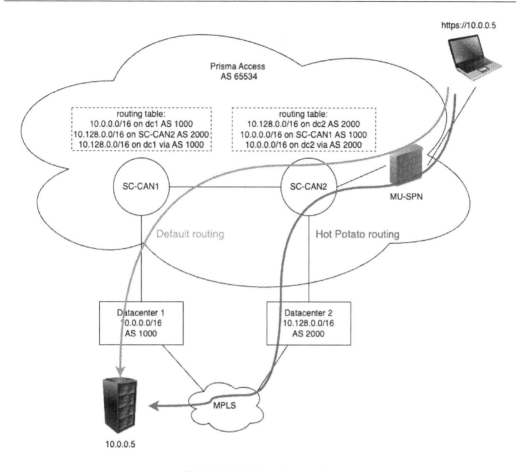

Figure 3.16 – Hot potato routing

Backbone Routing

Backbone Routing will determine if asymmetric routing will be allowed and if load sharing (this is *not* load balancing) should be enabled:

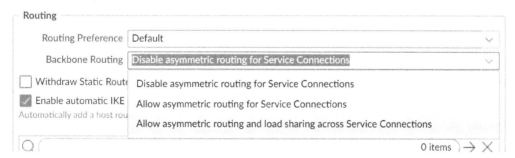

Figure 3.17 – Backbone Routing

Depending on how the SC-CANs are connected and how routing is achieved, there may be a need to allow asymmetric routing. By default, asymmetric routing is not allowed, which means routing needs to be set so that each node only connects to a set of subnets and there is no overlap or backend routing that could cause packets to use multiple paths. This scenario will represent the most common cases where an SC-CAN is connected to one data center and another SC-CAN is connected to a different data center.

Allow asymmetric routing for Service Connections will allow asymmetric flows, meaning packets egressing one SC-CAN and coming back via a different SC-CAN, to happen. This could happen where a customer has, for example, an additional backbone where routing may change dynamically or two Layer 2 connected data centers.

Allow asymmetric routing and load sharing across Service Connections can be enabled if multiple service connections are established with a single data center for bandwidth optimization.

Finally, the **ZTNA Connectors** tab lets you configure the subnet that's used for the STNA connectors, as well as the subnet used for the applications:

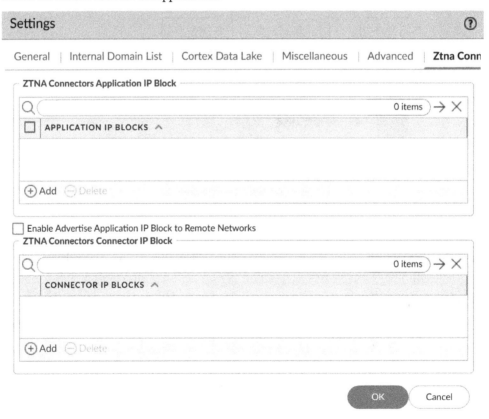

Figure 3.18 – The ZTNA Connectors tab

Once you're done configuring the settings, make sure you click **OK** to save the changes.

Service Operations

Under **Service Operations**, on the right-hand side of the **Service Setup** landing page (see *Figure 3.9*), we can find a lot of useful features to control the service infrastructure:

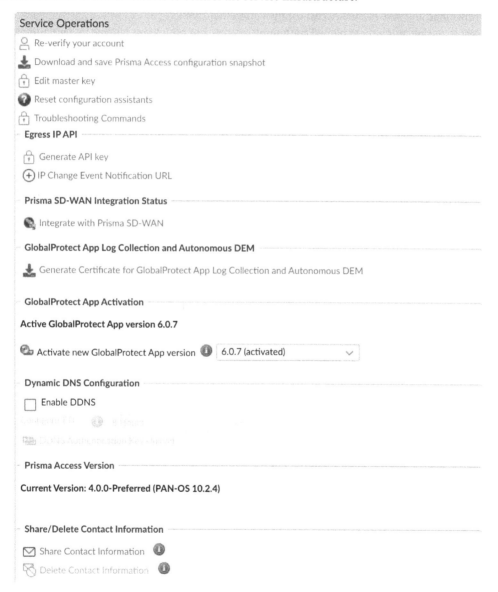

Figure 3.19 – Service Operations

Let's review what these options can do:

- **Re-verify your account** is used to (re)submit a one-time key from the **customer support portal (CSP)**. This can be useful if the connection between Panorama and the Prisma Access tenant needs to be restored. This can be necessary after Panorama has been restored after a failure, for example.

- **Download and save Prisma Access configuration snapshot** lets you export a saved configuration snapshot, similar to **export named configuration snapshot**, which you can find under **Panorama | Setup | Operations**.

- **Edit Master key** works like the firewalls and Panorama master key and lets you set a new master key for Prisma Access. The master key is used to encrypt all certificate private keys and administrator passwords.

- **Reset Configuration assistants** resets all the wizards that pop up when you first access Prisma Access so that you can run them once more.

- **Troubleshooting Commands** lets you collect some useful runtime information, as shown in the following screenshot. You can run a check to verify the status of the logging service to CDL or fetch the routing table associated with a specific SC-CAN or RN-SPN. If EDLs are being used, you can also check their output from here to ensure they're being populated properly:

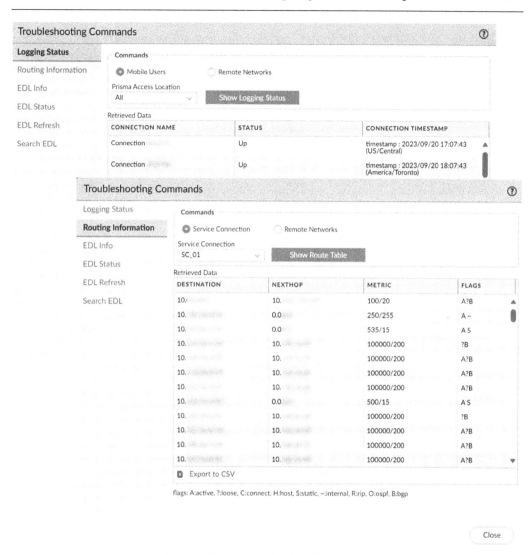

Figure 3.20 – Troubleshooting Commands

- **Generate API key** lets you generate an API key that can be used to fetch the current list of active IP addresses used by all the SPNs, the list of reserved IPs for MU-SPNs, and so on. **IP Change Event Notification URL** can be configured with a server URL where a notification is sent in case an IP change happens in your Prisma Access environment so that you are made aware that you need to retrieve a fresh list of IP addresses.

- **Integrate with Strata SD WAN** lets you connect an existing Strata SD-WAN environment to Prisma Access.

- **Generate Certificate for GlobalProtect App Log Collection and Autonomous DEM** generates a client certificate that must be used by clients that have the ADEM plugin active on their GlobalProtect agent. The client certificate is set in the GlobalProtect portal agent configuration and is used to authenticate the client against the ADEM cloud tenant for telemetry collection.

- **GlobalProtect App Activation** lets you select which GlobalProtect agent version is installed for the clients if automated updates are enabled in the GlobalProtect portal app configuration.

- **Dynamic DNS configuration** can, when enabled, send an nsupdate message to the internal **Dynamic DNS (DDNS)** server to map the hostname and tunnel IP for a mobile user. nsupdate is sent to the primary DNS server (which needs to support nsupdate) that's been configured in Panorama's DNS server list in **Panorama | Setup | Services | Primary DNS Server**.

- **Prisma Access Version** will simply display which version of Prisma Access your tenant is on currently.

- **Share/Delete Contact Information** lets you share contact details with Palo Alto so that they can contact you regarding the Prisma Access service.

These commands will help you control settings that would traditionally be available from the CLI or via the GlobalProtect configuration. The service infrastructure is now ready for additional components to be added.

Summary

In this chapter, you learned about the prerequisites for, and how to configure, the service infrastructure. You are now able to set up a Prisma Access tenant both via the Strata Cloud Manager and Panorama management interfaces.

In the next chapter, we will learn how to set service connections and will go into finer detail about how these SC-CANs work and how they should be deployed

4

Deploying Service Connections

Now that we've prepared the Service Infrastructure, we are ready to start learning about and deploying **Service Connection Corporate Access Nodes (SC-CAN)** to connect the data centers to Prisma Access. **Service connections** represent the backbone that connects the core of a customer's network to the users and branch offices in faraway locations and enables the customer to provide business continuity in case of failure. Service connections are used to attach data centers and private applications to the Prisma Access Cloud so that they are optimally available to users across the globe.

In this chapter, we're going to cover the following main topics:

- What is the use case for service connections?

- Provisioning SC-CAN in cloud-managed Prisma Access

- Provisioning SC-CAN in Panorama

Technical requirements

A basic understanding and working knowledge of setting up IPSec VPN tunnels and dynamic routing using **Border Gateway Protocol (BGP)** is required for readers to follow along with the creation of service connections in this chapter. An understanding of cloud-based routing and compute nodes is required.

What are service connections used for?

As we already touched upon at the beginning of this book, service connections, or SC-CANs, represent a data center connection, an extension of the data center into the cloud. Because of this function, the SC-CAN has some distinctive characteristics, some shared with **remote network security processing nodes (RN-SPN)**, some unique to SC-CAN.

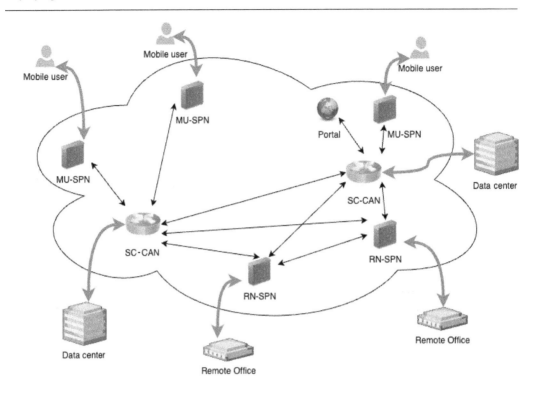

Figure 4.1 – Prisma Access overall architecture

A service connection is established by creating an IPSec VPN tunnel between a Prisma Access CAN and a data center. The resulting tunnel is a service connection. All traffic up and down between the data center and Prisma Access will traverse this VPN tunnel.

Unlike an SPN, there is no security enforcement on the CAN. Therefore, even though the remote VPN peer can be any IPSec-capable device, it is recommended to have a security-capable device such as a **next-generation firewall** (**NGFW**) that can enforce security policies and perform deep packet inspection in the data center.

Each SC-CAN provides 1 Gbps of throughput, but access to the internet is not possible through a service connection. This bandwidth can be used for mobile users connected to a MU-SPN, or remote networks connected to an RN-SPN to access resources in a data center. Service connections can also be used to transport sessions between different data centers that each have a service connection, meaning all SC-CANs can carry sessions among one another.

Service connections also serve as routing nodes and route reflectors in a region, and enable mobile users to connect to remote networks and vice versa.

Service connections also serve as User-ID redistribution agents as they collect all the user-to-IP mapping information from the connected MU-SPN. This means that if there are multiple MU-SPN locations active in a region, and one SC-CAN, the SC-CAN is the single source for User-ID redistribution.

SC-CANs are provisioned in several locations inside a region. The location should be chosen to be closest to the data center connecting to it. The location will also determine which MU-SPN connects to it, as an MU-SPN always connects to the geographically closest SC-CAN, to reach the infrastructure network.

For example, in Europe, there is a location available in each country. If your data center is located in the Netherlands, activate a service connection in the Netherlands location.

If no data center needs to be connected in a region, but MU-SPNs are provisioned that do need to connect to RN-SPNs in or outside the region, or a data center in a different region, an SC-CAN in the region is recommended to provide a low latency connection as traffic is routed through the geographically closest SC-CAN, which could mean connections inside Europe first need to traverse to an SC-CAN in the US if none are available in Europe.

Each SC-CAN will have a primary VPN tunnel and can be configured with a backup IPSec tunnel, which can be connected to, for example, a secondary ISP link in the data center. This backup tunnel will be active and can establish BGP peering, but will not carry any other sessions until the primary tunnel is down.

Provisioning an SC-CAN in cloud-managed Prisma Access

You may have noticed in the last chapter that the Panorama-managed Service Infrastructure had many more options available than the cloud-managed counterpart. This is because most of those options have been moved under the service connections in cloud-managed Prisma Access.

To start configuring a service connection in the cloud management interface, access the Prisma Access app via `https://apps.paloaltonetworks.com`. Once the dashboard has loaded, navigate to **Workflows** | **Prisma Access Setup** | **Service Connections** and you will be presented with a page similar to the following screenshot:

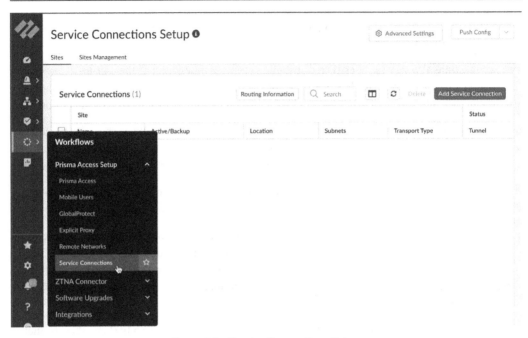

Figure 4.2 – Service Connections Setup

Let's first take a look at **Advanced Settings** by clicking the **Advanced Settings** button at the top on the right-hand side. You will see that you have similar options available as you do in Panorama:

- **BGP Routing Preferences**: You have two options under this:

  - **Default** will simply apply BGP features as they are designed. Routing can be manipulated by prepending the AS path or by setting a higher or lower **multi-exit discriminator** (**MED**) (the MED functions somewhat like a metric, providing your router with a measure of preference where traffic should be sent on multiple connected paths. The AS path is slightly different as it applies a distance to a route that can be used to discourage usage of a path unless there is no alternative.)

  - **Hot Potato Routing** will alter routing so packets are egressed out of the closest viable service connection; that is, if an MU-SPN is connected to an SC-CAN that has a route to a subnet pointing towards its connected data center, and a more preferred route to a next SC-CAN, it will still egress packets directly towards the data center.

- **Enable automatic IKE peer host routes for Remote Networks and Service Connections**: This will add a static route pointing to the default route, out to the internet, for each connected RN-SPN or SC-CAN peer. This can be useful in case the remote peer uses a public IP as an IPSec peer IP but also advertises the subnet this peer's public IP belongs to inside the tunnel, which could cause routing issues.

- **Withdraw Static Routes if Service Connection or Remote Networks IPSec tunnel is down**: By default, static routes configured on RN-SPN or SC-CAN tunnels will remain in the routing table even when the associated connection is down. Enabling this feature will remove the static routing and sessions may take an alternative path to the same destination.

- **Backbone Routing**: You have three options under this:

  - **Disable Asymmetric routing for Service Connections** requires any given session to flow only via one service connection.

  - **Allow Asymmetric routing for Service Connections** can be enabled in case packets may egress and ingress via different service connections. This could be due to hot potato routing, or routing preferences on the customer backbone.

  - **Allow Asymmetric routing and load sharing across Service Connections** can be enabled when multiple SC-CANs are bundled to increase bandwidth towards a single data center.

- **Outbound Routes for the Service** lets you set up to 500 IP subnets that will be installed on all SPNs and CANs as routes directly to the internet.

- **Traffic Steering** is a policy-based forwarding adaptation inside Prisma Access that lets you forward sessions that match a traffic steering rule directly to a service connection, bypassing all routing.

The default **Advanced Settings** should look like the following screenshot:

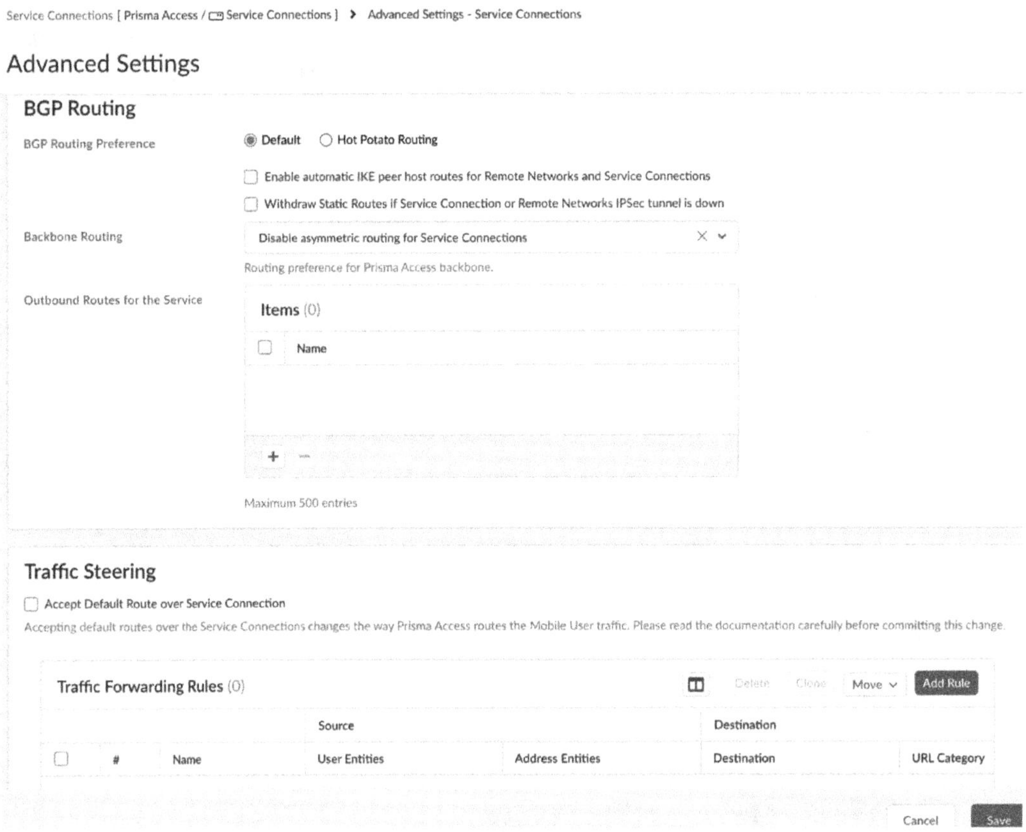

Service Connections [Prisma Access / ▢ Service Connections] ▶ Advanced Settings - Service Connections

Advanced Settings

BGP Routing

BGP Routing Preference	◉ Default ○ Hot Potato Routing
	☐ Enable automatic IKE peer host routes for Remote Networks and Service Connections
	☐ Withdraw Static Routes if Service Connection or Remote Networks IPSec tunnel is down
Backbone Routing	Disable asymmetric routing for Service Connections ✕ ⌄
	Routing preference for Prisma Access backbone.

Outbound Routes for the Service

Items (0)

☐   Name

＋ －

Maximum 500 entries

Traffic Steering

☐ Accept Default Route over Service Connection

Accepting default routes over the Service Connections changes the way Prisma Access routes the Mobile User traffic. Please read the documentation carefully before committing this change.

Traffic Forwarding Rules (0)   ▥   Delete   Clone   Move ⌄   Add Rule

			Source		Destination	
☐	#	Name	User Entities	Address Entities	Destination	URL Category

Cancel   Save

Figure 4.3 – Advanced Settings

Click **Cancel** to leave this page, or **Save** if you made any changes already. Let's create a service connection by clicking the **Add Service Connection** button you already saw in *Figure 4.1*:

The main page for a fresh service connection can be seen in the following screenshot:

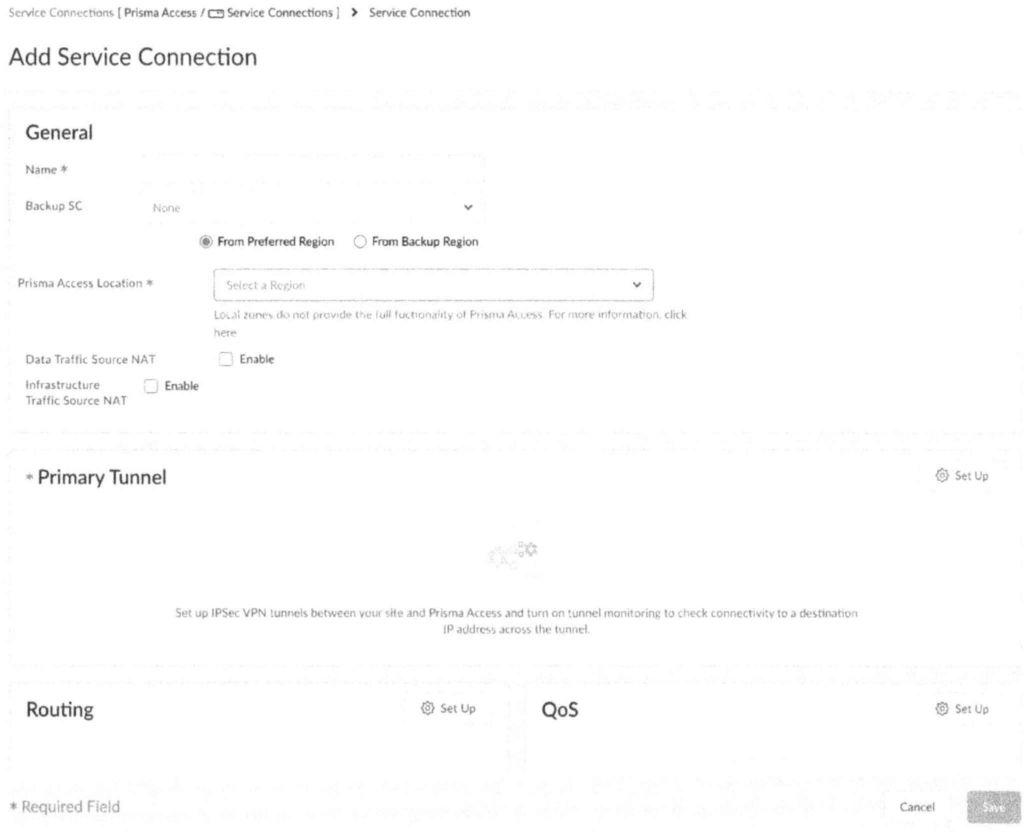

Service Connections [Prisma Access / ▭ Service Connections]   ❯   Service Connection

Add Service Connection

General		
Name *		
Backup SC	None	⌄
	◉ From Preferred Region ○ From Backup Region	
Prisma Access Location *	Select a Region ⌄	
	Local zones do not provide the full fuctionality of Prisma Access. For more information, click here	
Data Traffic Source NAT	☐ Enable	
Infrastructure Traffic Source NAT	☐ Enable	

* **Primary Tunnel**   ⚙ Set Up

Set up IPSec VPN tunnels between your site and Prisma Access and turn on tunnel monitoring to check connectivity to a destination IP address across the tunnel.

Routing   ⚙ Set Up   QoS   ⚙ Set Up

* Required Field   Cancel   Save

Figure 4.4 – Adding Service Connection

The following things can be configured:

- **Name** is a descriptive name for the service connection, such as **DC1** or **AWS-Private-Cloud**.
- **Backup SC** lets you set a fallback service connection if this service connection fails. This setting will *only* be used in case **Hot Potato Routing** is selected in **Advanced Settings**.
- **From Preferred Region** are locations in Google Cloud compute locations.
- **From Backup Region** will show you a list of locations AWS compute locations.

- **Prisma Access Location** lets you choose in which of the 114 locations this service connection needs to be deployed. **Data Traffic Source NAT** is used in traffic steering. Without NAT enabled, the dedicated service connection for traffic steering will use the organization's source addresses while with NAT enabled the service connection will use the User-ID agent address of the service connection.

- **Infrastructure Traffic Source NAT** can be enabled to hide all infrastructure connections headed for the traffic steering dedicated service connection behind the User-ID agent of the service connection.

Next, we can start creating the IPSec connections.

Primary tunnel

To create the primary VPN connection, click **Set Up** in the **primary tunnel**. This will prompt a popup on the right side of the screen that lets you configure all the appropriate attributes for the tunnel:

- **Tunnel Name** should be a descriptive name.

- **Branch Device Type** lets you select one of several vendors for compatibility.

- **Authentication** can happen through a **preshared key** or a **certificate** that is installed on both peers in the tunnel.

- **IKE local** and **peer identification** is used as an alternative identification, which will be a necessary setting if the remote peer is, for example, behind a NAT device, is using an internal IP address in its phase1 header, or there is an IP conflict with another tunnel. This setting is not strictly necessary if the remote peer has a public IP.

- **Branch Device IP Address** can be a **static IP** or a **Dynamic** IP. In the case of the latter, it is advisable to select **IKE Passive Mode** so Prisma Access does not initiate connections.

- **Tunnel Monitoring** can be enabled to send pings every three seconds to a remote IP. After five failures, the tunnel will be brought down.

- **Proxy ID** can be configured to limit the subnets that are allowed to traverse the tunnel. Each Proxy ID pair will generate a set of **security associations (SAs)** for said pair of subnets. Proxy IDs may also be required when the remote peer is a policy or community-based VPN system. Route-based VPN devices are capable of setting up a tunnel without any routes needing to be provided during the negotiation phase. Policy-based VPN devices such as Cisco or Check Point VPN communities require subnet pairs to be part of the negotiation. For these latter cases, the subnet pairs can be added in the Proxy ID configuration.

In the following figure, you'll see an example configuration for a VPN tunnel to my main data center:

Figure 4.5 – Createing an IPSec tunnel

To configure the IKE parameters or IPSec Crypto map, there are two links at the bottom that will lead you to create a new profile. Let's start with **IKE Advanced Options**. The first page lets you set **IKEv1 only**, **IKEv2 preferred**, or **IKEv2 only** modes. You can also create a new IKE crypto profile. From the dropdown, you can select multiple pre-created profiles, but select **Create New** and choose your own parameters. When you click **Save**, the new profile will automatically be selected in the previous screen, so select **Save** here as well:

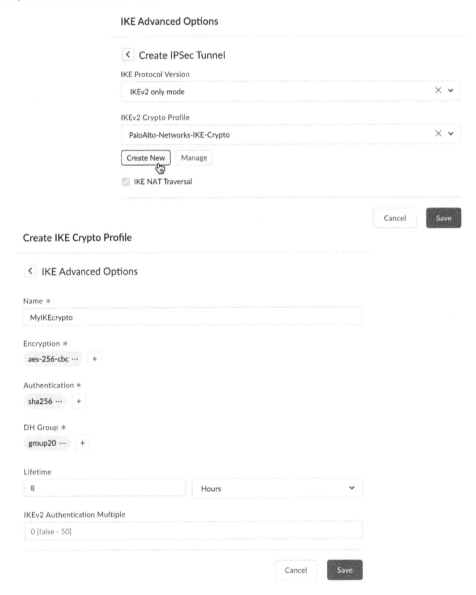

Figure 4.6 – IKE Advanced Options

When you've clicked **Save** on the **IKE Advanced Options** page, you will be taken back to the **Create IPSec Tunnel** page. Now, select the **IPSec Advanced Options** link and create a fresh IPSec Crypto profile. Click **Save** twice when you're done:

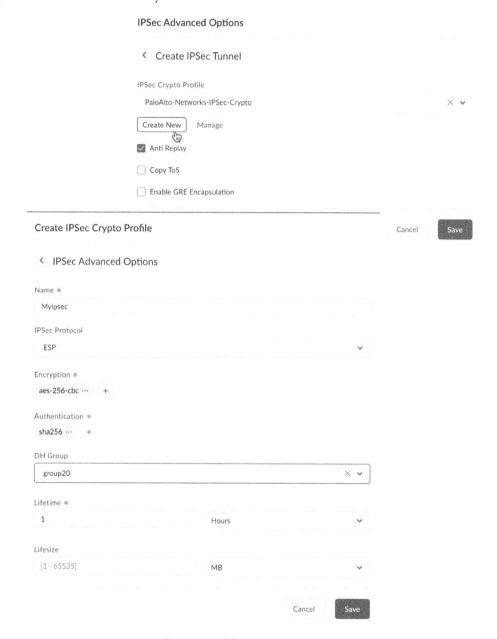

Figure 4.7 – IPSec Advanced Options

You have now configured the primary IPSec tunnel. Click **Save** again to be taken back to the service connection configuration. You will now see the first tunnel listed in the service connection and a new **Set Up Secondary Tunnel** button to create a backup tunnel. Go through the same steps as before:

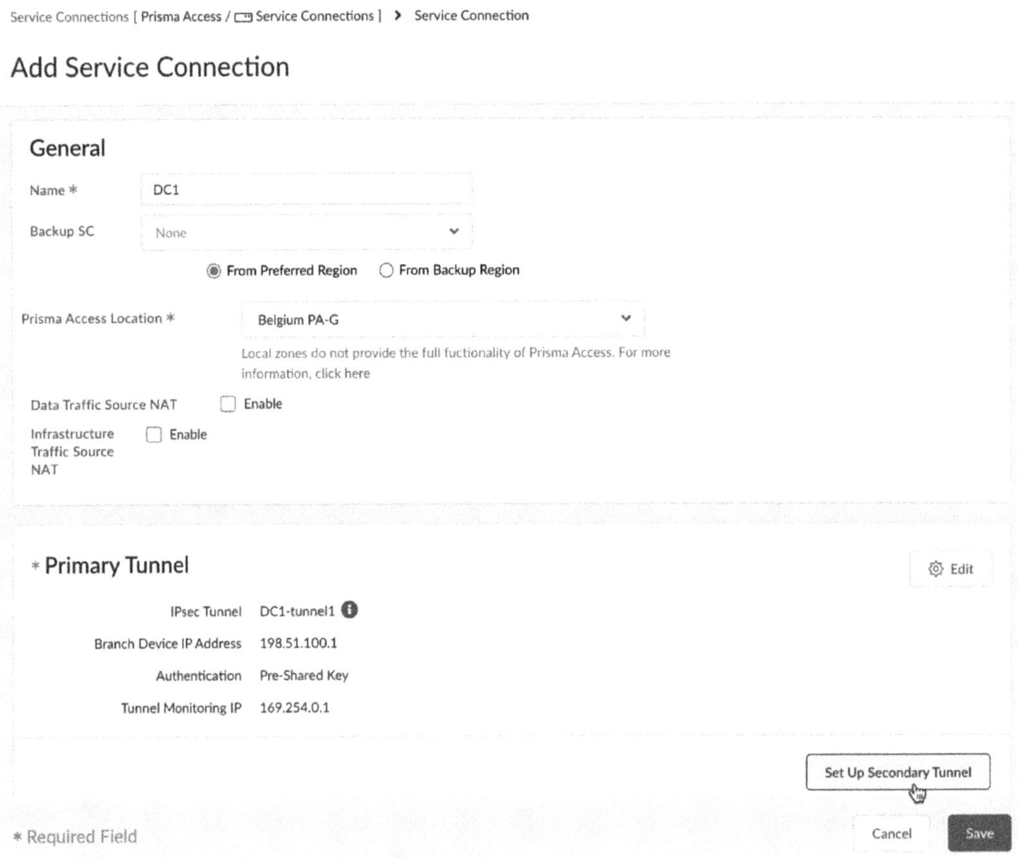

Service Connections [Prisma Access / 🖵 Service Connections] ❯ Service Connection

Add Service Connection

General

Name *	DC1
Backup SC	None ⌄

◉ From Preferred Region   ○ From Backup Region

Prisma Access Location *   Belgium PA-G ⌄

Local zones do not provide the full fuctionality of Prisma Access. For more information, click here

Data Traffic Source NAT   ☐ Enable

Infrastructure Traffic Source NAT   ☐ Enable

* Primary Tunnel   ⚙ Edit

IPsec Tunnel	DC1-tunnel1 ⓘ
Branch Device IP Address	198.51.100.1
Authentication	Pre-Shared Key
Tunnel Monitoring IP	169.254.0.1

Set Up Secondary Tunnel

* Required Field   Cancel   Save

Figure 4.8 – A service connection with one tunnel

Once the secondary tunnel has been created, your service connection should look similar to the following screenshot:

Figure 4.9 – A service connection with two IPSec tunnels

The next step is to configure routing. Click the **Set Up** button in the routing section to get into the routing configuration.

There are two routing options available. Static routes can be added for simplified routing: all sessions matching a subnet will be sent *down* a service connection toward the data center. These subnets will be distributed on the infrastructure so all other nodes are made aware that this route exists here and sessions will be routed towards this SC-CAN. Only a smaller subnet in a different SC-CAN will route traffic toward the other SC-CAN. Click the plus + button to add all the subnets that should be routed towards the data center:

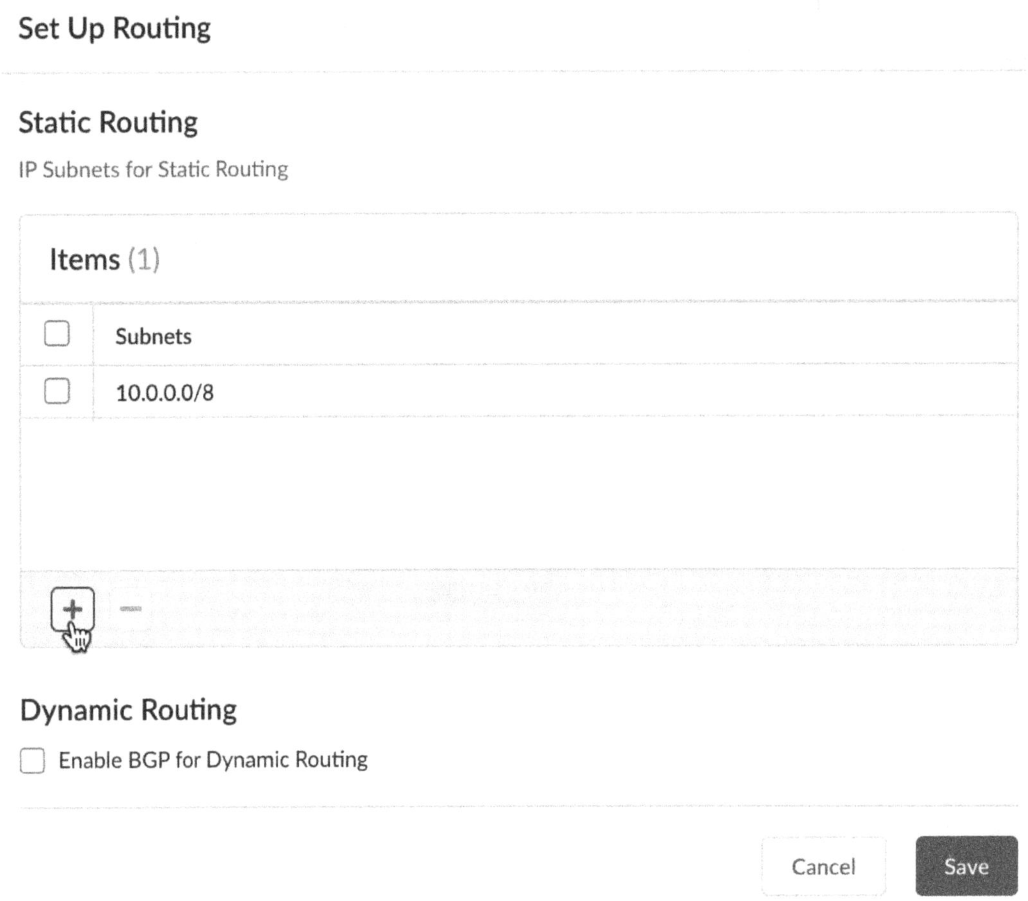

Set Up Routing

Static Routing

IP Subnets for Static Routing

Items (1)

	Subnets
☐	10.0.0.0/8

Dynamic Routing

☐ Enable BGP for Dynamic Routing

Cancel   Save

Figure 4.10 – Static Routing

The second routing option is **Dynamic Routing** using BGP. By checking the **Enable BGP for Dynamic Routing** box, the BGP options will become available.

There are a few options available that will influence the way the Prisma Access BGP peer behaves:

- **Summarize Mobile User Routes before advertising** will summarize the mobile user subnets into the larger supernets you will configure on the MU-SPN (different subnets can be configured per location or region; we'll see more about this in *Chapter 6*). Without summarization, Prisma Access will advertise individual /24 subnets.

- **Advertise Default Route**: If the data center is advertising a default route, this route can also be advertised into the infrastructure, which will make all internet-bound traffic route via this service connection instead of breaking out locally on the SPN

- **Use Different BGP Peer for Secondary Tunnel**: By default, the secondary WAN connection will simply be used as secondary transport if the primary fails, so all the BGP attributes (source IP, peer IP, AS number, etc.) remain identical. If the secondary WAN tunnel connects to a different VPN device with different IP addresses for BGP peering, this option will unlock the option to configure the secondary BGP attributes in the **Secondary WAN** tab.

- **Add No-Export Community** is disabled by default, but can be set to **Enable-in**, **Enable-out**, or **Enable-both**:

  - **Enable-in** will set no-export to routes learned from the remote peer, so they're not advertised to other SC-CAN or SPN

  - **Enable-out** will set no-export to the routes advertised to the remote peer so it doesn't share these routes further down to its peers

  - **Enable-both** will set no-export to learned and advertised routes

- To not share Prisma Access subnets with the remote peer, enable **Do Not Export Routes**. If this option is not checked, the SC-CAN will advertise all the routes it has learned from other SC-CANs, remote networks connected to RN-SPNs, and all mobile user pool subnets and local routes to the remote peer.

Configure the peer IP address and **autonomous system** (**AS**) number used by the remote peer for BGP peering. The local IP address can be any address you choose. An example BGP configuration can be seen as follows:

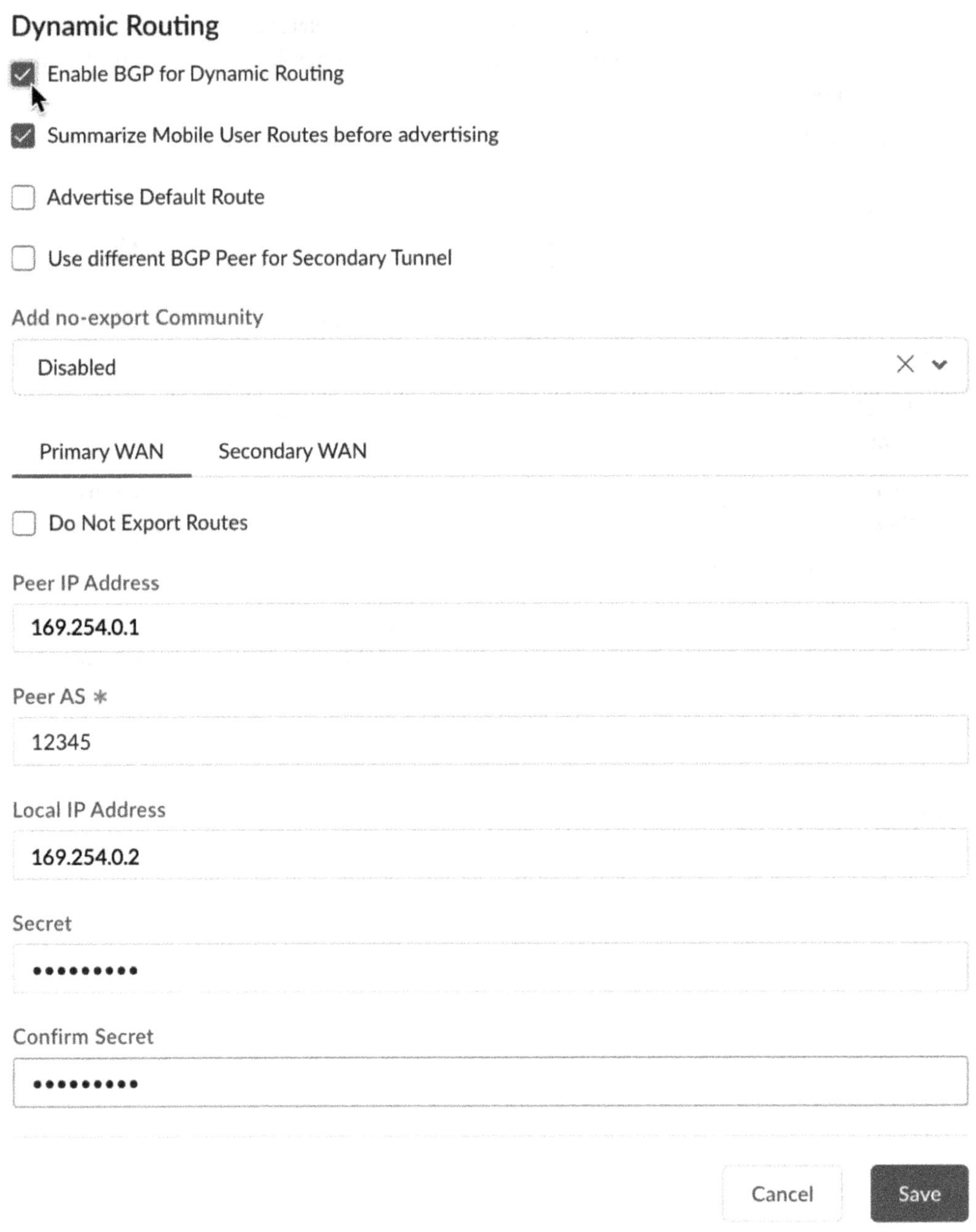

Dynamic Routing

☑ Enable BGP for Dynamic Routing

☑ Summarize Mobile User Routes before advertising

☐ Advertise Default Route

☐ Use different BGP Peer for Secondary Tunnel

Add no-export Community

Disabled	✕ ▾

Primary WAN   Secondary WAN

☐ Do Not Export Routes

Peer IP Address

169.254.0.1

Peer AS *

12345

Local IP Address

169.254.0.2

Secret

•••••••••

Confirm Secret

•••••••••

Cancel   Save

Figure 4.11 – BGP configuration

Click **Save** to save the routing configuration. If you like, you can also create a **Quality of Service** (**QoS**) profile for this service connection by clicking the **Set Up** button in the QoS section as you saw in *Figure 4.8*.

If this is the first time you have configured QoS, you'll need to create a new profile, or you can select a previously created profile if you have done this before.

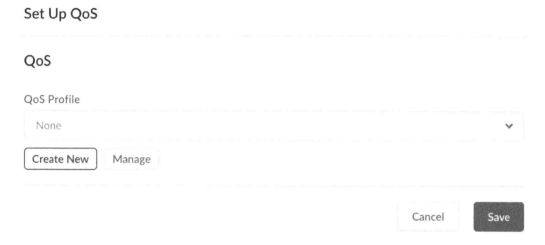

Figure 4.12 – Creating a new QoS profile

All you do next is define a profile that sets the parameters for one or more classes – these settings will be applied to certain sessions we define in QoS rules. You can create up to eight classes and set limitations and guarantees for each class, as you can see in the following screenshot:

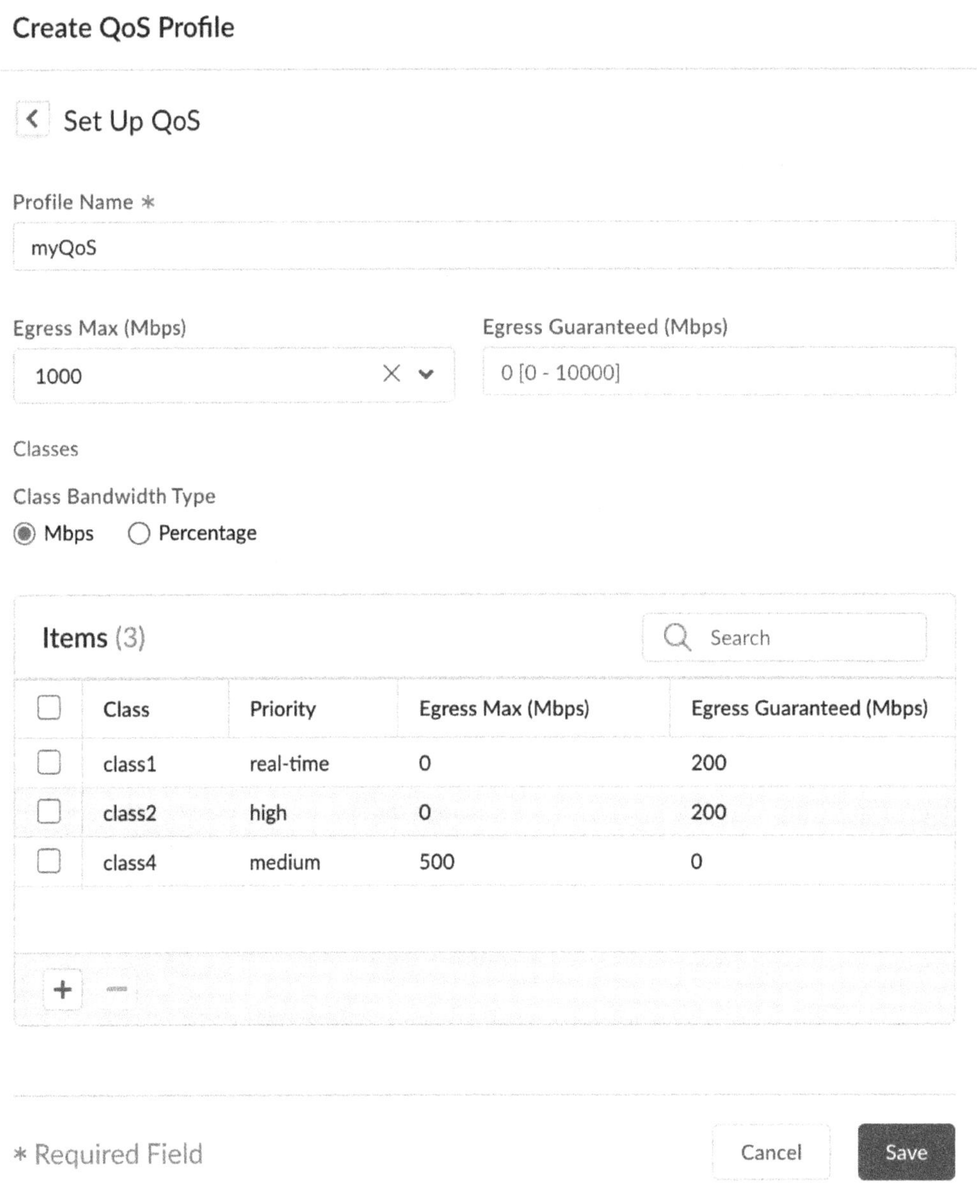

Create QoS Profile

< Set Up QoS

Profile Name *

myQoS

Egress Max (Mbps)

1000   X ˅

Egress Guaranteed (Mbps)

0 [0 - 10000]

Classes

Class Bandwidth Type

◉ Mbps   ◯ Percentage

Items (3)   Q Search

	Class	Priority	Egress Max (Mbps)	Egress Guaranteed (Mbps)
☐	class1	real-time	0	200
☐	class2	high	0	200
☐	class4	medium	500	0

\+ —

* Required Field   Cancel   Save

Figure 4.13 – QoS

You can set a maximum egress value, which limits the total throughput that will be allowed through this service connection. This can be useful if you want to use percentages for the classes, or if the remote data center has less than 1 Gbps bandwidth available.

Each of the eight classes can be set to a **low**, **medium**, **high**, or **real-time** priority. The priority will determine which session gets higher priority when queueing needs to happen due to congestion. **Egress Max** determines the total maximum bandwidth a class is allowed to consume while **Egress Guaranteed** ensures a class has access to at least the configured bandwidth.

A class with only a guarantee has exclusive access to the guaranteed bandwidth but can also use more as long as it doesn't interfere with the guarantee of other classes. As long as there are no sessions of a class that has a guarantee set, the bandwidth that would normally be reserved is available to other classes. Click **Save** to save the QoS profile, then click **Save** again to save the service connection configuration. You can now go ahead and configure the remote end.

Let's take a look at the Panorama side.

Provisioning an SC-CAN in Panorama

When configuring a service connection in Panorama, a few different steps need to be taken. The service connection itself needs to be provisioned, but the IKE Gateway and IPSec tunnel also need to be created. The latter can be accomplished by creating them from the traditional location in **Panorama** | **Templates**, or via the provisioning popup that allows you to create objects on the spot. I'll recommend creating the IKE Gateway and IPSec tunnel beforehand, so the service connection provisioning step is a little less cluttered.

First, navigate to **Templates** | **Network** and switch the template to the `Service_Conn_Template`. Next, open **Network Profiles** | **IKE Crypto**. You'll notice Palo Alto has already created a couple of default profiles for some well-known vendors, and a generic profile as you can see in the following screenshot:

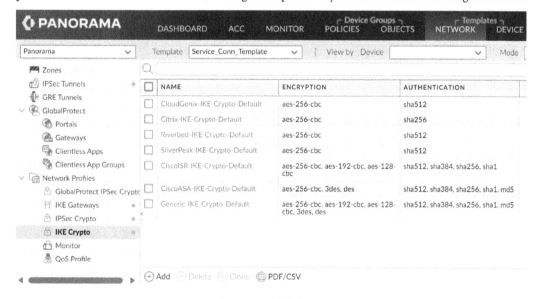

Figure 4.14 – IKE Crypto

We will, of course, create a fresh IKE Crypto profile so we can choose the best options to suit our requirements.

The following options are available:

- **DH GROUP**: 1, 2, 5, 14, 19, or 20

- **AUTHENTICATION**: non-auth, md5, sha1, sha256, sha384, or sha512

- **ENCRYPTION**: des, 3des, aes-128-cbc, aes-192-cbc, aes-256-cbc, aes-128-gcm, or aes-256-gcm

- **Lifetime**: Minimum 3 minutes, maximum 365 days (default is 8 hours)

- **IKEv2 Authentication Multiple**: 0 - 50

Select the parameters that best suit your needs:

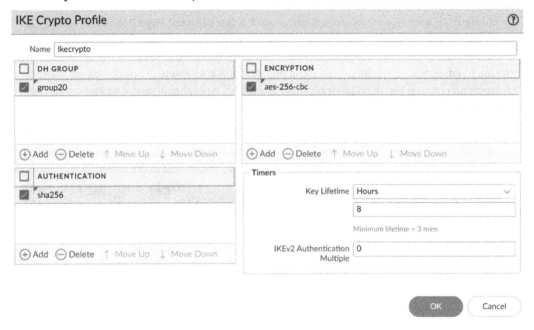

Figure 4.15 – IKE Crypto

Go ahead and also create a fresh IPSec Crypto profile in **Network Profiles | IPSec Crypto**.

The following options are available:

- **DH Group**: 1, 2, 5, 14, 19, or 20.

- **AUTHENTICATION**: non-auth, md5, sha1, sha256, sha384, and sha512.

- **ENCRYPTION**: des, 3des, aes-128-cbc, aes-192-cbc, aes-256-cbc, aes-128-gcm, and aes-256-gcm.

- **Lifetime**: Minimum 3 minutes, maximum 365 days (default is 1 hour).

- **Lifesize** is disabled by default. Can be set from 1 KB to 65535 TB. This option will trigger a rekey once a certain amount of data has been transferred rather than wait for the lifetime to expire.

Select the parameters that best suit your needs:

Figure 4.16 – IPSec Crypto

The next step is to configure the IKE Gateway that will represent the remote peer at the data center. You may need to perform this process twice if a secondary WAN link will be used for redundancy. Navigate to **Network Profiles | IKE Gateways** and you'll see several vendor templates have been prepared here as well:

Figure 4.17 – IKE Gateways

Click **Add** to create a new gateway object and provide the following information:

- A descriptive **Name**.

- Set **Version** to **IKEv1**, **IKEv2 preferred**, or **IKEv2 only**.

- **Peer IP Address Type**: **IP** or **Dynamic**. If the data center has a static IP, select **IP** and put the IP in the **Peer Address** field. Otherwise, select **Dynamic** in which case the IP field will disappear.

- **Authentication**: The default setting is a pre-shared key, which you can enter in a field right below the **Authentication** option. If you'd like to use a certificate instead, first generate and load the certificate via **Template** | **Device** | **Certificate Management** | **Certificates**.

- **Local Identification**: This can be **None**, **FQDN**, **IP Address**, **KEYID**, or **UserFQDN**. This is used to identify the Prisma Access side of the connection by a different means than the IP address used in the IKE header. In the case of a single tunnel, this can be set to **None** (default). In the case of a secondary WAN tunnel, it may be useful to set a value here as the Prisma Access side IP address will be identical for both tunnels, which may be an issue for the remote peer.

- **Peer Identification** follows the same principle as **Local Identification**. If the remote peer has a static IP address, the setting may be left in its default (**None**), but if the remote peer is behind a NAT gateway or has a dynamic IP address, an identification will be needed so Prisma Access will accept a connection with this peer.

Your gateway object should look similar to the following screenshot:

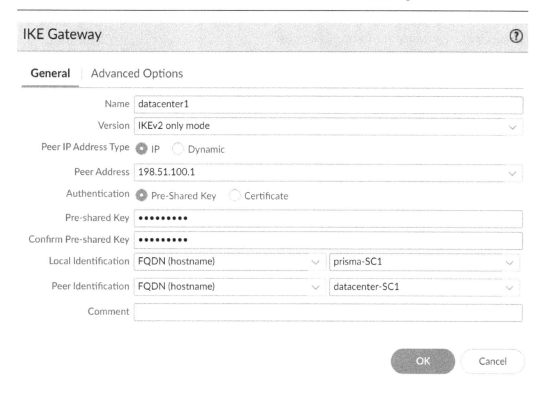

Figure 4.18 – IKE Gateway

In **Advanced Options**, you can set a few more options:

- **Enable Passive Mode** will tell Prisma Access to not initiate the IPSec connection. It will only act as a responder. This can be a useful setting in case the remote peer has a dynamic public IP address, or for troubleshooting purposes as the responder will see more detailed logs than the initiator.

- **Enable NAT Traversal** can be set to accept IKE connections over UDP/4500, which is used in case a peer is behind a NAT device.

- **IKE Crypto Profile** is where you set the crypto algorithm profile you created earlier.

- **Strict Cookie Validation** enforces the use of IKE_SA_INIT containing a cookie by the initiator. With this setting disabled (default), the initiator will only be forced to send IKE_SA_INIT containing a cookie when the number of half-open SAs exceeds the **Cookie Activation Threshold** global setting.

- **Liveness Check**: In IKEv2, each packet is a liveness check, but if the connection has been idle for the configured **Interval** number of seconds, Prisma Access will start sending empty informational packets to serve as liveness checks.

The following is an example of **Advanced Options**:

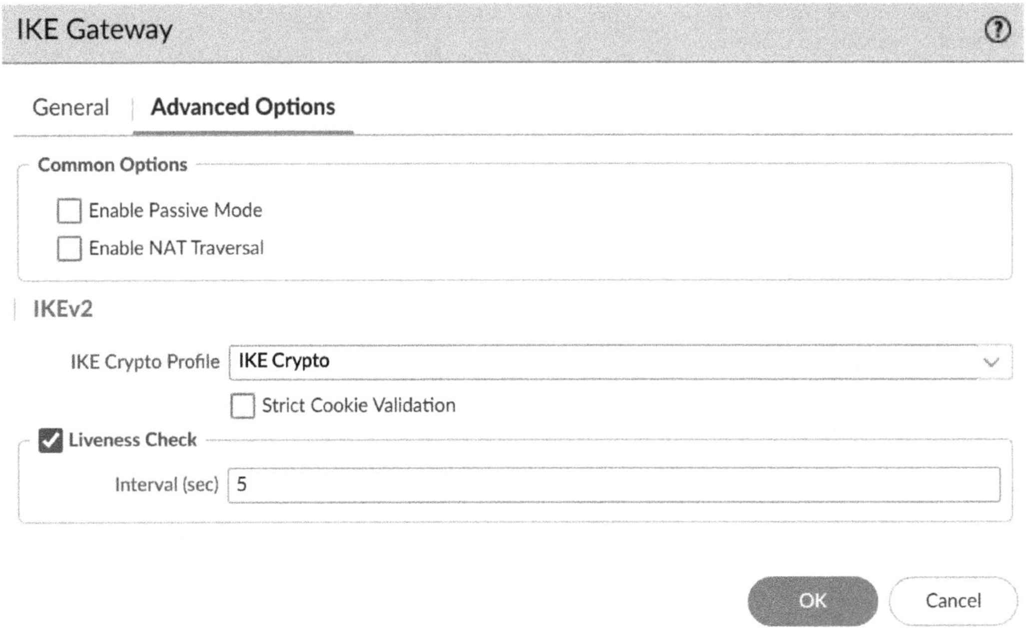

Figure 4.19 – Advanced Options

Don't forget to create a second IKE Gateway in case there will be a secondary WAN tunnel.

Once the IKE Gateway is created, the IPSec tunnel can be created. Navigate to **Templates | Network | IPSec Tunnels** where you will find the same preconfigured vendor templates we saw earlier:

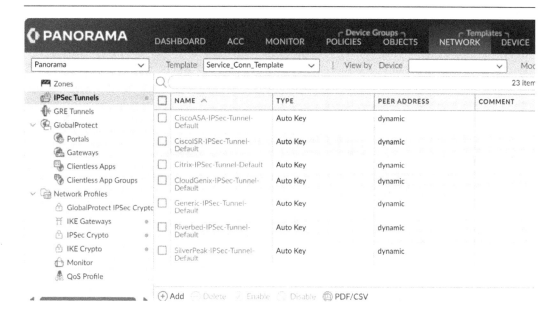

Figure 4.20 – IPSec Tunnels

Click **Add** at the bottom to create a fresh IPSec Tunnel object and fill out the following fields:

- **Name** should be an easily identifiable name.

- **Type** cannot be changed in the service connection template.

- **IKE Gateway** should be the corresponding IKE Gateway object we created earlier.

- **IPSec Crypto Profile** should be changed from **Default** to the new one we created earlier.

- **Enable Replay Protection** is enabled by default. It helps prevent replay attacks where someone who was able to intercept encrypted traffic reuses those same packets in an attempt to insert something malicious into the tunnel.

- **Type of service** (**TOS**) headers can be copied by checking the **Copy ToS Header** box so they are preserved across the tunnel, which might be useful if packet prioritization happens across the entire backbone and needs to traverse Prisma Access as well.

- **Add GRE Encapsulation** allows for a GRE header to be added for interoperability with a remote peer that requires GRE encapsulation.

- **Tunnel Monitoring** can be enabled to ping the remote peer every 3 seconds for a failure threshold of 5. This means if 5 pings are missed over 15 seconds, the tunnel will be put in a down state and failover can happen to the secondary WAN link.

> **Note**
> In Prisma Access, tunnel monitoring uses the same source IP address for all tunnels. This is usually the last IP on the infrastructure subnet. The destination IP can be anything the remote peer supports.

Your IPSec Tunnel object should look similar to the following screenshot:

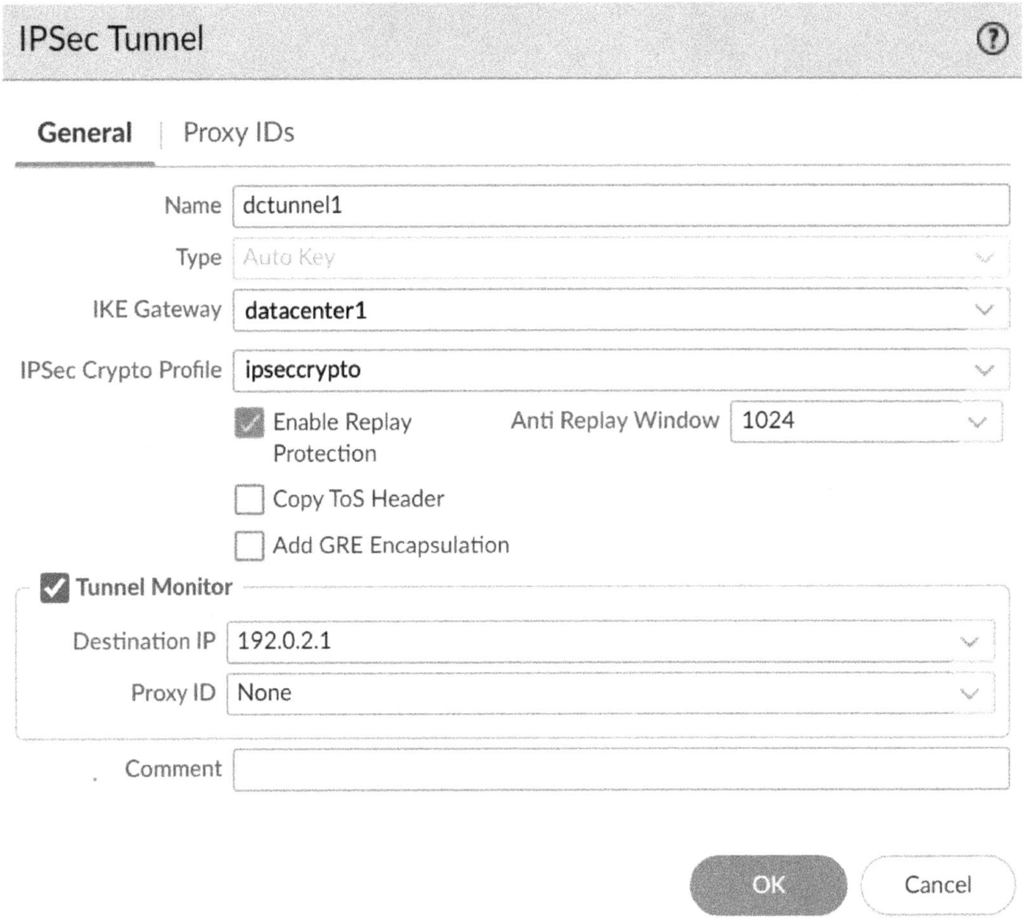

IPSec Tunnel   ⑦

General | Proxy IDs

Name	dctunnel1
Type	Auto Key ⌄
IKE Gateway	datacenter1 ⌄
IPSec Crypto Profile	ipseccrypto ⌄

☑ Enable Replay Protection   Anti Replay Window `1024` ⌄

☐ Copy ToS Header

☐ Add GRE Encapsulation

☑ **Tunnel Monitor**

Destination IP	192.0.2.1 ⌄
Proxy ID	None ⌄

Comment	

OK   Cancel

Figure 4.21 – Creating an IPSec Tunnel object

Repeat the process if you want to create a secondary WAN (backup) tunnel.

The next step is to create the actual service connection, so navigate to **Panorama | Cloud Services | Configuration | Service Connection**. You'll get an overlay that shows you where to configure things. Close the overlay and you'll land on the **Service Connection Onboarding** page:

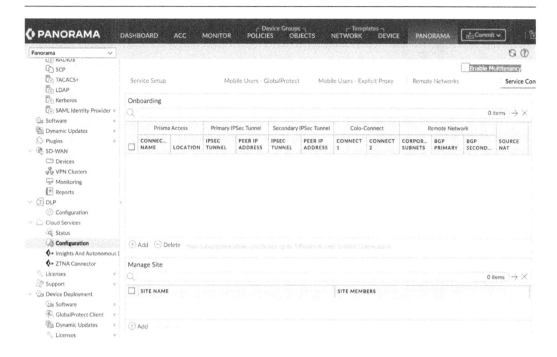

Figure 4.22 – Service Connection Onboarding

Click the **Add** button to onboard a new service connection. You will get a popup where you can configure all the parameters for the service connection:

- **Name**: Give the service connection a descriptive name.

- **Location**: Select the compute node region where the SC-CAN should be deployed. Place the SC-CAN as close to the data center location as possible. For cloud environments, verify the region of your cloud tenant so the SC-CAN can be deployed in or close to the same region.

- **IPSec Tunnel** will be the primary VPN tunnel used by the service connection to pass traffic to and from the connected data center.

- **Backup SC** selects a backup SC-CAN for hot potato routing.

- **Enable Secondary WAN** can be enabled to set a backup tunnel in case the primary tunnel fails.

- **Enable Data Traffic Source NAT** will NAT all the mobile user IP pool subnets and will prevent advertising all these subnets to the data center.

- **Enable Infrastructure Traffic Source NAT** will NAT all connections originating from an infrastructure IP so the infrastructure subnet does not need to be advertised to the data center.

- **IP Pool** is the pool of IP addresses that will be used in case one or both of the NAT options are enabled.

- **Static Routes** allows you to set static routes for any subnet hosted at the data center.

The onboarding popup should look similar to the following screenshot:

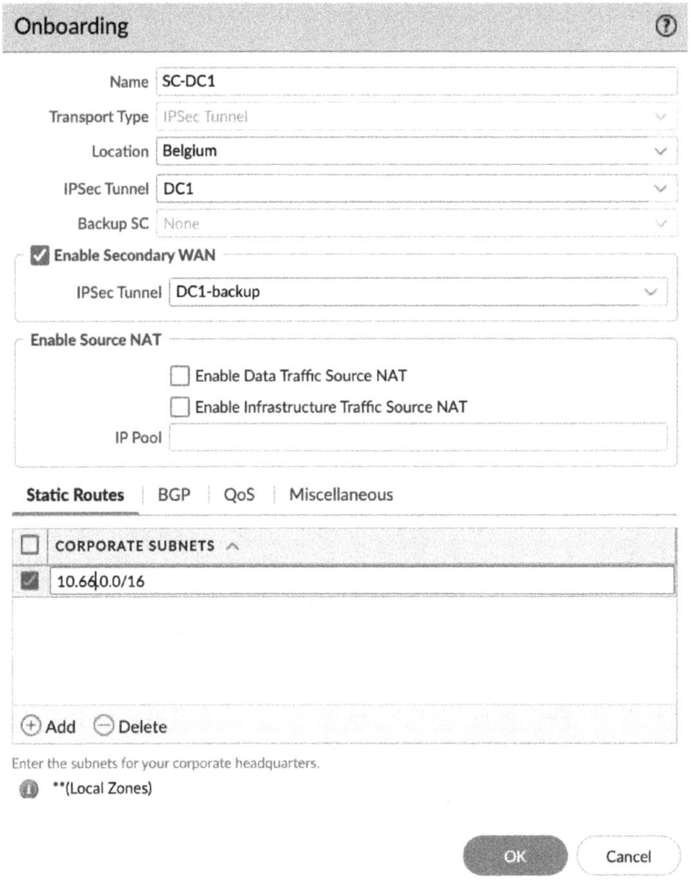

Figure 4.23 – Onboarding a service connection

Instead of or in addition to static routing, you can enable BGP dynamic routing to dynamically distribute routing information into or out of your data center. The following configuration options are available:

- **Add no-export community** is disabled by default but can be enabled on the outbound redistribution.

- **Summarize Mobile User Routes before advertising** will summarize the mobile user IP pool addresses into their regional subnets rather than individual /24 subnets.

- **Don't Advertise Prisma Access Routes** will prevent the Prisma Access BGP peer from advertising routes toward the data center.

- **Exchange IPv4 routes over IPv4 peering** is the default setting for an IPv4-only environment. If IPv6 should also be included, this setting can be changed to **Exchange IPv4 routes over IPv4 peering and IPv6 routes over IPv6 peering** or in an IPv6-only environment (or, for example, where IPv4 routes are static and IPv6 are set up via BGP), this can be changed to **Exchange IPv6 routes over IPv6 peering**.

Fill out the **Primary WAN** information, such as the peer AS and peer and local IP addresses. If a secondary WAN tunnel is configured, by default the **Same as Primary WAN** box will be checked. Uncheck it if the secondary tunnel uses different parameters. A typical BGP configuration for a service connection will look like the following screenshot:

Figure 4.24 – BGP configuration

In the **QoS** tab, you can enable QoS and add a profile that defines limits and guarantees for up to eight classes. Following is an example of a QoS profile that defines three different classes with two having a guaranteed reservation of 200 Mbps and class4, which is the default class for all traffic, being limited to 400 Mbps combined maximum:

Figure 4.25 – The QoS tab

Lastly, in the **Miscellaneous** tab, you can select **Disable Traffic Logging on Service Connection**. This setting should only be enabled in case asymmetric flows between multiple SC-CANs are generating excessive logs:

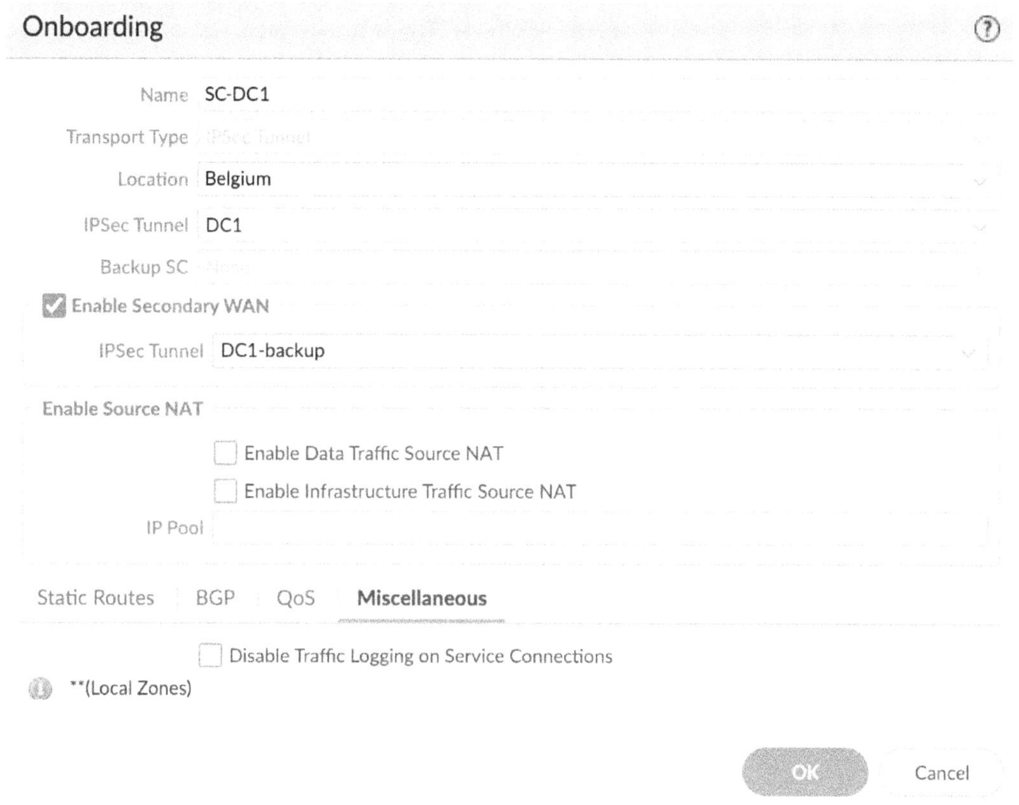

Figure 4.26 – The Miscellaneous tab

To commit these changes and provision the SC-CAN, click **Commit | Commit and Push**. In the **Commit and Push** popup, click **Edit Selections** to alter the **Push Scope Selection** settings. There, navigate to the **Prisma Access** tab and make sure the **Service Setup** box is checked. Click **OK** and then **Commit and Push**; the SC-CAN will now start the provisioning process. At this time, you can go grab a coffee as the process of provisioning a new compute node can take up to an hour:

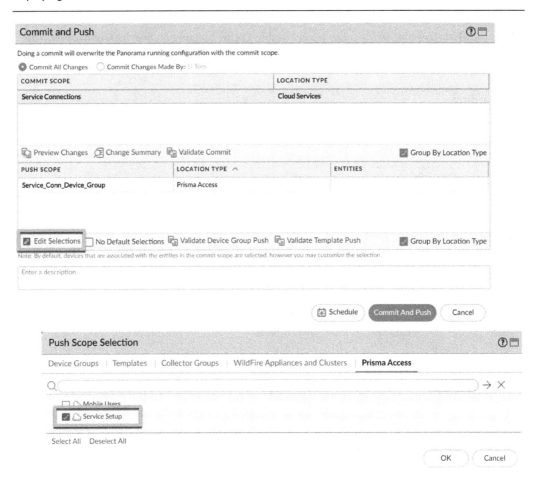

Figure 4.27 – Commit and Push

You can keep track of the provisioning process in the **Status** tab of **Cloud Services**. Once provisioning is completed, your status screen should look similar to the following screenshot:

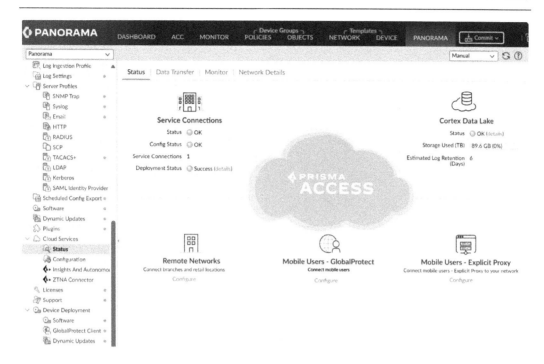

Figure 4.28 – Cloud Services | Status

You have now set up your first service connection. You can repeat the process for any additional SC-CANs you need to deploy.

Summary

In this chapter, we learned how to set up service connections or SC-CANs via cloud management and via Panorama. Service connections are used to connect your data center or cloud environment to the Prisma Access infrastructure so mobile users, remote networks, and even other data centers can access resources hosted in the data center.

Each service connection has 1 Gbps of bandwidth available, and multiple SC-CANs can be combined to increase the bandwidth for a given data center. SC-CAN does not have security enforcement, so the remote peer should ideally be an NGFW so security policies can be applied there.

In the next chapter, we will be learning about RN-SPN, which enables branch offices to be connected to the cloud and leverage the service connections to access private applications, and have secured, local, internet breakout.

Part 2: Configure Mobile User and Remote Network Security Processing Nodes

In this part, all the functionality of Prisma Access is unlocked. This part has the following chapters:

5

Configuring Remote Network SPNs

In this chapter, we will learn about **remote network security processing nodes** (**RN-SPNs**). We'll see that there are some major differences between RN-SPNs and what we learned about SC-CANs in the previous chapter. We will learn the difference between the trust and the untrust zones and how security is applied in SPNs. This chapter will help you to understand which locations require an SC-CAN connection, an RN-SPN, or both.

In this chapter, we're going to cover the following main topics:

- Deploying RN-SPNs in Strata Cloud Manager
- Deploying RN-SPNs in Panorama

Technical requirements

For this chapter, a basic working experience with Palo Alto firewalls is helpful, as topics such as security zones and IPSec configuration will be very similar to what is configured on the hardware of a VM firewall.

Before we can get started, we need to verify if the appropriate licenses have been attached to the tenant so that RN-SPNs can be spun up. On the Strata Cloud Manager, the licenses are listed on the **Overview**, which is the first page you see when you access `https://stratacloudmanager.paloaltonetworks.com/`.

At the bottom right side, you should see an allotment of Mbps, which can be used for RN-SPNs. The screenshot below shows a tenant that has 200 Mbps available for remote networks:

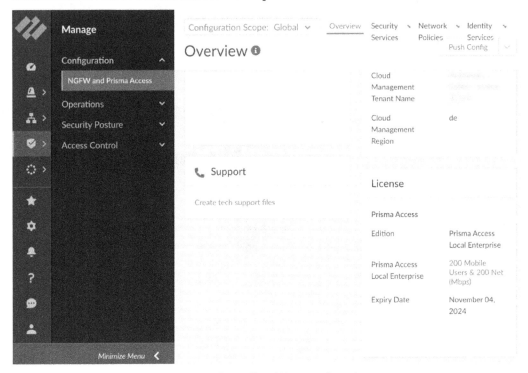

Figure 5.1 – Strata Cloud Manager Overview

In Panorama, you can find the licenses in **Panorama | Licenses**.

The following is a screenshot of licenses in Panorama:

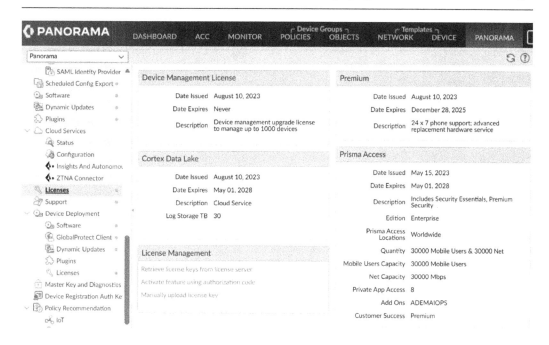

Figure 5.2 – Licenses in Panorama

Depending on the bandwidth you have available and the locations you want to deploy remote networks, the available quota may need to be distributed across different locations.

Each location that is onboarded will share its allotted bandwidth across all connected remote network connections. If, for example, Belgium is onboarded with 600 Mbps and five branch offices are connected to the RN-SPN, all five branch offices will share the full bandwidth. As we saw in *Chapter 1*, if more than 1,000 Mbps is assigned to a location, multiple RN-SPNs will be deployed, and the bandwidth will be divided evenly among the nodes. In this case, each branch office connection will need to be assigned to one of the available RN-SPN, also referred to as **IPSec termination nodes**.

Deploying RN-SPNs in Strata Cloud Manager

Before we can start establishing a connection with a branch office, we first need to assign bandwidth to a location. Once the bandwidth is assigned, a new RN-SPN will be spun up. This process usually takes around 45 minutes to complete but could take longer.

Assigning bandwidth to a location

The following is an example of bandwidth assigned to Belgium and Europe West in the Strata Cloud Manager in **Workflows | Prisma Access Setup | Remote Networks | Bandwidth Management**. Each location was given 50 Mbps, which is the minimum bandwidth you can assign to any location:

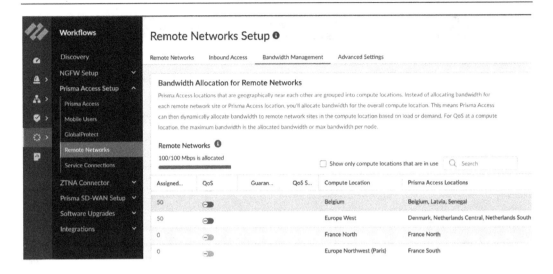

Figure 5.3 – Assigning bandwidth in Strata Cloud Manager

To add bandwidth to a location, search for the desired country and click the blue **0**. Input the desired bandwidth allotment and hit the *enter* key to confirm your configuration. The new location will now become available when you go to onboard a new remote network. If you want to decommission a location, simply set the bandwidth back to 0 and press the *enter* key. You will now be asked which node in that region to decommission.

Now that the bandwidth is assigned, we can move on to the advanced settings, where we can determine how DNS behaves.

Exploring advanced settings

Before we configure our first remote network, we can take a look at the advanced options to set up a **DNS proxy** for our remote networks. This will allow a remote network to subscribe to an internal DNS server that you control in the Prisma Access environment. So, internal domains are resolved by a corporate DNS server in a data center (routed via a service connection), and internet domains are resolved by a public DNS server.

As you can see in the following screenshot, the default configuration contains a **Worldwide** configuration with only the **Public Domains** column configured with the two Prisma Access default DNS servers. No configuration has been set yet in the **Internal Domains** section:

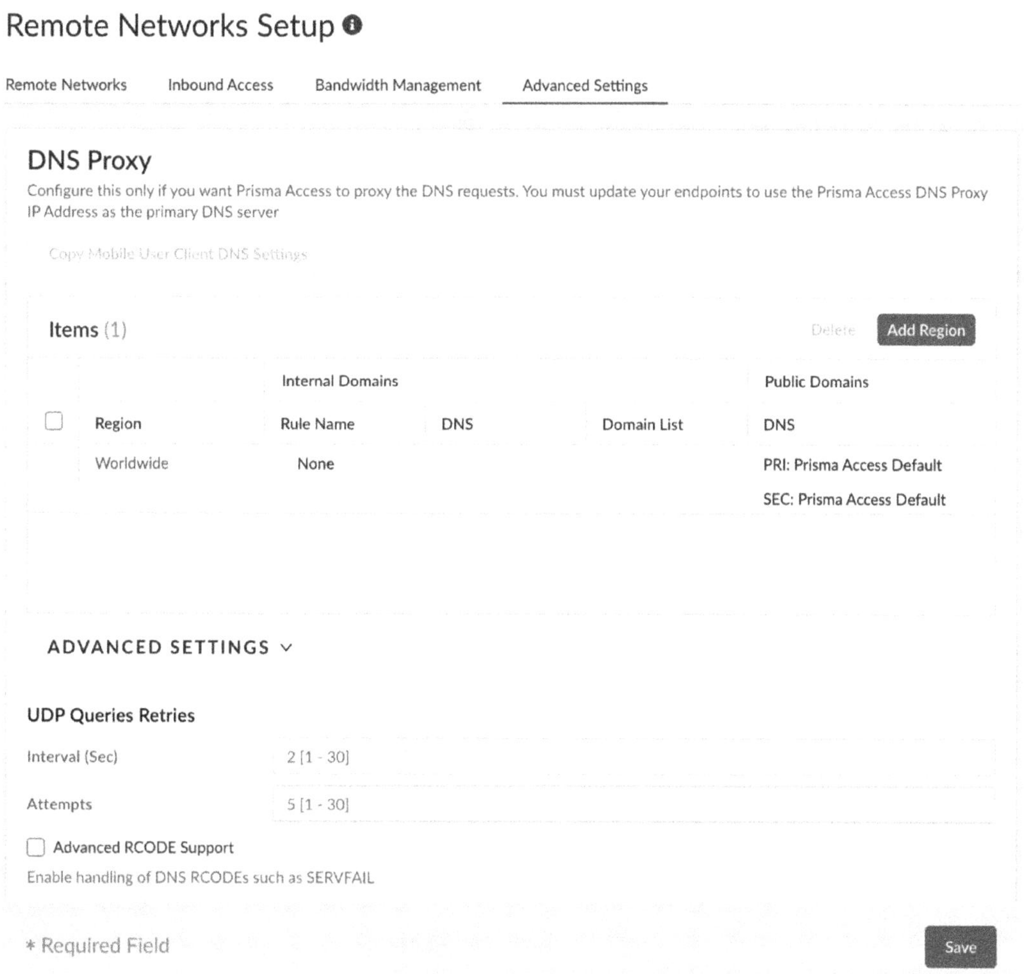

Remote Networks Setup ⓘ

Remote Networks   Inbound Access   Bandwidth Management   Advanced Settings

DNS Proxy

Configure this only if you want Prisma Access to proxy the DNS requests. You must update your endpoints to use the Prisma Access DNS Proxy IP Address as the primary DNS server

Copy Mobile User Client DNS Settings

Items (1)   Delete   Add Region

		Internal Domains			Public Domains
Region	Rule Name	DNS	Domain List	DNS
Worldwide	None			PRI: Prisma Access Default
				SEC: Prisma Access Default

ADVANCED SETTINGS ∨

UDP Queries Retries

Interval (Sec)   2 [1 - 30]

Attempts   5 [1 - 30]

☐ Advanced RCODE Support
Enable handling of DNS RCODEs such as SERVFAIL

* Required Field   Save

Figure 5.4 – Remote network DNS proxy configuration

The available choices are to configure a singular, **Worldwide** configuration that will apply to all remote sites. Apart from that, we can set one worldwide setting that applies to most regions and then create a specific, new regional configuration that changes the behavior only in a specific region. This can be useful if, for example, the same intranet **fully qualified domain names** (**FQDNs**) are used worldwide. However, each region uses a different set of servers and a different DNS server. As you can see in the following example, I've created a custom setting for **Africa, Europe & Middle East** (**EMEA**) to redirect DNS queries for pangurus.com and pangurus.lab to two internal DNS servers: 10.0.0.0.53 and 10.0.1.53.

Any DNS lookups for public records will be redirected to the default public DNS servers, but these can also be changed to an internal DNS server or a specific public DNS server if there is a preference:

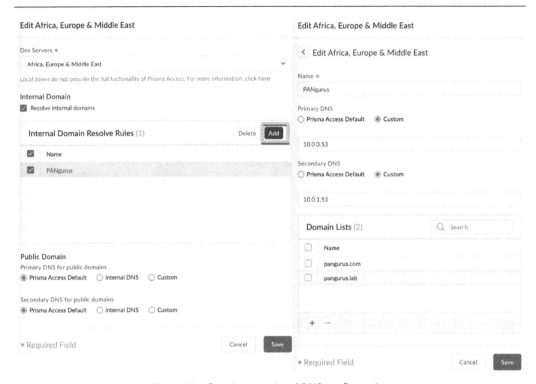

Figure 5.5 – Creating a regional DNS configuration

This will allow you to fully control the user experience globally or in individual regions. Currently, there are three major regions (Americas, EMEA, and Asia Pacific) and about 23 **compute nodes** with which to set the regional configuration. Once the DNS configuration has been set, we can go ahead and configure the first tunnels.

Configuring remote network tunnels

Now that one or more locations have been onboarded, we can start creating remote network connections. Go to **Workflows | Prisma Access Setup | Remote Networks | Remote Networks** and click **Add Remote Networks**.

You'll need to set the following things:

- **Site Name** can be any descriptive name for the remote network, such as the office location or a partner name.

- **Prisma Access Location** needs to be one of the countries to which you assigned bandwidth.

- **IPSec Termination Node** will be one of the RN-SPN nodes that was spun up after assigning bandwidth to a location. Depending on the volume of bandwidth you have assigned, more than one node may be available from the dropdown. You'll notice that the node is named as the location, followed by a type of fruit. This is the standard naming convention for all RN-SPNs spun up in Prisma Access.

- **Equal cost multi-path** (**ECMP Load balancing**): If left as **None**, you will be able to create a primary tunnel and a backup tunnel. If a site needs more bandwidth towards the internet (ECMP is only supported for internet traffic), setting ECMP to **Enabled** will allow the creation of up to four tunnels, where bandwidth is shared across all tunnels. If you set ECMP to **Enabled**, keep the following in mind:

  - ECMP is only supported for internet-bound connections.

  - **Border gateway protocol** (**BGP**) must be configured on remote networks that have been set to ECMP mode; **static routes are not supported**.

  - Tunnel monitoring should be disabled; link failover is controlled by BGP. The RN-SPN-side BGP peer will use a default **HoldTime** (the time before a route is removed when a tunnel is down) of 90 seconds but will adopt the value set on the remote peer. Consider lowering the HoldTime to 30 seconds and a **KeepAlive** of 10 seconds on the on-premises peer to improve failover time.

You will see a page similar to the following screenshot:

Add Remote Networks

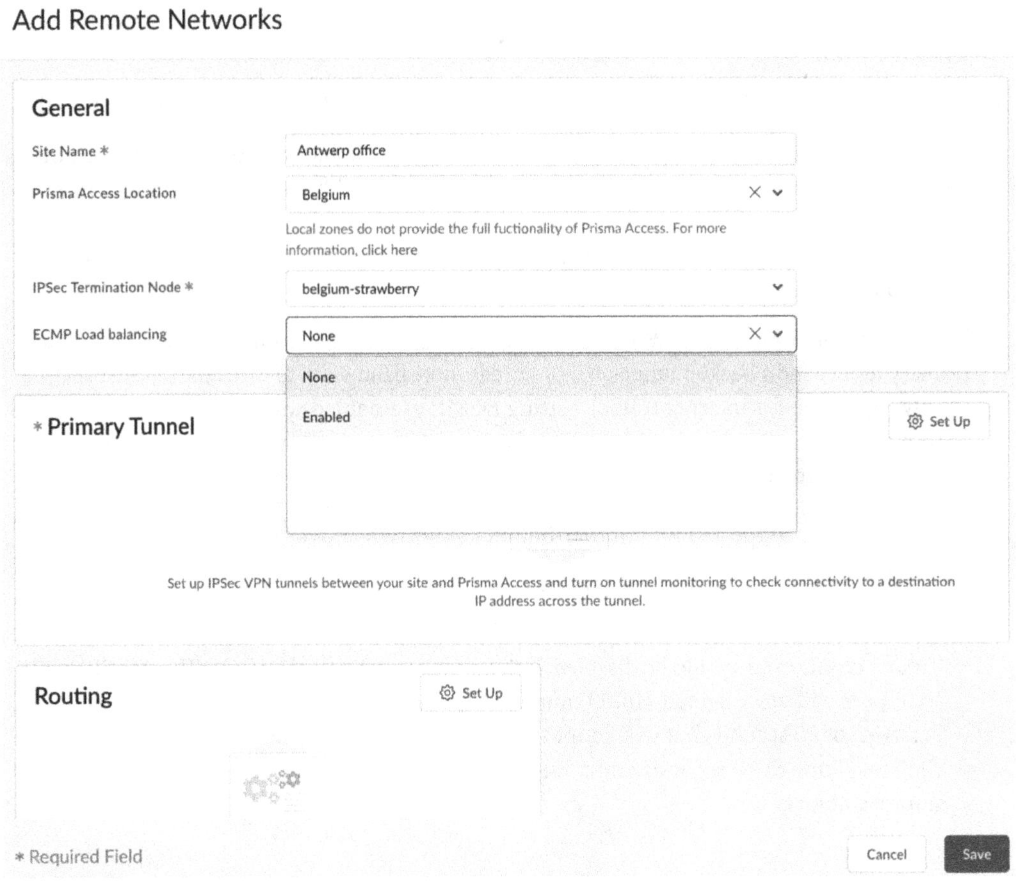

Figure 5.6 – Creating a remote network

When **ECMP Load balancing** is left as **None**, you can configure a **Primary Tunnel** by clicking the **Set Up** button.

When **ECMP Load Balancing** is **Enabled**, the name will change, and you will see **Tunnel 1** instead of **Primary**, indicating you can configure multiple active tunnels. An example of what you would see is shown in the following screenshots. On the left, we see the **Primary Tunnel** indicator; on the right, we have ECMP enabled so that we see **Tunnel 1**:

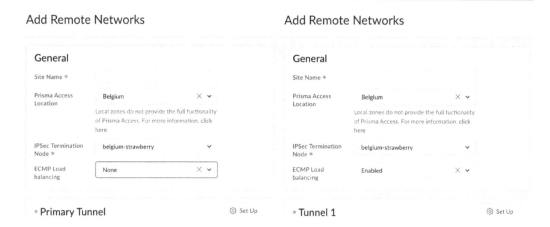

Figure 5.7 – ECMP disabled and enabled

Once you've chosen whether you need ECMP or not, you can start configuring the IPSec tunnel by clicking **Set Up**. You will see the basic configuration screen where you fill out the tunnel attributes:

- **Tunnel Name** should be a descriptive name, clearly indicating what this tunnel will be used for (for example, officeX-Primary, locationX-tunnel1, and so on).

- **Branch Device Type** gives you the option to indicate which remote vendor device will be used. This option will preload commonly used IKE and IPSec crypto profiles for the selected vendor, ensuring easy compatibility with the most frequently used default settings.

- **Authentication** can be set to a **Pre-Shared Key** or a **Certificate**.

- **IKE Identification** is useful in cases where the remote peer is on a dynamic IP, behind a NAT device, or when multiple tunnels are connected to the same location to better identify each tunnel.

- **Branch Device IP Address** lets you set the remote IP of the branch office VPN device or allows you to switch to the Dynamic setting if the remote office does not have a static IP (dynamically assigned by their ISP).

- **IKE Passive Mode** will set the Prisma Access side tunnel to never initiate a connection, only acting as a responder. This can be useful when the remote site is not always online, for example.

- **Tunnel Monitoring** can be enabled to ensure routes are deleted when the tunnel goes down.

- **Proxy IDs** can be configured to limit which IP subnet pairs are used to negotiate security associations. Proxy IDs may be required if the remote peer used a policy-based IPSec configuration or communities instead of a route-based IPSec.

The following screenshot demonstrates a configuration for a remote office that has a dynamic public IP address:

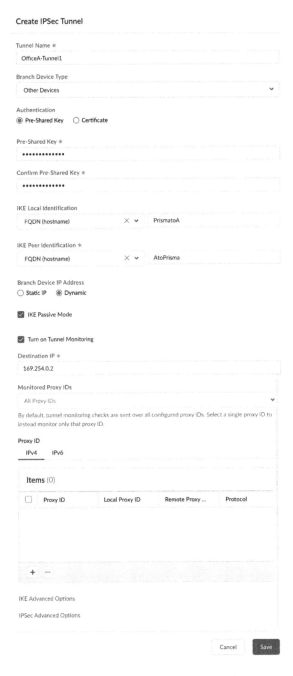

Figure 5.8 – Creating an IPSec tunnel

At the bottom of the IPSec configuration screen, we can go into the **IKE Advanced Options**, which allows us to set `IKEv1`, `IKEv2 preferred`, or `IKEv2 only`, and create a phase 1 crypto profile with the desired crypto parameters, and we can use **IPSec Advanced Options** to change the phase 2 crypto profiles:

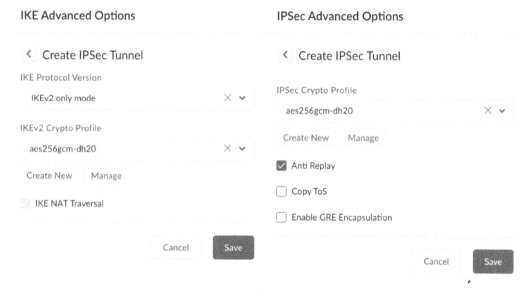

Figure 5.9 – Advanced Options

Click the **Save** button to store the new IKE **Advanced Options** and to save the **IPSec Advanced Options**. Then click **Save** once more to save the tunnel configuration.

Now that the first tunnel is configured, click **Save**, and you will return to the main screen to create the new remote network. In **Normal** mode, you can now go ahead and repeat the above process to create a backup tunnel. If ECMP is enabled, you can now create tunnels two through four:

Figure 5.10 – Creating a Secondary Tunnel or additional ECMP-enabled tunnels

After all the tunnels have been configured, routing needs to be configured so subnets are exchanged via dynamic routing or a remote subnet is set via a static route.

To start configuring routing, click the **Set Up** button next to routing (as you saw in *Figure 5.6*). The default routing configuration will look like the left side of *Figure 5.11*. If ECMP was enabled for the remote network, the routing configuration would look like the right side, lacking the static routing configuration:

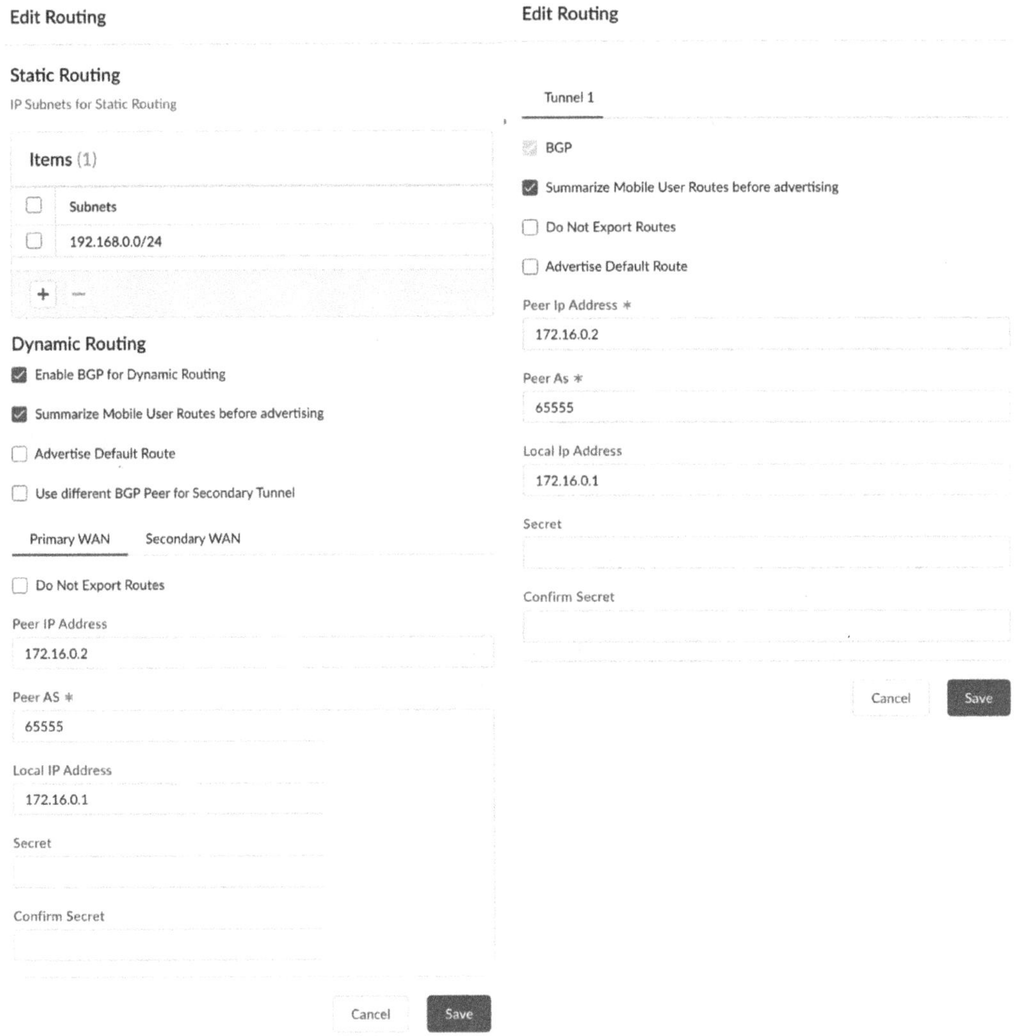

Figure 5.11 – Configuring routing

Click the **Save** button to store the **Routing** configuration, and then click on **Save** again to save the new remote network.

Since this is the first remote network, the RN-SPN still has to be spun up. Click **Push Config** and then click **Push** to open the **Push Config** dialog. Here, you can select the destination where your configuration changes need to be pushed. Because changes were made to the remote networks, this target will already be selected. Add a description of the change and click **Push** to commit the changes to Prisma Access and start the provisioning process:

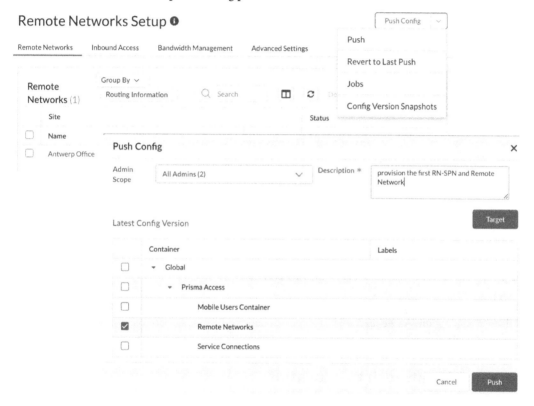

Figure 5.12 – Committing the configuration to Prisma Access

Once the Push has completed and the RN-SPN is provisioned, you will find additional information in the Remote Network Setup screen if you scroll to the right. The Service IP column will list the public IP to which the remote peer should establish its IPSec tunnel:

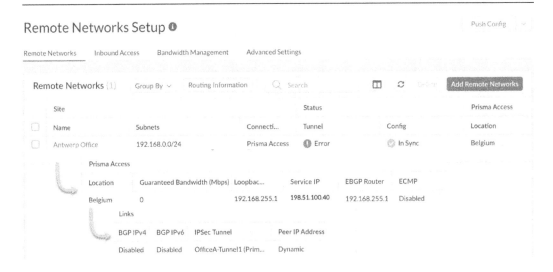

Figure 5.13 – Remote Networks details

Each RN-SPN will have one public IP to which **Remote Networks** can connect when you create multiple **Remote Networks** and attach them to the same IPSec termination node; the Service IP Column will list the same IP for all **Remote Networks**.

Let's take a look at setting up an RN-SPN via Panorama.

Deploying RN-SPNs in Panorama

Before we can start configuring IPSec tunnels to connect our remote networks, we first need to allocate bandwidth to a region. As we learned in *Chapter 1*, bandwidth is assigned to a region to deploy one or more RN-SPNs.

Assigning bandwidth to a location

Up to 1,000 Mbps assigned to a region will spin up a single node. Assigning more will provision multiple nodes and divide the assigned bandwidth evenly.

To start assigning bandwidth, navigate to **Panorama** | **Cloud Services** | **Configuration** | **Remote Networks** and edit **Bandwidth Allocation**. You will get the full list of all available locations, which you can filter by setting a preferred country name in the search field, as I have demonstrated in the following screenshot, where I filtered the output to show me Belgium so I could allocate 50 Mbps, the minimum value for a single RN-SPN:

Figure 5.14 – Allocating bandwidth

Next, we need to create security zones, which we'll use once we start building security rules. We will need two zones, one for the internet and one for internal connections.

Zone mapping

Navigate to **Templates | Network**, find **Remote_Network_Template**, open the **Zones** section, and create two zones.

As illustrated in the following figure, I created RN-Trust and RN-Untrust to signify the internal and external areas:

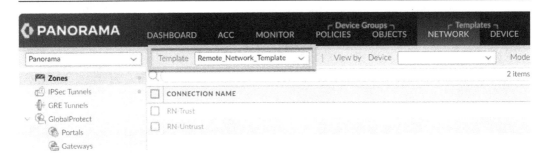

Figure 5.15 – Creating security zones

By default, any connections from or to **Remote Networks** (from or to an internal resource such as mobile users, other Remote Networks, or any data center behind a service connection) will be mapped as **RN-Trust to RN-Trust** in a security rule. Any connections that get routed out to the internet would be mapped as **RN-Trust to RN-Untrust**. In short, anything that stays inside the organization will be **RN-Trust to RN-Trust**, and anything going out to the internet is **RN-Trust to RN-Untrust**.

To achieve this, we also need to **register** the RN-trust zone as a trusted zone. Go back to **Panorama | Cloud Services | Configuration | Remote Networks** and edit **Zone Mapping**. You'll see that both zones are in the **UNTRUSTED ZONES** column. Select your trust zone and move it to the **TRUSTED ZONES** column:

Figure 5.16 – Zone Mapping

Next, we're going to configure the general settings.

Remote Network settings

In the **Settings** tab (**Panorama** | **Cloud Services** | **Configuration** | **Remote Networks** | **Settings**), we can first configure the template stack that will be used for the remote networks; the stack and template name cannot be changed, but additional templates can be added to the stack, containing the shared configuration used in other template stacks. The **Remote_Network_Template** template will always be at the top position and cannot be moved; other templates can be moved around. All of the RN-SPNs will share the same template stack.

We can also set the **Device Group** inheritance. By default, it will be set in the **Shared Parent Device Group**, but it can be moved into a different parent. All RN-SPNs will reside in the same **Device Group**.

For **user-ID**, a master device can be assigned. This should be a device where all relevant user-to-IP mappings are available and are set to be redistributed. Alternatively, user-ID can be fetched from the **cloud identity engine** (**CIE**). We'll see CIE in more detail in *Chapter 9*.

Overlapped Subnets can be enabled to accommodate remote networks that have the same subnet. Overlapping subnets can occur when multiple branch offices use the same local subnet or when onboarding a new partner who uses the same subnet as one or more of your branch offices.

Before configuring this setting, consider the following limitations:

- Remote networks with overlapping subnets will no longer be able to establish sessions with other remote networks, mobile users, or service connections.

- Other (non-overlapping) remote networks, mobile users, or service connections will no longer be able to establish sessions with other remote networks with overlapping subnets.

- Remote networks with overlapping subnets can only connect to the internet.

- Remote networks without overlapping subnets will not be impacted by enabling this setting.

The default **Settings** page will look like the screenshot shown in the following figure:

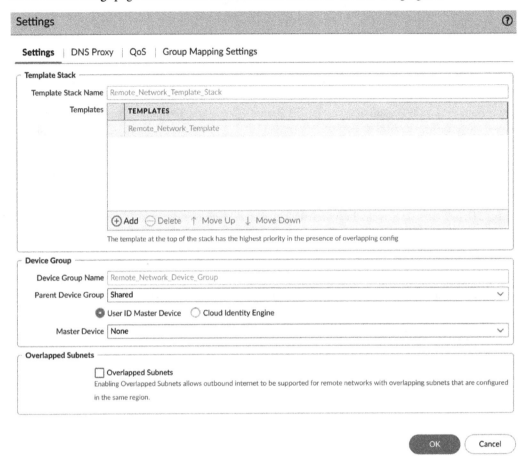

Figure 5.17 – Remote Network Settings

In the next tab, **DNS Proxy**, you can create DNS proxy rules. When a remote network is set to use the DNS proxy IP provided by Prisma Access, you can control how DNS lookups are performed by setting rules that redirect DNS lookups from internal domains to internal DNS servers. If multiple different sets of internal FQDNs exist, different rules can be created to redirect each set to a different internal DNS server without needing to configure complicated DNS settings on the client machine or in the remote network. All public DNS records will be resolved by the default public DNS server or by a server of your choice.

As you can see in the following screenshot, my DNS proxy rule is assigned to the **Worldwide** region. If different regions have different internal DNS servers, separate rules can be created for each region; so, users in the United States will be redirected to a DNS server in a US data center, and European users will be redirected to a DNS server in an EU data center to resolve internal FQDNs:

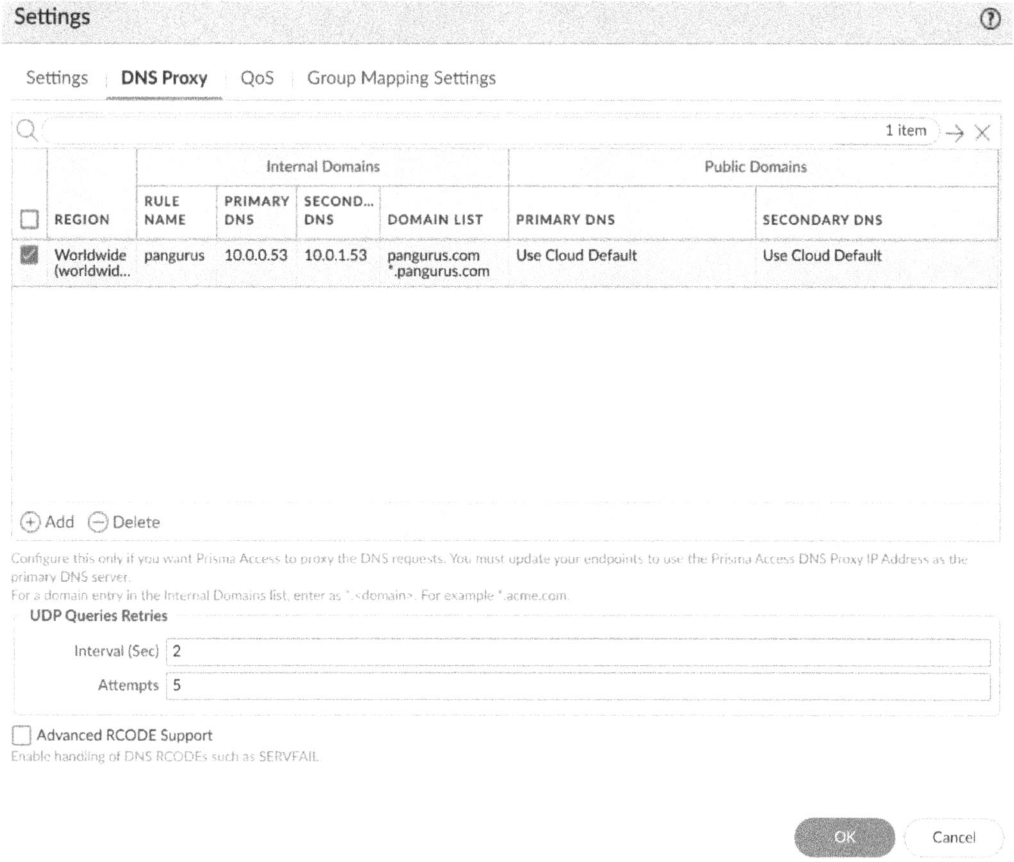

Figure 5.18 – Remote Network DNS Proxy

In the next tab, **QoS**, the quality of service can be enabled for each individual compute location. **QoS** can be used to set guarantees to ensure sufficient bandwidth is reserved for business-critical applications or impose limitations to prevent the available bandwidth from being saturated by undesirable or chatty applications:

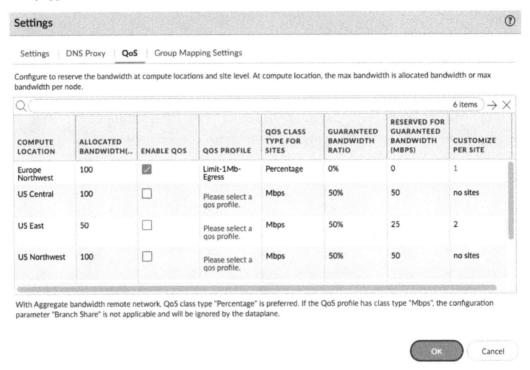

Figure 5.19 – Remote network QoS

The QoS profile can be created in **Templates | Network | Remote_Network_Template | Network Profiles | QoS Profile**.

You can limit the total bandwidth for each remote network the profile is assigned to– which can be useful to ensure no single remote network connected to an RN-SPN consumes all the bandwidth—by setting a value in **Egress Max**. Traffic can also be controlled more granularly by creating classes and setting an **Egress Max** or **Egress Guaranteed**:

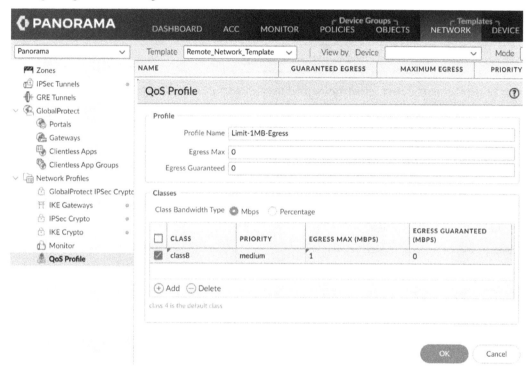

Figure 5.20 – QoS Profile

In the last tab of the remote network **Settings | Group Mapping Settings**, we can configure group mapping. This setting can be enabled to fetch active directory groups and their members, so we can build security rules based on group membership later on. In this part of the configuration, we determine which attributes need to be collected for the usernames inside the groups.

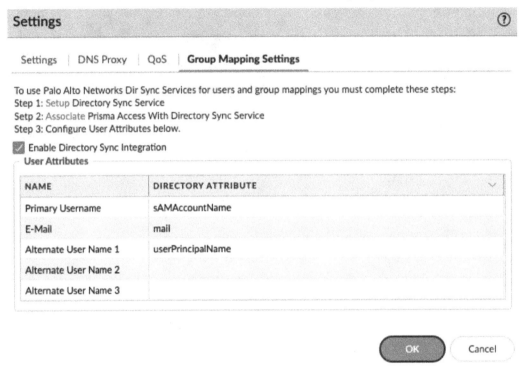

Figure 5.21 – Group Mapping Settings

Now that all the configuration has been prepared, we can start onboarding remote locations.

If you have not committed the configuration yet, you should push a commit to the remote network orchestrator so the RN-SPN to which we assigned bandwidth (earlier) can be provisioned.

Push the **Commit** button, and first commit to Panorama.

Once the commit job is completed, push **Commit** again and select **Push to Devices**. Click **Edit Selections** and open the **Prisma Access** tab. Select **Remote Networks** and click **OK**, followed by **Push**, to send the configuration up to Prisma Access.

Figure 5.22 – Push configuration to Remote networks

The process of provisioning the RN-SPN can take up to 45 minutes, so you may need to wait a bit. The provisioning progress can be seen in **Panorama | Cloud Services | Status**.

Configuring remote network tunnels

Before a remote network can be provisioned, we first need to create the IKE Gateway and IPSec Tunnel configuration. First, we will create the crypto sets for IKE (phase 1) and IPSec (phase 2) by navigating to **Templates** | **Network** | **Remote_Network_Template** | **Network Profiles** | **IKE Crypto** and **IPSec Crypto**. There are already a few preconfigured sets with common crypto settings for other vendors. However, it is recommended that you build your own crypto profiles. Whenever possible, try to use the strongest encryption that the peer will allow:

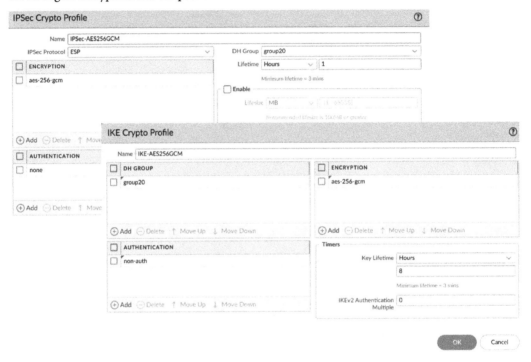

Figure 5.23 – Crypto profiles

Next, we can create the IKE Gateway in **Templates | Network | Remote_Network_Template | Network Profiles | IKE Gateways**. The IKE Gateway object contains all the configuration needed to establish an initial connection and establish Phase 1 of the IPSec negotiation:

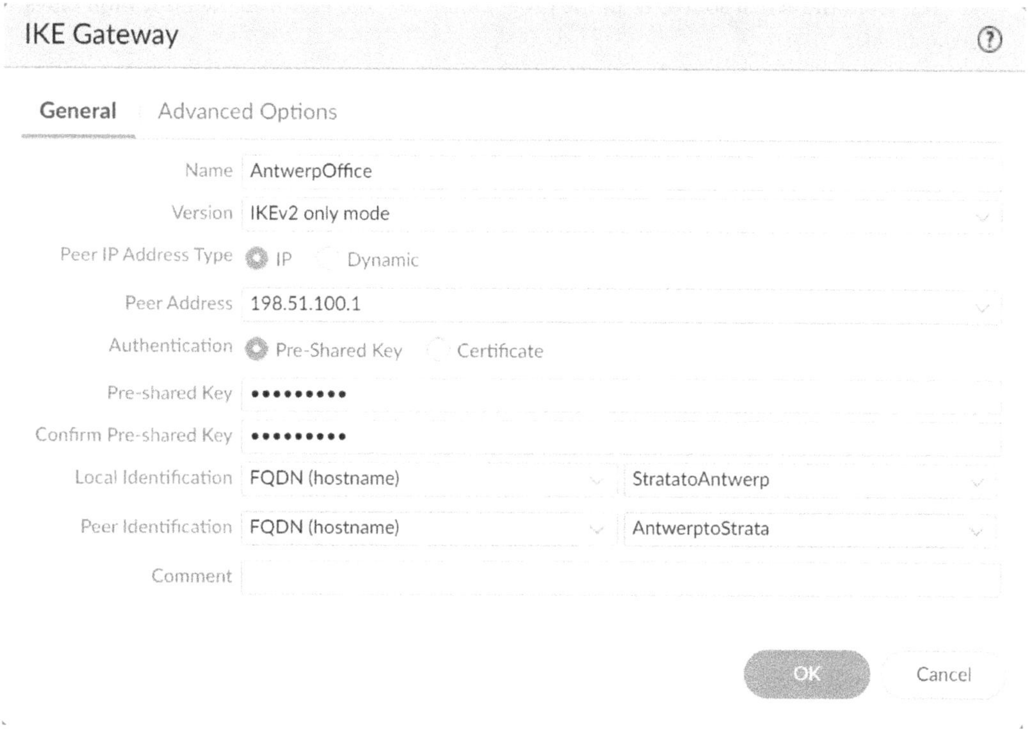

IKE Gateway   ⑦

General   Advanced Options

Name	AntwerpOffice
Version	IKEv2 only mode
Peer IP Address Type	⦿ IP ○ Dynamic
Peer Address	198.51.100.1
Authentication	⦿ Pre-Shared Key ○ Certificate
Pre-shared Key	•••••••••
Confirm Pre-shared Key	•••••••••

Local Identification	FQDN (hostname)	StratatoAntwerp
Peer Identification	FQDN (hostname)	AntwerptoStrata
Comment		

OK   Cancel

Figure 5.24 – IKE Gateway General settings

You can configure the following settings:

- **Name** should be a very descriptive name to easily identify the gateway, as you may have multiple gateway objects for the same location if you set up a secondary WAN link or load balanced connections.

- **Version** allows you to set IKEv1, IKEv2 preferred (allows downscaling to IKEv1), or IKEv2 only. It is recommended that you set the version to the IKEv2 only mode, as IKEv2 is faster, more secure, and more reliable than IKEv1.

- **Peer IP Address Type** can be set to **IP** for a peer with a static IP or to **Dynamic** for a peer who might be getting a DHCP address.

- **Authentication** can be set to **Pre-Shared Key**, or a certificate can be loaded.

- **Local** and **Peer Identification** will be useful to serve as additional identification if multiple tunnels connect to the same IP address (for example, a secondary WAN) or if the remote peer is behind a NAT gateway, causing the **security association** (**SA**) header to have a different IP address from the actual source IP in the protocol header. The following Identification types are available:

  - None

  - FQDN (hostname)

  - IP address

  - KEYID (binary format ID string)

  - User FQDN (email address).

In the **Advanced** tab, we can configure the following settings:

- **Enable Passive Mode** sets Prisma Access to only respond to incoming connections. This can be a useful setting if the remote peer is not online all the time.

- **Enable NAT Traversal** should be set if the remote peer is behind a NAT device. This allows for the use of IPSec packets over UDP 4500 instead of protocol 50.

- For IKEv1 legacy connections, we can select the **Exchange mode** to **auto**, **aggressive**, or **main**. The **auto** mode will automatically try to determine the exchange mode. The **main** mode is the most secure mode, as it encrypts the identity of both peers but requires six messages to be transmitted before peering is established. **Aggressive** mode sends the identity in clear text but only requires three messages to establish a connection. The **Main** mode may not function properly if one of the peers has a dynamic IP address.

- In the IKEv2 settings, we can enable **Strict Cookie Validation** if the remote peer supports this added security feature, and we can change the interval or disable the **Liveness** check.

- **IKE Crypto Profile** is the crypto profile that will be used for this remote peer:

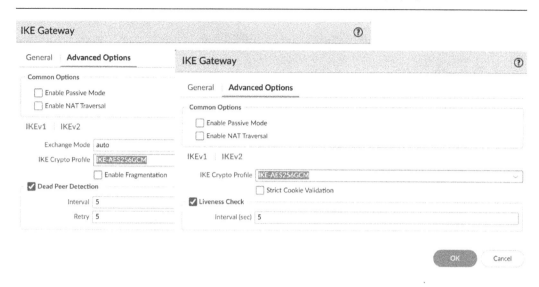

Figure 5.25 – IKE Gateway Advanced Options

Next, we need to create an IPSec Tunnel object for the phase 2 configuration for the remote network. Navigate to **Templates | Network | Remote_Network_Template | IPSec Tunnels**. Then, create a new tunnel object:

- **Name:** Select an easily identifiable name, just as we did for the IKE gateway

- **IKE Gateway:** Select the IKE Gateway you just created and one that matches this IPSec tunnel

- **IPSec Crypto Profile:** Select the new crypto profile

- **Tunnel Monitor:** Enable this if the remote side has a pingable tunnel interface (or loopback, and so on)

> **Important note**
>
> All tunnel monitoring originating from Prisma Access will use the same source IP address. So, in cases where there are multiple tunnels, such as secondary WAN links, to the same remote network, ensure there are no potential routing issues on the remote site that could cause tunnel monitoring to fail. In such cases, you may need to disable tunnel monitoring.

The following figure depicts the IPSec Tunnel configuration:

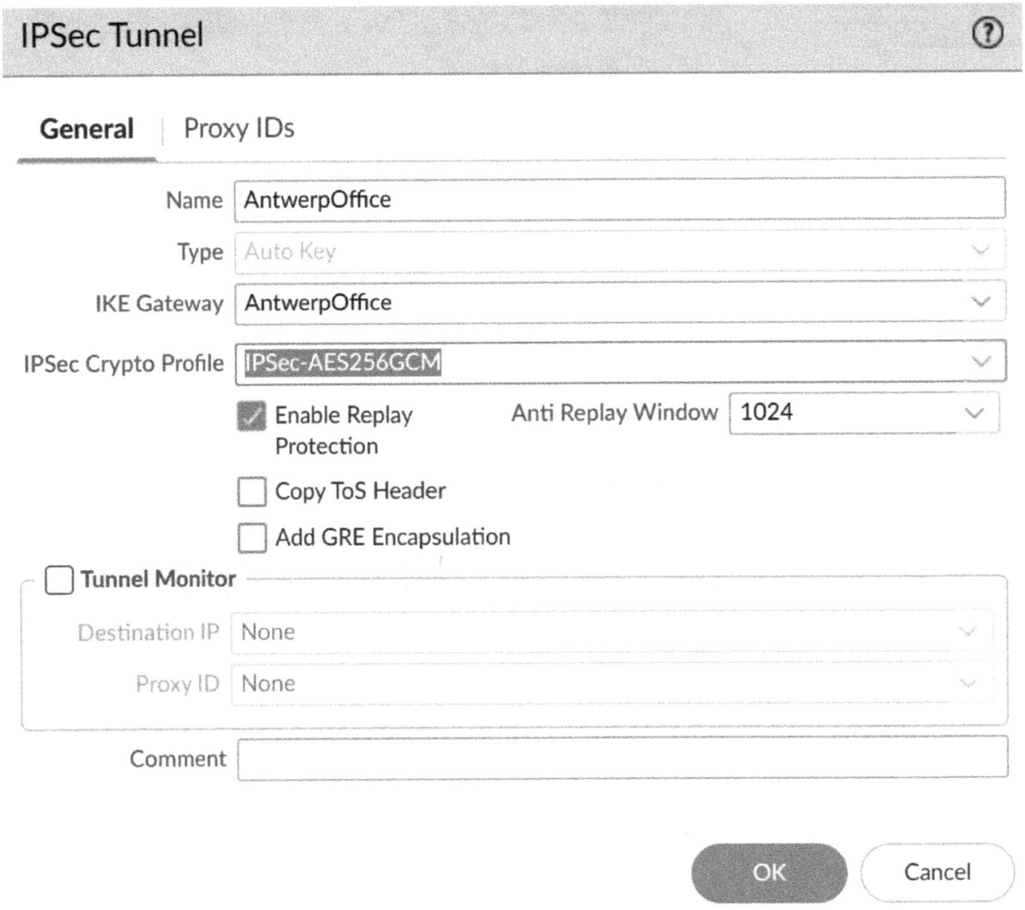

Figure 5.26 – IPSec Tunnel configuration

Repeat the preceding process for each remote network and each IPSec tunnel that needs to be onboarded.

From what we have learned in this section, you should have been able to create at least one IKE gateway and IPSec tunnel, so now we can start onboarding IPSec tunnels into the Prisma Access remote networks.

Onboarding remote networks

Remote networks can now be onboarded by adding them via **Panorama | Cloud Services | Configuration | Remote Networks | Onboarding**.

When creating a new onboarding, you will need to select the **Location** that was assigned bandwidth earlier. Once the location has completed its provisioning, a new **IPSec Termination Node** will become visible. Depending on the amount of bandwidth assigned to the location, one or more available IPSec termination nodes will appear. If more than one is available, select the appropriate node for this remote network connection.

Select the appropriate **IPSec Tunnel**, and if a backup link will be used, enable and select the **Secondary WAN** tunnel.

A remote network will also need to be configured with either a static route (towards the remote network) or the BGP configuration, which must be completed to ensure peering can be established and routes exchanged.

To enable BGP, you need to do the following:

- Check the **Enable** box.

- By default, the mobile user `supernet` is divided into /24 (255.255.255.0) subnets. These subnets can be summarized back into the regional or global IP pools, so only one or a handful of routes are advertised towards the remote network when enabling **Summarize Mobile User Routes before advertising**.

- **Advertise Default Route** can be enabled to advertise the IP address of the RN-SPNs as a default route towards the remote network, ensuring all traffic is sent into the tunnel.

- **Don't Advertise Prisma Access Routes** prevents the strata routing table from being shared with the remote network.

The onboarding process should look like the following screenshot:

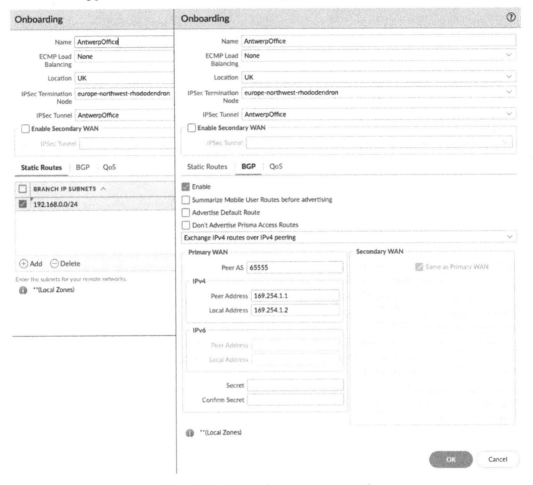

Figure 5.27 – Onboarding a remote network

To increase available bandwidth, **equal cost multi-path** (**ECMP**) can be enabled by selecting Enable with Symmetric Return in the **ECMP Load balancing** dropdown. **ECMP Load Balancing** will allow you to bundle up to four IPSec tunnels to a remote network, and each tunnel must be configured with BGP peering; **ECMP Load balancing** does not support static routes. Remote networks that have ECMP enabled can only be used for internet access; they will not be able to connect to other Prisma Access-connected resources:

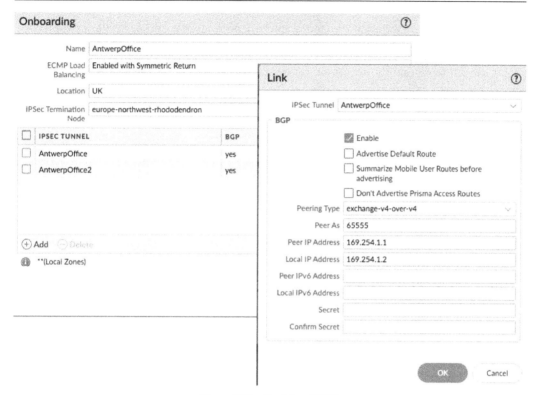

Figure 5.28 – Enabling ECMP

Once the onboarding configuration is complete, click **OK** and then **Commit | Commit to Panorama**. After the commit to Panorama is completed, push **Commit** and **Push to Devices**. As we saw in *Figure 5.22*, make sure the remote networks are selected and then push the configuration up to the infrastructure.

To obtain the public IP address for the RN-SPN, navigate to **Panorama | Cloud Services | Status Network Details | Remote Networks** and find the remote network name. **SERVICE IP ADDRESS** is the public IP address used by this IPSec termination node and must be configured as a peer IP on the remote network VPN device:

Figure 5.29 – Network Details

Once the remote peer has been fully configured and BGP peering is established (in this case, BGP is enabled), the BGP status link will show you the Prisma Access side details for BGP peering.

You are now able to repeat this process for each branch office and will be able to use static routing when it is best suited and when you will need BGP to learn and advertise routes.

Summary

In this chapter, we learned all about configuring **remote network security processing nodes** (RN-SPNs) and saw how we should go about creating secure IPSec VPN tunnels on the Strata Cloud Manager and on Panorama. In the next chapter, we will take a look at how **mobile user security processing nodes** (MU-SPNs) are provisioned and deployed.

6

Configuring Mobile User SPNs

In this chapter, we're going to go through the steps needed to select locations and then deploy MU-SPNs in the regions where they are needed. We will learn about **GlobalProtect** (**GP**) and how it can be set to accommodate different end user requirements.

In this chapter, we're going to cover the following main topics:

- Design considerations and understanding gateway selection
- Selecting regions and provisioning MU-SPNs
- Configuring the portal

Technical requirements

The topics covered in this chapter resemble a traditional GP deployment, so previous experience deploying a GP portal and gateway will be very helpful in comprehending the components we will be covering in this chapter.

Design considerations

Before we start setting up an array of MU-SPNs all over the world, some things need to be considered. When deploying a traditional GP design with several gateways spread across the world, a GP agent will collect a list of all available gateways from the (single) portal and test connectivity with all of them, then proceed to connect to the fastest one.

In Prisma Access, this mechanism has been changed quite a lot.

Gateway selection

First, a GP agent will connect to the portal. The portal is the node that serves configuration to the GP endpoint and provides gateways for the endpoint to connect to. It is also used when clientless applications are made available to users. Due to the nature of cloud computing, the URL that's used for the portal can be attached to different nodes in different regions of the world. At the time of writing, there are three portal nodes – one in the Americas, one in EMEA, and one in APAC – all responding to the same FQDN. So, the GP agent connects to the node closest to the user. Depending on which theatres have any locations active in them, all or just some of the portals will be active in that theatre – that is, if only European locations have been provisioned, only the European portal node will be active. They're geolocated in the US East, Ireland, and Singapore.

When the GP agent connects to the portal, its country of origin is determined, and a list of available gateways is provided. That list of gateways will have different priorities that are very different from the regular GP deployments:

- **Priority 1**: This is the highest priority and is reserved for the in-country gateway. This will ensure that GP always tries to connect to an in-country resource, which will typically provide the best user experience both in terms of latency and things such as geolocated language settings on websites.

- Priorities 2 and 3 are not used in Prisma Access.

- **Priority 4**: This is a lower priority where a gateway is provided as a regional backup in case the in-country MU-SPN is responding very poorly or is unavailable. These locations can't be selected and are predetermined, so an MU-SPN should be provisioned in that location to ensure fallback is available. The regional backups are as follows:

  - **EMEA**: Netherlands Central

  - **APAC**: Hong Kong, Japan Central, or Japan South

  - **Americas**: US Northwest

- **Priority 5**: This is an even lower priority. It is available for global *last resort* fallback locations. These will be used by any endpoint that is unable to connect to the in-country or regional backup nodes. These locations are also predetermined and must be provisioned to provide the last resort fallback capability:

  - Hong Kong

  - Japan Central

  - Japan South

  - Netherlands Central

  - US Northwest

- Bahrain

- France North

- Ireland

- South Africa West

- South Korea

Ideally, these three priorities give the user the best experience while providing fallback options in case an in-country MU-SPN is unavailable. This also means that the MU-SPNs that are provisioned need to match the countries where users usually reside.

> **Note**
>
> You may have noticed that, for example, Netherlands Central appears both on prio4 and prio5. This is because Netherlands Central is both a regional and a global fallback. Other regions will fall back to Netherlands Central if their regional fallback fails.

When a user is in a country where there is no local MU-SPN, the regional and global gateways will be used for gateway selection.

The selection process formula for the available gateways is as follows:

$$Weight = \frac{(RTT - lowest\ RTT) \times 100}{range*} + 100 + priority \times 20.$$

* Range = lowest to highest RTT difference e.g. 100 - 500 range = 400

RTT is the TLS handshake time in ms.

So, for example, for a user in Belgium, we have these two gateways:

- Belgium RTT 40 ms

- Regional fallback Netherlands central RTT 20 ms

The weight for Belgium is $((40 - 20) / 20) \times 100 + 100 + (1 \times 20) = 220$.

The weight for Netherlands Central is $((20 - 20) / 20) \times 100 + 100 + (5 \times 20) = 200$.

Even though the Belgian MU-SPN is in-country, the Netherlands MU-SPN has a lower weight. So, GP will connect to the Netherlands to achieve optimal user experience.

It's important to note that GP will connect to MU-SPN in regards to the hierarchy (in-country, regional fallback, or global fallback) and the gateway's responsiveness (TLS RTT). If no in-country MU-SPN is available, the regional and global backup will be polled and not the closest country where an MU-SPN is available.

For example, a user in Italy would fall back to Netherlands Central if no MU-SPN in Italy was enabled, even though an MU-SPN in the neighboring country of Switzerland may exist.

Another interesting side effect of cloud computing is the use of **compute locations** and **edge locations**. Not every country has a data center where processing takes place; instead, larger regional hubs (compute nodes) provide compute services for smaller locations where only connectivity is provided. In most cases, this does not influence any behavior as backbone connectivity is fast across the globe and geolocation is provided by merit of cloud magic: the connectivity IP lives on the Google infrastructure in-country. So, connectivity from the endpoint goes directly to the in-country GCP POP, but the compute takes place elsewhere. Internet breakout retains the geolocated IP that's closest to the user for optimal performance.

Some countries have more than one location in them – for example, Germany. Germany Central is the compute node, whereas Germany North and South are edge locations. In terms of gateway selection, such edge locations are disregarded as there is an in-country compute node, which means Germany North and Germany South can only be selected manually (if manual gateway selection is enabled and the locations have been provisioned).

A complete list of all compute modes and their edge locations can be found here: `https://docs.paloaltonetworks.com/prisma-access/administration/prisma-access-overview/list-of-prisma-access-locations`.

When an endpoint connects to an MU-SPN, it will receive an IP address from an IP pool.

IP pools

Similar to how GP receives an IP from the IP pool assigned in the gateway of a traditional deployment, GP will also receive an IP from a pool in Prisma Access. The main difference between a traditional gateway and Prisma Access MU-SPNs is that instead of an IP pool per gateway, MU-SPNs are assigned subnets from a larger pool per region. IP pools can be provisioned in a worldwide pool, a theater (Americas, EMEA, or APAC), or a regional pool assigned to a compute location. The minimum pool size is /23, but you will need to provide a pool that exceeds the number of users you plan to onboard.

Each onboarded MU-SPN will take a minimum of one /24 subnet from the regional or worldwide pool. If more users than there are free IP addresses in the subnet connect to an MU-SPN, additional /24 subnets will be assigned. When calculating the number of IP addresses and subnets needed, consider that an MU-SPN that hosts 10 users will also take a /24 slice from the pie, and users may log on from multiple devices, which will take up additional IP addresses.

If regional and worldwide IP pools are configured, MU-SPNs will first take subnets from the regional pool and will start taking subnets from the worldwide pool if the regional pool is depleted:

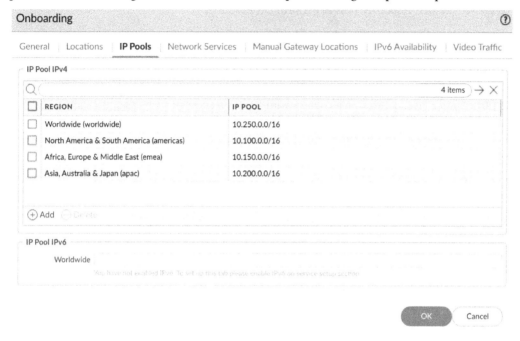

Figure 6.1 – Regional and worldwide IP pools

Make sure the IP pools do not overlap with other subnets used inside the organization as that could cause routing issues. All IP pools are advertised across the infrastructure and potentially out to SC-CANs and remote networks via BGP.

MU-SPN autoscaling

There may be locations that attract far more users than what is optimal for a single node to handle. Contrary to RN-SPNs that are assigned bandwidth, MU-SPNs do not come with a bandwidth limitation. They are, however, somewhat limited in the number of users that can connect to a single node.

To accommodate a large number of users at the same time, additional nodes may need to be deployed to ensure optimal user experience. When a threshold of connected users is reached, an **autoscale** event will take place. This autoscale event will kick off when the original node reaches a threshold of about 1,200 users. A new node is activated and after it becomes active, new users will be routed to the new node. Both nodes will accept incoming connections via the same FQDN, which is controlled via a DNS routing algorithm to distribute load.

At the time of writing, Palo Alto Networks uses **Route 53**, a service by AWS that leverages monitoring of destinations that share the same FQDN so that load can be distributed among all participating servers based on their responsiveness to perform DNS routing.

The provisioning process takes up to 45 minutes. So, in case of a large surge of users, the first batch of users may all end up on the first node as they connect while the second node is still booting up. If the second node reaches the tipping point, an additional node is spun up, and so on. This chain of events can take a while, so it is not optimal for a region that consistently has a large number of users (for example, headquarters in a country with 10,000 users). For such cases, you can reach out to Palo Alto to request a certain location that has an appropriate number of nodes pre-provisioned each morning to take on the load and spun down each night when the users return home. You will be asked to provide appropriate proof for each region this is requested for.

Let's take a look at how we set up MU-SPN via Strata Cloud Manager.

Configuring MU-SPN in Strata Cloud Manager

To start using Mobile User access, we need to enable **GlobalProtect**. This can be found in **Workflows | Prisma Access Setup | Mobile Users**.

Once enabled, the Mobile User volume will be assigned, at which point you can access the GP setup via the button or a newly appeared menu item – that is, **GlobalProtect in Workflows | Prisma Access Setup | GlobalProtect**:

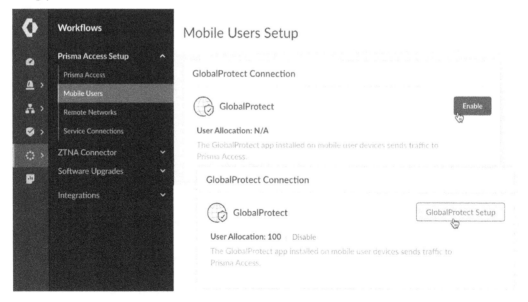

Figure 6.2 – Enabling GlobalProtect Connection

We'll start by setting up the infrastructure settings.

Infrastructure

Click **Set Up Infrastructure Settings** on the **Infrastructure** page to start configuring the infrastructure:

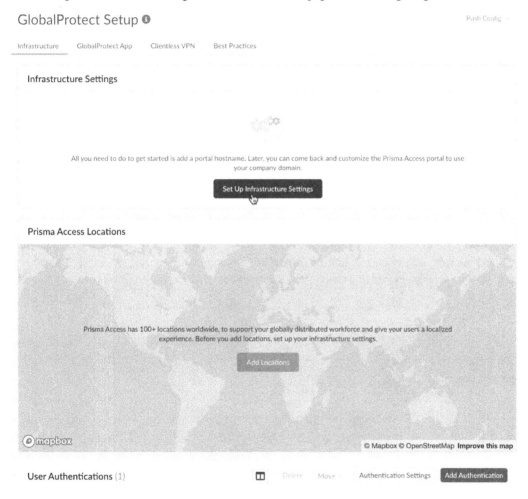

Figure 6.3 – Set Up Infrastructure Settings

Regarding **Infrastructure Settings**, we can configure the FQDN that will be used as the portal address. Palo Alto provides a free subdomain to gpcloudservice.com. If you want to use an FQDN that is linked to your corporate domain name, you can create the appropriate FQDN here as well and import the server certificate for the FQDN. This certificate should be signed by a public **Certificate Authority** (**CA**) such as GoDaddy, Globalsign, or Digicert as it will be used on the public-facing portal.

In the public DNS record for your corporate portal FQDN, you must set the `gpcloudcervice.com` subdomain as a CNAME value, as illustrated here:

```
% dig a globalprotect.pangurus.com

; <<>> DiG 9.10.6 <<>> a globalprotect.pangurus.com
;; global options: +cmd
;; Got answer:
;; ->>HEADER<<- opcode: QUERY, status: NOERROR, id: 37047
;; flags: qr rd ra; QUERY: 1, ANSWER: 1, AUTHORITY: 1, ADDITIONAL: 1

;; OPT PSEUDOSECTION:
; EDNS: version: 0, flags:; udp: 512
;; QUESTION SECTION:
;globalprotect.pangurus.com.        IN      A

;; ANSWER SECTION:
globalprotect.pangurus.com.        300    IN      CNAME
pangurus.gpcloudservice.com.
```

The **Default Domain** setting will let you use the free subdomain. Switching to **Custom Domain** will let you add the appropriate details. Click the **Import** button to upload the server certificate. Make sure you include the private key and, if possible, add the certificate chain in the certificate file:

GlobalProtect [Prisma Access / Mobile Users Container / 🖳 GlobalProtect]   ❯   Infrastructure Settings - GlobalProtect

Infrastructure Settings

Portal Name

By default your portal is always accessible via a gpcloudservice.com domain based on your portal host name. You can also use your custom domain to access your portal

Portal Name Type	◯ Default Domain ◉ Custom Domain
Portal HostName *	globalprotect.pangurus.com
Portal DNS CName *	pangurus .gpcloudservice.com
	Add a CNAME record for your Portal HostName pointing to Portal DNS CName in your DNS server.
Portal Certificate *	pangurus ⌄
	Import

Figure 6.4 – Portal domain

Next is the **Client DNS** configuration. This section controls if and how internal domains should be resolved. By default, all DNS queries are sent out to a public DNS server. However, some domains may need to be resolved by an internal DNS server for a private record:

Client DNS

By default, each region uses worldwide DNS settings. You can also customize the DNS settings per region.

Items (1)   Delete **Add Region**

		Internal Domains			Public Domains
	Region	Rule Name	DNS	Domain List	DNS
	Worldwide	pangurus domain	PRI: 10.0.0.53	pangurus.com	PRI: Prisma Access Default
			SEC: 10.0.10.53		SEC: Prisma Access Default

ADVANCED SETTINGS ∨

UDP Queries Retries

Interval (Sec)   2 [1 - 30]

Attempts   5 [1 - 30]

☐ Advanced RCODE Support
Enable handling of DNS RCODEs such as SERVFAIL

Figure 6.5 – Client DNS

By default, there is a single item set for worldwide that points to Prisma Access's default DNS servers. You can edit it to add **Internal Domain Resolve Rules**. Each rule can contain a set of domains and their respective internal DNS servers. You can also opt to change public DNS resolvers to custom public DNS servers or set it so that public DNS records are also queried on the internal servers. This allows you to control which servers should resolve public FQDNs, as well as the internal domains.

Multiple **Internal Domain Resolve Rules** can exist, redirecting different domains to different DNS servers. This allows, for example, partner or joint venture domains to be resolved on their respective internal or public DNS servers.

If records should be resolved on regional DNS servers, multiple client DNS profiles can be created for each region. If no regional profile exists, the worldwide profile will be used. You can also add a DNS suffix list for each region, or worldwide:

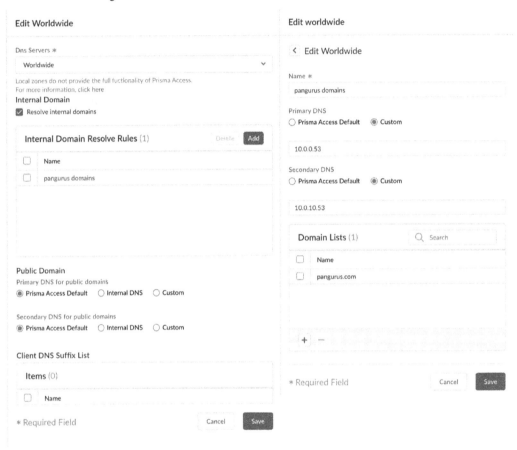

Figure 6.6 – Configuring proxy DNS

Click **Save** when you're done configuring each region to store your changes. Next, we need to add the IP pool. These are the IP addresses the MU-SPNs have at their disposal to assign to connected users. As we saw earlier in this chapter, each MU-SPN will be assigned a minimum of one /24 subnet, potentially more if over 253 users connect to a single location. We can set up a single worldwide IP pool, which is great for a small deployment. But for larger environments, it may be best to assign each region its own IP pool:

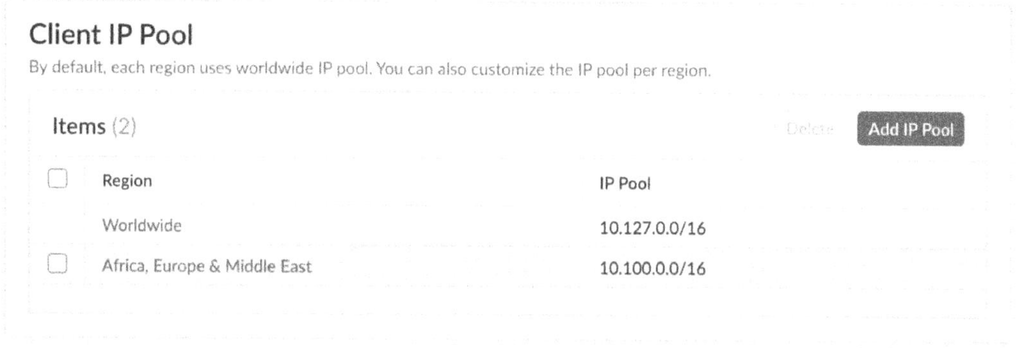

Figure 6.7 – Client IP Pool

In the following section, we have a setting that creates an IPv6 sinkhole. Enabling this option creates an IPv6 DNS sinkhole address and an IPv6 next hop sinkhole that are sent to the GP endpoints as part of their connection parameters. These sinkhole addresses will ensure no IPv6 connections can be established.

If the sinkhole is not enabled, there are two possible options for IPv6:

- **IPv6 can be enabled inside the tunnel** so that all IPv6 connections pass by the security enforcement of the MU-SPN out to the internet and potentially onto the backbone. A security policy needs to be created to account for IPv6.

- **IPv6 can be disabled on the infrastructure**, but this will cause all IPv6 connections originating from the endpoint to bypass the tunnel and break out locally, which can pose a severe security risk. If IPv6 is not allowed on the backbone, the IPv6 sinkhole should be enabled to prevent endpoints from connecting to any IPv6 addresses.

> **Note**
>
> In Panorama, the IPv6 sinkhole setting can be enabled by running the following command from the CLI:
>
> ```
> > set plugins cloud_services mobile-users ipv6 yes
> ```

If a legacy NetBIOS name service is used to identify internal resources, WINS server addresses can be enabled for each region or worldwide.

Lastly, the gateway FQDNs can be retrieved here once locations are selected and MU-SPNs are provisioned. This will happen after the following step of selecting locations and committing that change, which will trigger the provisioning process.

These FQDNs will likely be needed by the SAML IdP as an identifier (entity ID) to be allowed to broker authentications:

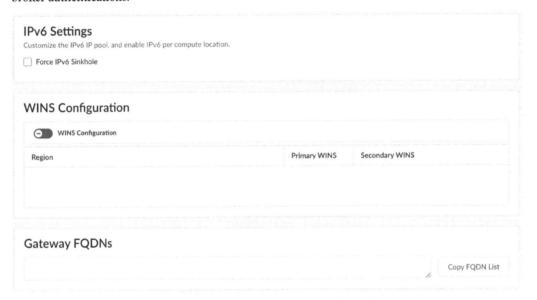

Figure 6.8 – IPv6 sinkhole and WINS configuration

Click **Save** to save your configuration. Once you've done this, you will be brought back to the previous screen. You will now be able to add locations by clicking **Add Locations**, which will take you to an overview of available regions:

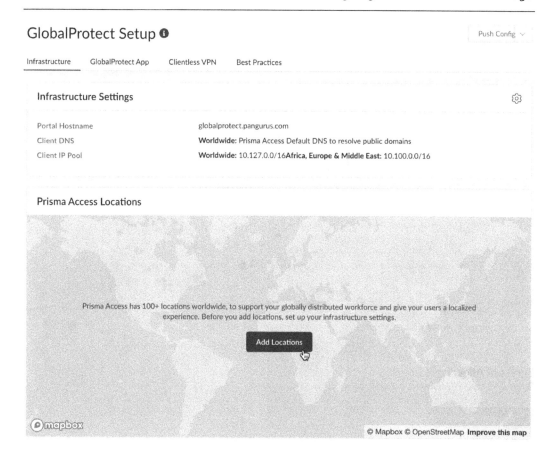

Figure 6.9 – Adding locations

When you select a specific region, you will be shown a map with all the available locations in the selected region. Select the desired locations by clicking the black + sign for each respective location you wish to add. The location should display a green checkmark when activated. You can select individual countries or click the **Select All** button at the top to activate all locations at once. Click **Save** and repeat this process for each region where gateways need to be made available:

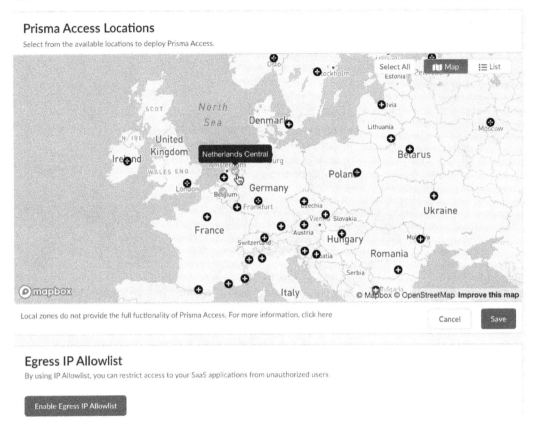

Figure 6.10 – Selecting gateway locations

When you have saved the last set of locations, go back to the GP **Setup** screen and commit the configuration by clicking **Push Config | Push** in the top-right corner. Add a description and ensure **Mobile Users Container** and **GlobalProtect** are selected and then click **Push** to send the config out. The provisioning process can take up to 45 minutes, so this is a good moment to take a break.

The Egress Allowlist can be enabled to control which outbound IP addresses can be used by MU-SPNs to access private SaaS applications.

By default, each active location will have two IP addresses – one active and one standby as each MU-SPN is essentially an active/passive cluster. These two IP addresses may switch their active/passive status during upgrade events. Autoscale events will also provision additional IP addresses at a location as a new MU-SPN is spun up to add capacity for users.

If your organization has private SaaS applications that require an access list containing allowed source IP addresses, enabling the Egress Allowlist will prevent Prisma Access from activating IP addresses that have not been approved by you first. This does require monitoring on your part as new IP addresses will not be used, potentially blocking autoscaling, until they have been approved.

Once the commit has been completed and the locations have been provisioned, you can go back to the Prisma Access locations and enable the Egress Allowlist. It will initially return a list of all the active and passive node IP addresses. Click **Migrate** to enable the IP allowlist:

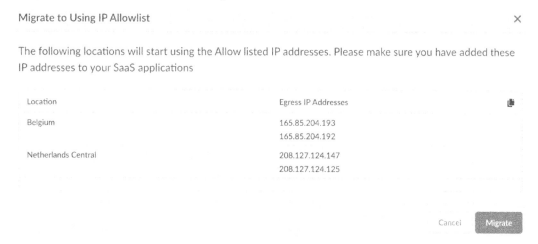

Figure 6.11 – Enabling the IP allowlist

Once the allowlist is active, you'll need to onboard all the IP addresses by clicking the **Pending - Confirm Egress IPs** link:

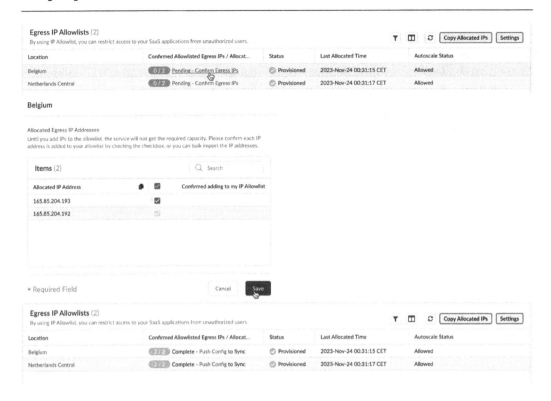

Figure 6.12 – Selecting allowlist IP addresses

Click **Save** to save the egress IP allowlist. Another commit is needed to push the change out to all the MU-SPN nodes.

With the nodes provisioned, you can also go back to the **Infrastructure** settings and retrieve the FQDN for all the nodes:

Gateway FQDNs

Figure 6.13 – Gateway FQDNs

With these FQDNs, you can prepare the SAML IdP for the next step, where we'll configure authentication. The default setting includes an authentication method for local users, which we'll replace with SAML. Under **Authentication Settings**, we can add a certificate profile to enable client certificate authentication and we can choose to block quarantined devices from logging on. If this setting is disabled, quarantined devices will be allowed to connect and a security policy can be used to limit access to internal resources:

User Authentications (1)
2/2 Failed Practice Checks
Authentication Settings
Add Authentication
#
Authenticate User From
Authentication Method
Authentication Profile
Certificate Profile
1
Any OS
Local Users
Local Users
Authentication Settings
Certificate Profile
None
Create New
Manage
This certificate profile is shared with other authentication method on Mobile Users.
Block Login
Block Login for Quarantined devices
Cancel
Save

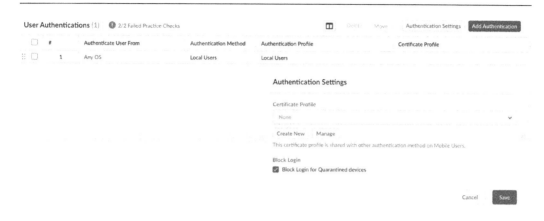

Figure 6.14 – Default authentication

Click **Add Authentication** to start creating a new authentication profile:

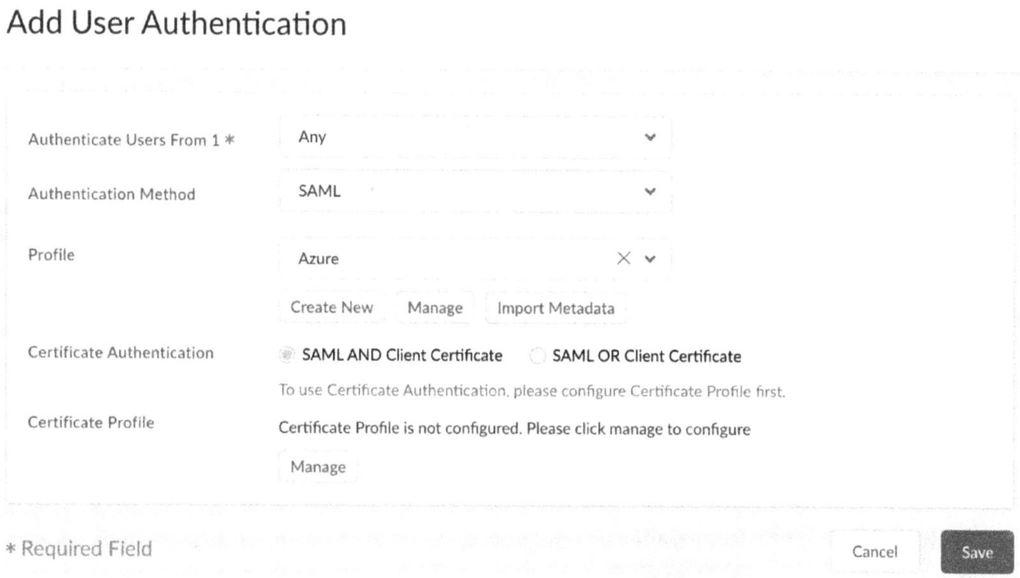

Add User Authentication
Authenticate Users From 1 *
Any
Authentication Method
SAML
Profile
Azure
Create New
Manage
Import Metadata
Certificate Authentication
SAML AND Client Certificate
SAML OR Client Certificate
To use Certificate Authentication, please configure Certificate Profile first.
Certificate Profile
Certificate Profile is not configured. Please click manage to configure
Manage
* Required Field
Cancel
Save

Figure 6.15 – Adding user authentication

In the authentication profile, you can limit the operating system to which this profile applies. The following operating systems can be set:

- **Any** for all operating systems
- **Android**
- **Browser** for browser-based clientless connections
- **Chrome**
- **IoT**
- **Linux**
- **Mac**
- **Satellite** for Palo Alto firewalls that have an IPSec tunnel configured as satellite
- **Windows**
- **WindowsUWP**
- **iOS**

We can also select the authentication method. We'll select SAML. The following options are available:

- **Local Users**.
- **SAML**.
- **RADIUS**.
- **LDAP**.
- **TACACS+**.
- **Kerberos**.
- **Cloud Identity Engine**.
- **Multiple Authentication Profiles in a Sequence**. Any authentication method can be added to a sequence except SAML or CIE

If a certificate profile was added in the **Authentication Settings** area, as seen in *Figure 6.15*, or you clicked **Manage** and added a new profile, the following options can be considered:

- **SAML AND Client Certificate**, which will require an endpoint to have a client certificate and provide SAML authentication
- **SAML OR Client Certificate**, which allows an endpoint to connect using only the client certificate or by providing SAML authentication

Once we've selected the operating system and authentication method, we can create a new profile. With SAML, we can also import the metafile provided by the IdP:

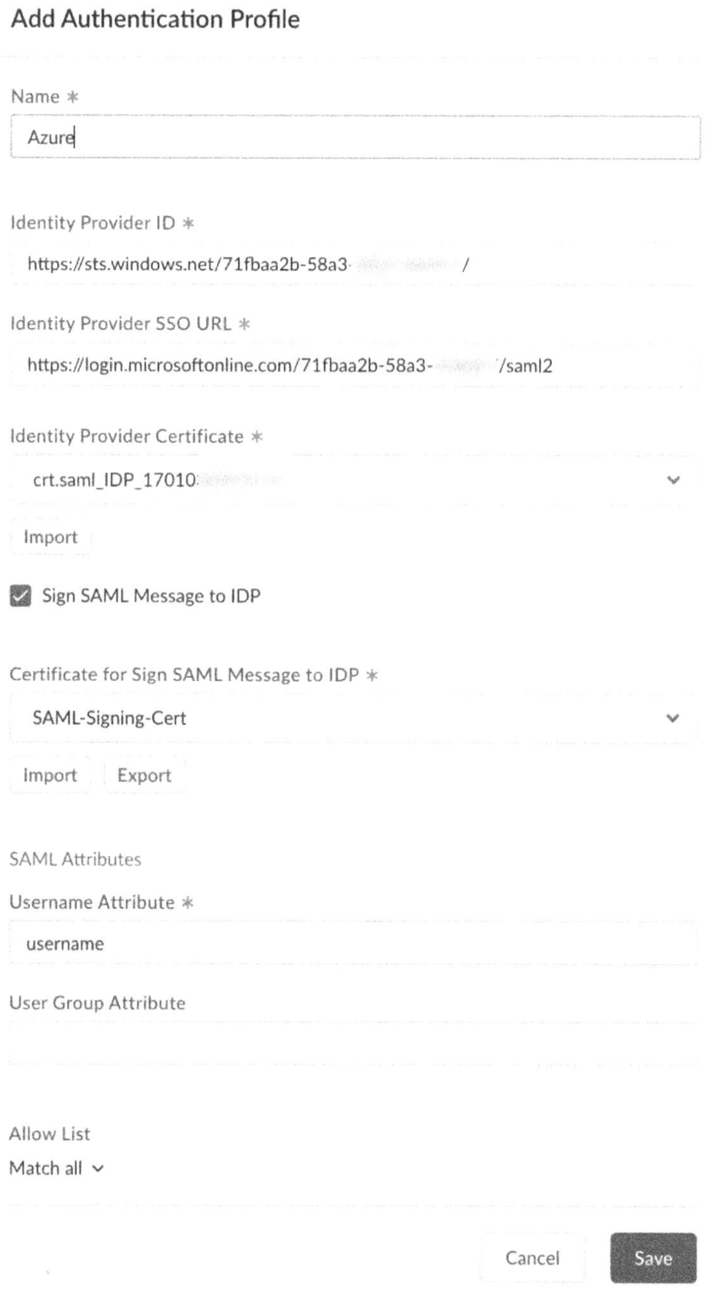

Add Authentication Profile

Name *

Azure

Identity Provider ID *

https://sts.windows.net/71fbaa2b-58a3- /

Identity Provider SSO URL *

https://login.microsoftonline.com/71fbaa2b-58a3- /saml2

Identity Provider Certificate *

crt.saml_IDP_17010

Import

☑ Sign SAML Message to IDP

Certificate for Sign SAML Message to IDP *

SAML-Signing-Cert

Import   Export

SAML Attributes

Username Attribute *

username

User Group Attribute

Allow List

Match all ⌄

Cancel   Save

Figure 6.16 – Adding Authentication profile

The SAML attributes can be tweaked to match the attributes used by the IdP. Save the new authentication profile and delete the default profile:

Figure 6.17 – Deleting the Local Users profile

Now that the infrastructure is set up, we can create the agent configuration. This will determine how the GP agent behaves.

GlobalProtect app

In the next tab, we can set the GP application behavior and tunnel settings. Both sections have a default configuration set already, which we can edit or replace with a new profile:

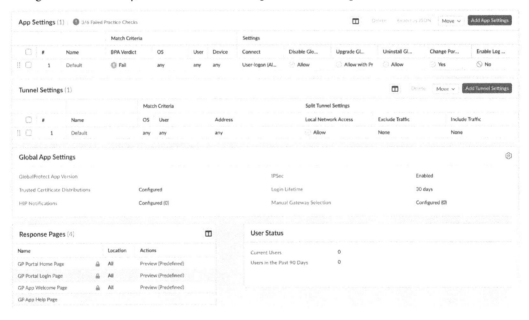

Figure 6.18 – GlobalProtect app settings

App Settings

App Settings controls which agent configuration is distributed to clients. Multiple different **App Settings** profiles can be created to create a personalized user experience for each type of user or device.

Under **App Settings**, open the **Default** profile or **Add App Settings**.

Match Criteria

The first section is **Match Criteria**. Especially if multiple profiles are configured, this is where you determine who or what will match this specific profile. A single profile can be used for everyone, but it is possible to create different profiles based on the endpoint operating system, username or AD group membership, a matching endpoint serial number, or a client certificate installed on the endpoint.

The following endpoint operating systems can be selected:

- **Android**
- **Chrome**
- **IoT**
- **Linux**
- **Mac**
- **Windows**
- **WindowsUWP**
- **iOS**

A certificate profile can be configured by uploading a CA certificate to match client certificates.

You can also add a registry entry or Plist check, which will verify if an entry exists inside the registry or Plist on a system:

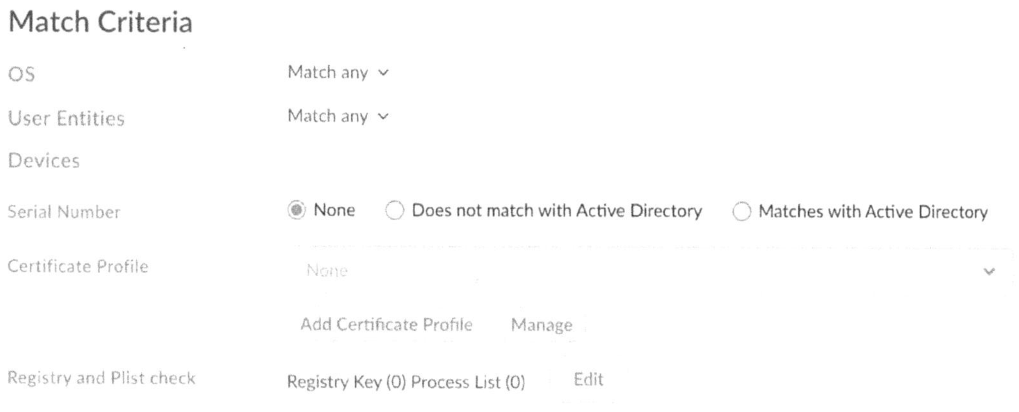

Match Criteria

OS	Match any ∨
User Entities	Match any ∨
Devices	
Serial Number	⦿ None ○ Does not match with Active Directory ○ Matches with Active Directory
Certificate Profile	None ∨
	Add Certificate Profile Manage
Registry and Plist check	Registry Key (0) Process List (0) Edit

Figure 6.19 – Match Criteria

In the next section, we will take a look at authentication cookies. These can be used to control if and how users are authenticated automatically. You can find these below **Match Criteria**.

Authentication Override

By default, **Authentication Override** is enabled and set to 24 hours. This means that once a user logs on, they will receive an authentication cookie that allows them access to the portal to retrieve configuration for 24 hours, regardless of the SAML conditional access. The app settings only pertain to configuration via the portal, and not connectivity via a gateway MU-SPN. So, it is safe to leave this setting enabled and even extend it to a longer timeframe. This will prevent users from being asked for credentials just to retrieve configuration:

Figure 6.20 – Authentication Override

The next section is the actual configuration that dictates how the GP application will behave. Scroll down to see the **App Configuration** area.

App Configuration

The first setting you'll see here is the **Connect** option, which contains four modes:

- **Always on**: Every time the user logs on, GP connects to Prisma Access.
- **Pre-logon**: A connection is established as soon as the endpoint is booted, even before the user is logged on.
- **On-demand**: This allows the user to choose when to connect.
- **Pre-logon, then on-demand**: The connection is established before the user is logged on. Once the user logs on, the connection becomes on-demand.

By default, all users are allowed to disable GP, which allows them to interrupt the always-on mode. This mode can be set to one of the following:

- **Allow**: With this setting, the user is allowed to disable GP, letting them access the internet directly without a tunnel.

- **Disallowed**: This prevents the user from disabling the GlobalPrtoect agent.

- **Allow with comment**: The user must leave a comment stating why they disabled GP. Preconfigured reasons can be provided in the **Display the following reasons to disconnect GlobalProtect (Always-on mode)** field. The reason is logged.

- **Allow with passcode**: The user needs to know the passcode that was set in the configuration to be able to disable GP.

- **Allow with ticket**: The user must reach out with a ticket number.

The maximum number of times the user is allowed to use the disable function can be controlled by setting a value in **Max Times User Can Disable** with a maximum value of 25 (0 means this setting is disabled and there is no restriction to how many times a user is allowed to disable GP). This number of disables is stored on the client machine's UserOverrides registry key under `HKEY_CURRENT_USER\Software\Palo AltoNetworks\GlobalProtect\Setting`.

How long GP remains disabled can also be controlled by setting **Disable Duration (min)** to a value up to 65,535 minutes, after which GP will automatically re-enable and connect if the connect method is set to always on. This setting does not apply to other connection methods as those allow the user to decide when to connect.

User-initiated **uninstall** of the GP application can be **allowed**, **disallowed**, or **allowed with password**.

The GP application can be updated in the following ways:

- **Allow when the user accepts the upgrade prompt**: This is the default setting. When a new GP package is made available from the infrastructure, the user will be notified that a new version is available, and they can upgrade at their convenience.

- **Disallow**: Upgrades are not allowed; the software package is controlled through an external software management tool.

- **Allow manually**: Upgrades can be performed by the user.

- **Allow transparently**: When a new software package is made available, it is automatically and invisibly installed the next time the user logs on.

- **Allow when the user is in the corporate network**: The package will be upgraded when the GP agent detects it is internal via the internal host detection.

- **Allow User to Change Portal** allows users to add additional portals, or delete the current one. This can come in handy if a legacy or parallel portal exists, or if partners also offer GP connectivity.

- **Enable Autonomous DEM and GlobalProtect App Log Collection for Troubleshooting** sets the agent to download the ADEM plugin if the license has been activated.

- The **Welcome Page** option allows you to load a small HTML page that displays when users connect. This can be handy to share the AUP/EULA or broadcast a MOTD:

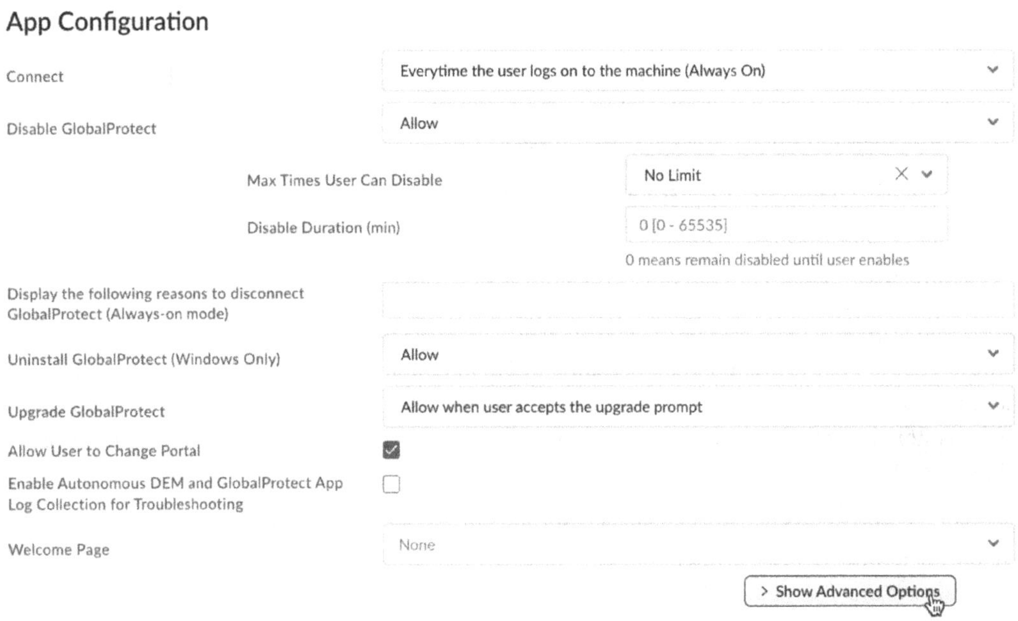

App Configuration

Connect	Everytime the user logs on to the machine (Always On) ⌄
Disable GlobalProtect	Allow ⌄
Max Times User Can Disable	No Limit × ⌄
Disable Duration (min)	0 [0 - 65535]
	0 means remain disabled until user enables
Display the following reasons to disconnect GlobalProtect (Always-on mode)	
Uninstall GlobalProtect (Windows Only)	Allow ⌄
Upgrade GlobalProtect	Allow when user accepts the upgrade prompt ⌄
Allow User to Change Portal	☑
Enable Autonomous DEM and GlobalProtect App Log Collection for Troubleshooting	☐
Welcome Page	None ⌄

> Show Advanced Options

Figure 6.21 – App Configuration

Additional configuration can be revealed by clicking the **Show Advanced Options** button. Here's a list of the available options:

- **Apps:**

  - **GlobalProtect App Config Refresh Interval (hours)**: 1 to 168 hours; the default is 24. This is the frequency at which the GP application will fetch a fresh version of its configuration.

  - **Show GlobalProtect in System Tray**: This is enabled by default. It can be used to hide GP from view.

  - **Send HIP Report Immediately if Windows Security Center (WSC) State Changes (Windows Only)**: This is enabled by default. HIP checks run on a preconfigured timer and will update the HIP status only at that time. The WSC can detect changes to some processes (Windows Firewall and Windows Defender) immediately and update the HIP status immediately.

- **Show Status Panel at Startup (Windows Only)**: This will open the GP status panel every time the user logs on. This setting is disabled by default.

- **Persist for User Input**: This will maintain the status panel while the user logs on. This setting is disabled by default.

- **User behavior**:

  - **Allow user to Sign Out from GlobalProtect App**: This is enabled by default. Disabling this option will prevent the user from logging off, which can prevent them from bypassing security.

  - **Allow user to extend GlobalProtect User Session**: This can be enabled to allow the user to extend the current session. By default, a session can be active for 30 days before it is forcibly terminated or restarted. If this maximum lifetime is shortened but you want to allow the user to extend their session without being disconnected, this setting can be enabled.

  - **Allow User to Use Advanced View**: This is enabled by default. Disabling this setting will change the user's GP to a simplified view.

  - **Allow User to Dismiss Welcome Page**: This is enabled by default.

  - **Have User Accept Terms of Use before Creating Tunnel**. A **Terms of Use (ToU)** page can be loaded and presented to the user. This setting will require the user to accept the terms before they're able to connect.

  - **Allow User to Rediscover Network**: This is enabled by default. This setting allows the user to manually rediscover their network connection, which can be helpful if the user is roaming or switching networks from Wi-Fi to wired frequently.

  - **Allow User to Resubmit Host Profile**: This is enabled by default. The HIP profile is checked every hour by default. If a user runs into an issue that blocks them from accessing any resources due to, for example, a missing patch, this setting allows them to resubmit their host profile after applying the patch so they don't need to wait until the automatic update happens.

  - **Allow User to Continue with Invalid Portal Server Certificate**: By default, the agent will not connect to the portal if the certificate is invalid for any reason – for example, if it has expired. Enabling this setting will allow the agent to connect regardless of the certificate state. This can be useful if, for example, a self-signed certificate is used to test something.

- **Authentication**:

  - **Use Single Sign-on (Windows)**: This is enabled by default. This setting will carry the **single sign-on (SSO)** credentials for authentication to GP.

  - **Use Single Sign-on for Smart card PIN (Windows)**

  - **Use Single Sign-on (Mac)**

- **Clear Single Sign-on Credentials on Logout (Windows Only)**: This is enabled by default. This setting clears the SSO credentials from GP's cache after the user logs off.

- **Use Default Authentication on Kerberos Authentication Failure**: enabled by default. If Kerberos authentication fails, authentication will fall back to default authentication.

- **Use Default Browser for SAML Authentication**: By default, SAML authentication will trigger an embedded browser in GP to complete the authentication process. Enabling this setting will call the system default browser instead.

- **Client Certificate Lookup Store**: By default, certificate lookups will be done in the **User and Machine** stores. This can be changed to only look up certificates in the user or machine store.

- **SCEP Certificate Renewal Period (days)**: 0 to 30 days, but 7 days by default. If the following setting is set to SCEP client certificates, this setting controls the renewal period for client certificates.

- **Client Certificate**: By default, the client certificate is set to none. However, this setting can be changed to local, which will require a client certificate signed by an uploaded CA certificate to be installed on the endpoint, or **SCEP** which allows for auto-enrollment for client certificates.

- **Save User Credentials**. This option allows credentials submitted in GP to be saved. So, if the user logs off and on again, the credentials will still be there. There are four options:

  - **Yes**

  - **No**

  - **Save Username Only**

  - **Only with User Fingerprint**

- **Extended Key Usage OID for Client Certificate**: An OID can be added here to identify the correct client certificate property required to log on.

- **Retain Connection on Smart Card Removal (Windows Only)**: Enabled by default.

- **Custom Password Expiration Message (LDAP Authentication Only)**: When authentication is set to LDAP, the user can be notified via GP that their password is about to expire.

- **Change Password Message**: A custom notification can be added here, instructing the user to change their password if it is about to expire.

- **VPN**:

  - **Automatic Restoration of VPN Connection Timeout (min)**: 0 to 180 minutes; the default is 30 minutes. This setting controls how long GP will try to reconnect after the tunnel has been disconnected due to network issues. With the default setting, GP will give up on trying to reconnect after the tunnel has been down for 31 minutes. 0 minutes turns off the reconnect attempts.

- **Wait Time Between VPN Connection Restore Attempts (sec)**: 1 to 60; the default is 5. This is the time between reconnect attempts.

- **User Switch Tunnel Rename Timeout (sec)**: 0 to 600 seconds; the default is 0. 0 turns this feature off and retains the locally logged-on user's username. Setting a higher time will control how long a user has to authenticate while establishing a **Remote Desktop Protocol (RDP)** connection before the user ID associated with this tunnel is changed to the RDP user's username.

- **Pre-Logon Tunnel Rename Timeout (sec) (Windows Only)**: -1 to 7,200; the default is -1. This setting determines how the pre-logon tunnel is handled by the gateway:

  - -1 does not timeout the pre-logon tunnel; it is simply renamed to the logged-on user's username.

  - 0 will immediately terminate the pre-logon tunnel when the user logs on, and a new tunnel is created for the user.

  - 1 to 7,200 will have the pre-logon tunnel remain connected for the specified amount of time. If the user logs on with their own username the tunnel is reassigned to the user, if the user does not log on, the tunnel will be timed out after the set amount of time

- **Preserve Tunnel on User Logoff Timeout (sec)**: 0 to 600; the default is 0. This setting keeps the tunnel active for several seconds after the user logs off, which can be useful for post-logoff scripts, for example.

- **Automatically Use SSL When IPSec Is Unreliable (hours)**: 0 to 168; the default is 0. This setting will force the usage of SSL for the configured amount of time after the agent falls back from IPsec to SSL due to IPsec reliability issues.

- **Connect with SSL Only**: This will disable IPSec for the users matching this profile, and resort to SSL/TLS only.

- **Split-Tunnel Option**: The default setting is **Network Traffic Only**, but this can be changed to **Both Network Traffic and DNS**. The former will perform DNS lookups for all domains via the tunnel and only break out the actual traffic according to the split tunneling configuration. The latter will perform DNS lookups for the split tunnel domains on the local DNS rather than the tunnel DNS.

- **Enhanced Split-Tunnel Client Certificate Public Key**: A split tunnel file can be hosted elsewhere, in which case the client certificate public key can be added here so that the client can connect to the web server.

- **Enforcement**:

  - **Endpoint Traffic Policy Enforcement**: This setting can be enabled to prevent traffic on the physical interface of an endpoint when it is connected to GP. There are four options:

    - **Disabled**: This is the default setting

    - **Enforce for TCP/UDP traffic (based on IP Address Type)**: This setting enforces policy for TCP/UDP based on the tunnel IP version – that is, IPv4 or IPv6

    - **Enforce for all TCP/UDP traffic**: This setting enforces policy for TCP/UDP, regardless of the IP version

    - **Enforce for all traffic**: This enforces policy for all protocols, regardless of the IP protocol version

  - **Allow traffic to specified hosts/networks when Enforce GlobalProtect Connection for Network Access is enabled and GlobalProtect Connection is not established**: Up to 10 IP addresses or network segments can be added that will be accessible even if **Enforce GlobalProtect Connection for Network Access** is enabled, which would normally block all connections.

  - **Allow traffic to specified FQDN when Enforce GlobalProtect Connection for Network Access is enabled and GlobalProtect Connection is not established**: Up to 40 FQDNs can be added that will be accessible even if **Enforce GlobalProtect Connection for Network Access** is enabled, which would normally block all connections.

  - **Captive Portal Exception Timeout (sec)**: 0 to 3,600 seconds; the default is 0. This setting gives the user a grace period to log onto a captive portal (such as in an airport or hotel) before **Enforce GlobalProtect Connection for Network Access** is enforced.

  - **Automatically Launch Webpage in Default Browser Upon Captive Portal Detection**: A custom URL can be entered here that will be launched in the default browser when GP detects a captive portal is present in the network the endpoint is connected to, to trigger the captive portal.

  - **Traffic Blocking Notification Delay (sec)**: 5 to 120; the default is 15. This is the amount of time GP waits before displaying the traffic-blocking notification after establishing a connection to the network.

  - **Display Traffic Blocking Notification Message**: This is enabled by default.

  - **Traffic Blocking Notification Message**: A custom traffic-blocking notification message can be entered here.

  - **Allow User to Dismiss Traffic Blocking Notifications**: This is enabled by default.

  - **Display Captive Portal Detection Message**: This is disabled by default. Enable it to show a notification that a captive portal exists in the network the user is connected to.

- **Captive Portal Detection Message**: A custom message can be displayed when GP detects a captive portal in the network.

- **Captive Portal Notification Delay (sec)**: 1 to 120, the default is 5. This is the amount of time GP waits before displaying a notification it detected a captive portal in the network.

- **Enable Advanced Internal Host Detection**: This can be enabled so that the client will also verify the internal gateway's certificate after performing a reverse lookup to determine if the host is on the internal network.

- **HIP Process Remediation Timeout (sec)**: 0 to 300; the default is 0. This setting can be enabled to allow GP a set amount of time to run a HIP remediation script.

- **Connection behavior**:

  - **GlobalProtect Connection MTU (bytes)**: 1,000 to 1,420; the default is 1,400.

  - **Maximum Internal Gateway Connection Attempts**: 0 to 100; the default is 0. This setting determines how many times GP will try to connect to an internal gateway when it detects it is on an internal network. With this setting set to 0, GP will keep trying.

  - **Portal Connection Timeout (sec)**: 1 to 600; the default is 5. This is the time a connection request to the portal times out due to no response.

  - **TCP Connection Timeout (sec)**: 1 to 600; the default is 5.

  - **TCP Receive Timeout (sec)**: 1 to 600; the default is 30.

- **DNS**:

  - **Resolve All FQDNs Using DNS Servers Assigned by the Tunnel (Windows Only)**: Enabled by default. Disabling this setting will allow Windows hosts to send DNS queries to the DNS server configured on the physical interface.

  - **Append Local Search Domains to Tunnel DNS Suffixes (Mac Only)**

  - **Update DNS Settings at Connect (Windows Only) (Deprecated)**: This setting is inherited from the old PAN-OS configuration and should no longer be used.

- **Proxy**:

> **Note**
> The GP agent can be used as an authentication client for the secure web gateway/explicit proxy, which removes the requirement for SSL decryption on all traffic and authentication cookies.

  - **Local Proxy Port**: 1024 to 65534; the default port is 9999.

- **Agent Mode for Prisma Access**:

  - **Tunnel**: This is the default mode. In this mode, GP acts as a normal VPN client and relies on the routing table to route traffic into the tunnel.

  - **Proxy**: In this mode, all traffic is controlled by proxy configuration and is either sent to the explicit proxy/secure web gateway or directly.

  - **Tunnel and proxy**: This is a hybrid mode where some traffic is sent to the SWG and some is sent into the tunnel.

- **Detect Proxy for Each Connection (Windows only)**: This is disabled by default, which causes auto-detect of the proxy once and use of the proxy for all subsequent connections. Enabling this setting will cause the proxy to be detected automatically for every connection.

- **Set Up Tunnel Over Proxy (Windows & Mac Only)**: Enabled by default. This lets GP detect proxy configuration and use the proxy to establish a connection. Disabling this option lets GP bypass local proxy configuration.

- **Forwarding Option**:

  - **Forwarding Profiles**: This lets you choose forwarding profiles for the proxy.

  - **Proxy Auto-configuration (PAC) file URL**: This is the default setting. Choose to use a PAC file to control traffic to the proxy.

  - **Forwarding profiles/Proxy Auto-Configuration (PAC) File URL**: This lets you select the forwarding profiles or enter the PAC file's URL.

- **MFA**:

  - **Enable Inbound Authentication Prompts from MFA Gateways**: This can be enabled so that additional MFA can be triggered on the GP agent.

  - **Network Port for Inbound Authentication Prompts (UDP)**: 1 to 65535; the default is 4501.

  - **Trusted MFA Gateways**: The gateway address (and port if not the default) of the redirect URL for MFA authentication.

  - **Inbound Authentication Message**: A default message is provided, but it can be customized to notify users about the MFA authentication.

  - **Suppress Multiple Inbound MFA Prompts (sec)**: 0 to 180; the default is 0 (disabled). In cases where multiple MFA authentication messages are received, the messages can be suppressed for the configured amount of seconds.

- **Troubleshooting**:

  - **Log Gateway Selection Criteria**: This creates additional logging about the gateway selection process a GP agent goes through.

  - **Run Diagnostics Tests for These Destination Web Servers**: Up to 10 URLs (FQDN or IP-based) can be added here. These will be used to measure download speeds. The Autonomous DEM license is required for this feature.

- **Device quarantine**:

  - **Device Added to Quarantine Message**: A message can be customized to notify users their device was placed in quarantine.

  - **Device Removed from Quarantine Message**: A message can be customized to notify users their device was removed from quarantine.

This concludes all the options available in the **App** section.

The next feature below the **App** section is **Internal Host Detection**, which enables you to let the GP agent self-disable if it detects it is inside a corporate network.

Internal Host Detection

GP can perform a reverse lookup of an IP address against its local DNS server's IN-ADDR-ARPA record to see if it receives an internal hostname. If the lookup matches the correct hostname, GP will remain disconnected, or connect to an internal gateway:

- **Internal Host Detection**: This enables IPv4 or IPv6

- **IP Address/Hostname(IPv4)** or **(IPv6)**: These options add the IP address for which a reverse DNS lookup is done and add the hostname that would be resolved if the client is using an internal DNS server

Gateways

- **External gateways**: By default, all Prisma Access gateways are available to all users. In the **Gateways** section, you can add individual MU-SPNs so that specific users/groups/devices are only allowed to connect to these. You can also add gateways hosted on physical chassis as additional (direct) gateways.

- **Internal gateways**: This can be enabled and internal gateways added if there is an internal gateway that's been configured on the corporate LAN. Agents will report their HIP status and username or create an IPSEC connection to the internal gateway.

- **Third-party VPN**: The Cisco Systems VPN Adapter or the Juniper Network Virtual Adapter can be added here to allow these VPN agents to connect to Prisma Access.

HIP Data Collection

- **Collect HIP Data**: This is enabled by default.

- **Max Wait Time**: This can be between 10 to 60 minutes; the default is 20. This is the time GP will wait for the HIP profile to complete before giving up.

- **Certificate Profile**: Here, a certificate profile can be added if HIP needs to check for a machine certificate.

- **Exclude Categories**: If this profile does not need to check certain HIP categories (for example, antivirus, firewall, disk encryption, and others), you can exclude them here.

- **Custom Checks**: These can be added to check if a certain registry entry exists for Windows, a Plist item exists for Mac, or a process is running for Windows, Mac, or Linux.

Once you've selected all the parameters you need for this profile, click **Save** to go back to the GP main page.

Next, we'll look at **Tunnel Settings**.

Tunnel Settings

The **Tunnel Settings** profiles determine how traffic is routed. You can create different profiles that, depending on the **match criteria**, determine the connectivity profile for a user or device.

The match criteria can be determined by the following criteria:

- **OS**:
  - Android
  - Chrome
  - IoT
  - Linux
  - Mac
  - Windows
  - WindowsUWP
  - iOS

- **User Entity**:
  - Pre-logon will only match connections being established by an agent in pre-logon mode before the user has logged on to their desktop

- Username or AD group

- **Region**: Depending on the source country a user connects from, a different tunnel profile can be loaded

- **IP Address**: This will only match if the user's source IP

In the following screenshot, I set the profile to only be matched if the user is connecting from Belgium or the Netherlands:

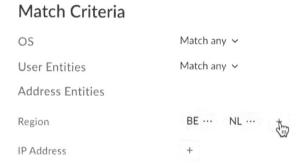

Match Criteria

OS	Match any ∨
User Entities	Match any ∨
Address Entities	
Region	BE ⋯ NL ⋯ +
IP Address	+

Figure 6.22 – Tunnel match criteria

The tunnel can also be configured to create and/or accept authentication override cookies. These cookies can be used to allow a user to reconnect within the specified timeframe without needing to re-authenticate. These cookies can also be shared with the portal (**App Settings**).

A common practice is to create and accept cookies on the portal and only create cookies on the gateway. That way, configuration can always be retrieved without needing to authenticate. However, setting up a tunnel requires authentication every time. The opposite can also be configured, where the portal creates cookies but does not accept them, but the gateway accepts cookies for authentication. Disabling cookies on both the portal and the gateway may lead to needing to authenticate twice when a user comes into the office in the morning, in which case the config is fetched and then a tunnel is created.

A different CA certificate can also be used for portal and gateway cookies so that they cannot be shared between the two.

For example, if you use the same CA certificate in the portal and gateway, cookies that are generated when a user authenticates to the portal can be used to authenticate against a gateway, bypassing other forms of authentication (SAML, LDAP, and so on). When different CA certificates are used, a cookie that's generated when authenticating to the portal will not allow the user to bypass authentication to the gateway, thereby requiring a new authentication method, which may then generate another cookie for the gateway.

As you can see, there are many different ways to leverage authentication cookies. In the following example, I have them set to be created when the user authenticates, and then remain active for 24 hours so that the user doesn't need to re-authenticate whenever they reconnect within those 24 hours:

Authentication Override

Authentication Override	☑ Generate cookie for authentication override
	☑ Accept cookie for authentication override
Certificate to Encrypt/Decrypt cookie	Authentication Cookie Cert ✕ ∨
	Import
Cookie Lifetime	24 Hours ∨

Figure 6.23 – Authentication Override

The behavior of the tunnel will mostly be dictated by the split tunnel configuration. **Split Tunneling** is used to split off certain connections to the local network or internet breakout instead of forwarding them over the tunnel to Prisma Access.

At the top of the following screenshot, you can see a checkbox for **Block direct access to local network**. Checking this box will prevent the endpoint from connecting to any other devices on the same remote network – for example, a user's home network printer, NAS, smart TV, and so on.

Next, we have **Exclude Traffic**, which allows us to specify the domain names or subnets split tunneling is enabled for. Here, I've excluded `pangurus.lab` and `198.51.100.0/24` from being tunneled and breaking out locally instead.

Below that, we can enable an **Include** list. This will specify exactly what should go into the tunnel. If you only want to reach the corporate data center, for example, and prefer to break out the internet locally, you can add the data center's subnet here; everything else will go out to the local ISP connection:

Split Tunneling

Local Network Access

You can control how GlobalProtect users on Windows, Mac and Linux access to local network

☐ Block direct access to local network

Exclude Traffic

Specify the mobile user traffic to exclude from Prisma Access policy inspection and enforcement. The GlobalProtect app does not route this traffic to Prisma Access and excludes traffic based on the application first, then the domain, and then the route.

Application   +

Domain

Domains (1)   Delete   **Add Domain**

	Domain	Ports
☐	pangurus.lab	

Route   198.51.100.0/24 ···   +

Customize Include Traffic

By default, the GlobalProtect app routes all traffic to Prisma Access except what's in the exclude list. Specify traffic that the GlobalProtect app should always route to Prisma Access, even when it meets exclude list criteria.

⬤✓ **Customize Include Traffic**

Application   +

Domain

Domains (0)   Delete   **Add Domain**

	Domain	Ports
☐	Domain	Ports

Route   +

Figure 6.24 – Split Tunneling configuration

We also have the option to quickly select a few video streaming applications that should be excluded from the tunnel to conserve bandwidth. If you deselect them, they will be routed into the tunnel, where they can still be blocked by a security policy or **Quality of Service** (**QoS**) limitations can be applied to them:

Exclude Video Stream Traffic

Choose not to send video streaming traffic from these applications to Prisma Access. This is a global setting and the match criteria for this rule does not apply.

☑ dailymotion   ☑ hulu-base   ☑ netflix-streaming   ☑ sling   ☑ vimeo-base   ☑ xfinity-tv   ☑ youku-base   ☑ youtube-streaming

Figure 6.25 – Exclude Video Stream Traffic

Click **Save** to save the tunnel configuration and return to the main GP page.

The next section is **Global App Settings**. Click the little cogwheel to the left to open these properties:

Figure 6.26 – Global App Settings

On the **General** page, we have various options.

At the top, we can select which **GlobalProtect agent version** is active. This version will be made available for users logging in to the portal via a web browser and will be installed on the already installed, but outdated, agent, depending on the install options selected in the **App Configuration** area.

Agent User Override Key is a password that can be shared with select users if disabling GP is set to require a password in the **App Configuration** area.

Trusted Application Distributions allows you to automatically install certificates into a connected endpoint user and machine store, which is useful for deploying your corporate PKI CA or a decryption CA.

Under **Connection**, you can limit the number of users that can be connected simultaneously, disable the use of IPSec if that's needed, and select the Crypto profiles for the GP tunnel.

Finally, **Timeout** determines how long a user is allowed to remain connected in one sitting and after how much time of inactivity the tunnel is logged out:

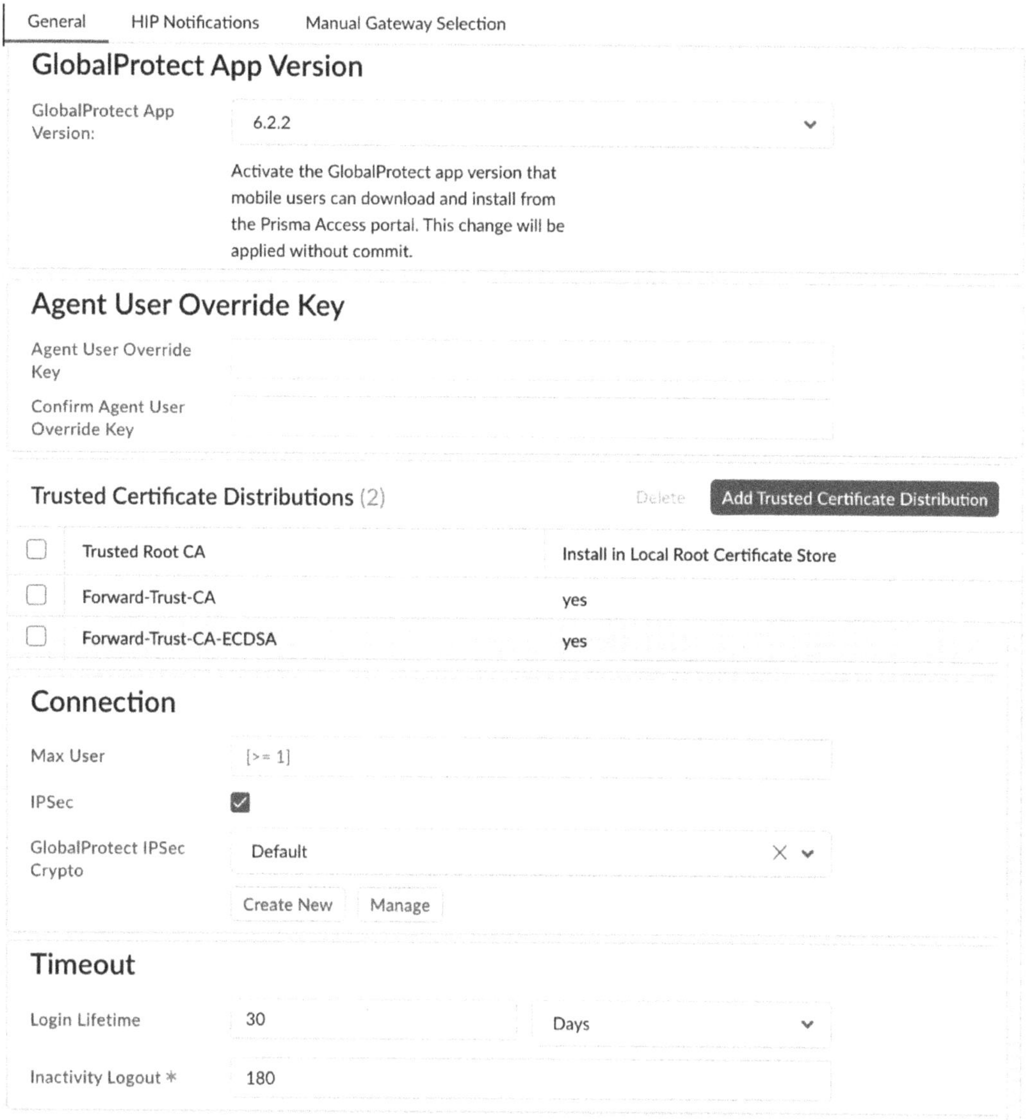

General   HIP Notifications   Manual Gateway Selection

GlobalProtect App Version

GlobalProtect App
Version:

6.2.2

Activate the GlobalProtect app version that
mobile users can download and install from
the Prisma Access portal. This change will be
applied without commit.

Agent User Override Key

Agent User Override
Key

Confirm Agent User
Override Key

Trusted Certificate Distributions (2)   Delete   Add Trusted Certificate Distribution

☐	Trusted Root CA	Install in Local Root Certificate Store
☐	Forward-Trust-CA	yes
☐	Forward-Trust-CA-ECDSA	yes

Connection

Max User   [>= 1]

IPSec   ☑

GlobalProtect IPSec   Default   ✕ ⌄
Crypto
                            Create New   Manage

Timeout

Login Lifetime   30   Days   ⌄

Inactivity Logout *   180

Figure 6.27 – App Global Settings

In the next tab, **HIP Notifications** can be enabled so that users are notified if they do, or do not, match a specific HIP check.

In the following screenshot, you can see a **Not Match Message** value that is set for the anti-malware machine check. The user will be notified if they fail the check, which means that their antivirus software isn't running or is outdated:

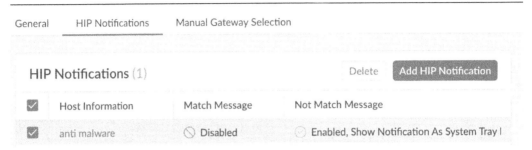

Figure 6.28 – HIP Notifications

In the last tab, **Manual Gateway Selection**, you can check a box next to each country that should be made available to the user for manual selection. This allows the user to select from a list of available gateways so that they can connect to the best gateway (in-country) or one of their preference (because they may need to be connected in or from a specific country for regulatory reasons):

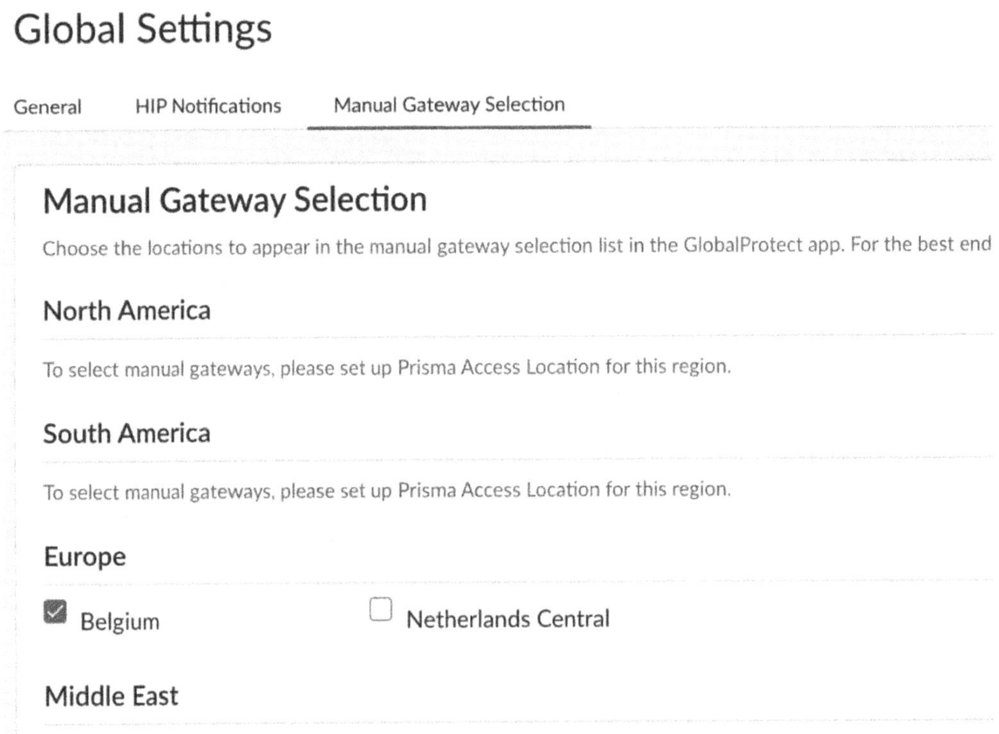

Global Settings

General   HIP Notifications   Manual Gateway Selection

Manual Gateway Selection

Choose the locations to appear in the manual gateway selection list in the GlobalProtect app. For the best end

North America

To select manual gateways, please set up Prisma Access Location for this region.

South America

To select manual gateways, please set up Prisma Access Location for this region.

Europe

☑ Belgium   ☐ Netherlands Central

Middle East

Figure 6.29 – Manual Gateway Selection

Click **Save** to store your changes and be taken back to the main GP page.

The last section is **Response Pages**. The default portal page and the default portal login pages can be changed so that, for example, the company logo and style are reflected. A **welcome page** can be displayed each time (or on occasion) whenever a user logs on to GP to notify them of important things, such as end user policies, upcoming maintenance work, and more.

The GP **help page** can also be updated so that the user can find company-specific information if they need assistance:

Response Pages (4)

Name	Location	Actions
GP Portal Home	All	Preview (Predefined)
GP Portal Login	All	Preview (Predefined)
GP App Welcome	All	Preview (Predefined)
GP App Help Page		

Figure 6.30 – Response Pages

With that, you have fully configured everything so that your users can connect. Click **Push Config** to commit your configuration to the MU-SPNs.

We will cover clientless VPNs in *Chapter 7*.

In this section, you learned how to set up MU-SPNs and the GP agent from Strata Cloud Manager. In the next section, we will learn how to do these same things from a Panorama-managed environment.

Configuring MU-SPNs in Panorama

To configure Mobile Users in Panorama, you must navigate to **Panorama | Cloud Services | Configuration | Mobile Users – GlobalProtect**.

We'll start by configuring the general settings by clicking the small cogwheel next to **Settings**, as indicated in the following screenshot:

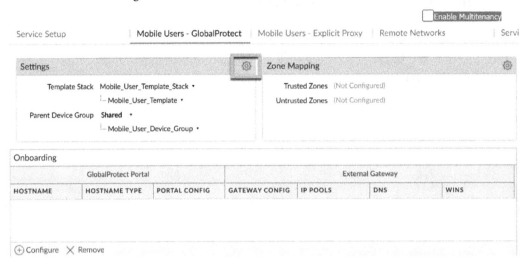

Figure 6.31 – Mobile Users – GlobalProtect

On the main **Settings** page, we can see `Mobile_User_Template_Stack`, `Mobile_User_Template`, and `Mobile_User_Device_Group`. These can't be renamed, and `Mobile_User_Template` can't be moved down to prioritize other templates. However, the **Parent Device Group** value for `Mobile_User_Device_Group` can be changed. In many cases, it is useful to create a parent device group for both `Remote_Network_Device_Group` and `Mobile_User_Device_Group` so that common rules can be created in a single parent rulebase. We'll see more about rulebases in *Chapter 8*.

At the bottom, we can choose to set a **User ID Master Device** value or use **Cloud Identity Engine** (**CIE**). This setting allows Active Directory groups containing usernames to be retrieved, which can then be used to grant or deny access in security rulebases or build GP profiles based on group membership. We'll dive into CIE in *Chapter 9*:

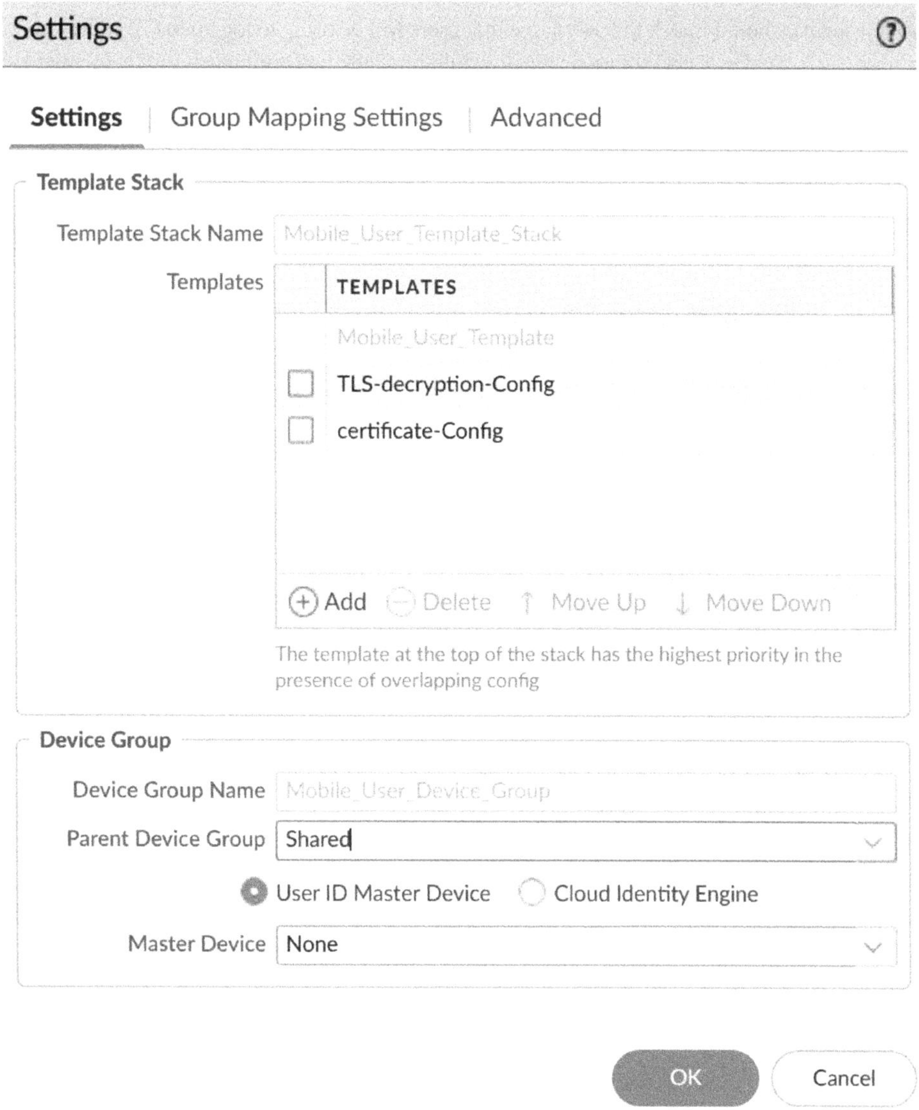

Settings

Settings | Group Mapping Settings | Advanced

Template Stack

Template Stack Name Mobile_User_Template_Stack

Templates

TEMPLATES

Mobile_User_Template

☐ TLS-decryption-Config

☐ certificate-Config

⊕ Add   ⊖ Delete   ↑ Move Up   ↓ Move Down

The template at the top of the stack has the highest priority in the presence of overlapping config

Device Group

Device Group Name Mobile_User_Device_Group

Parent Device Group Shared

◉ User ID Master Device   ◯ Cloud Identity Engine

Master Device None

OK   Cancel

Figure 6.32 – The Settings tab

In the **Group Mapping Settings** area, we can set the username attribute that's used when collecting group information from CIE. If LDAP is going to be used to retrieve group information, this needs to be configured the traditional way by going to **Mobile_User_Template** | **Device** | **User Identification** | **Group Mapping** rather than here. Only enable **Enable Directory Sync Integration** if you're going to use CIE.

The username format should match the username that users will be using to log on to GP. If they use their email address, `UserPrincipalName` or email would typically be configured. `sAMAccountName` can typically be used if LDAP authentication is used, but any other attribute can be configured if the IdP or directory service uses a custom format. In the following screenshot, I've added `cn` as an alternate as my directory service may sometimes return a common name due to the use of certificates:

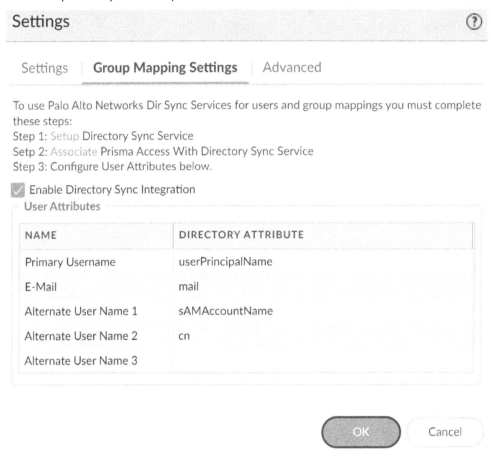

Figure 6.33 – The Group Mapping Settings tab

In the **Advanced** tab, we can enable a second portal. This can be useful if a GP portal only supports one set of authentication at a time. There are a few workarounds for this, such as filtering the authentication based on the host operating system or creating an authentication sequence. However, options such as SAML do not support an authentication sequence, which limits the options pretty quickly. The primary portal can be set up to authenticate everyone using SAML, with a secondary portal using the same FQDN but on port 8443 (for example, gp.mydomain.com and gp.mydomain.com:8443) with a different authentication mechanism as a fallback in case the SAML IdP suffers an outage:

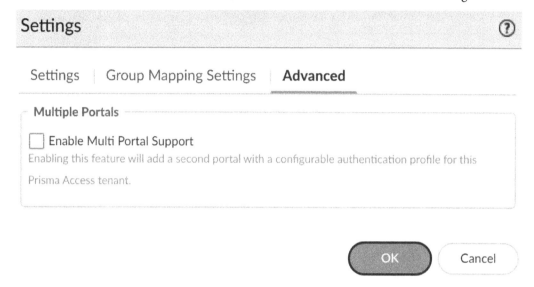

Figure 6.34 – The Advanced tab

Click **OK** once you're done configuring the settings.

To use a company domain for the portal address, we'll need a server certificate from a public CA.

Once you've received the certificate from your preferred public CA, upload the certificate and its chain (root, intermediary, and so on) by going to **Templates > Mobile_User_Template | Device | Certificate Management | Certificates** and then create an SSL/TLS profile containing the certificate by going to **Templates | Mobile_User_Template | Device | Certificate Management | SSL/TLS Service Profile**, as illustrated in the following screenshot:

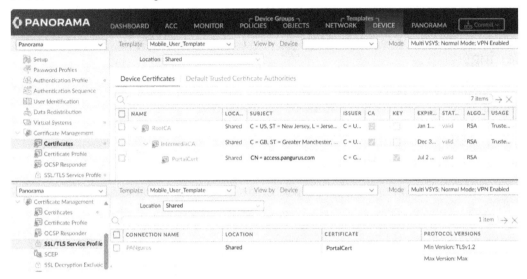

Figure 6.35 – Creating a portal TLS profile

Next, we will configure the onboarding section. Navigate back to **Panorama | Cloud Services | Configuration | Mobile Users – GlobalProtect**. Click **Configure** in the **Onboarding** section (see *Figure 6.32*):

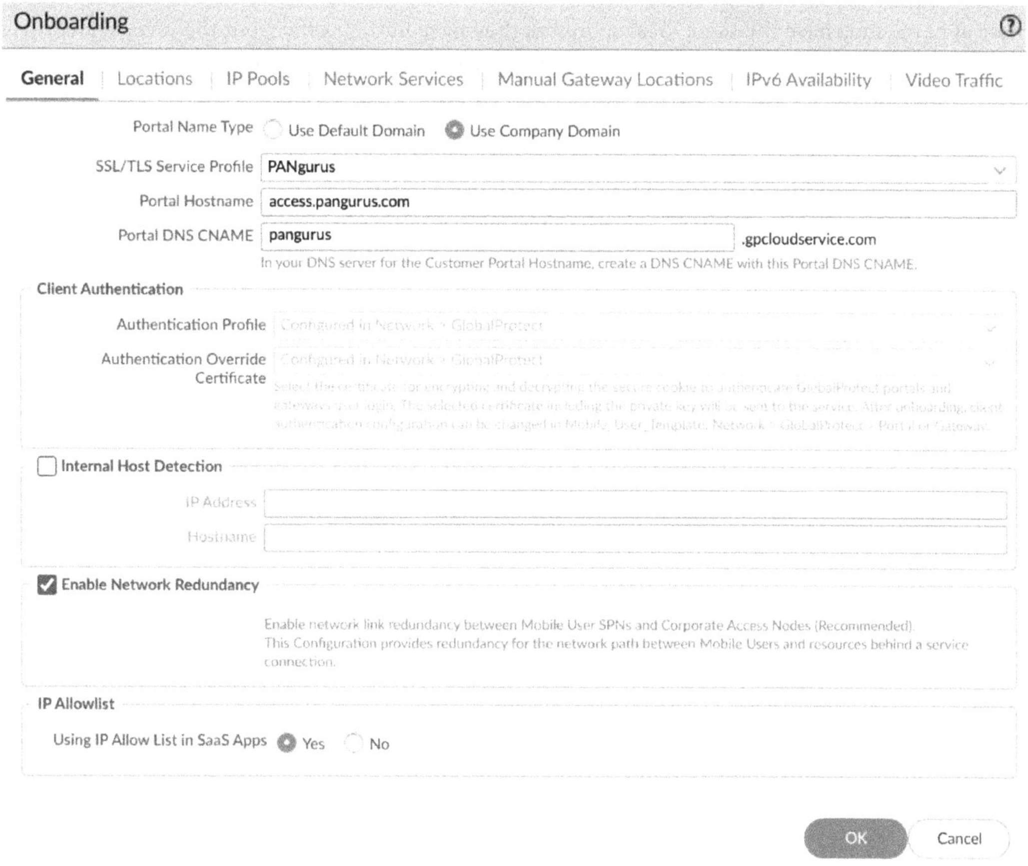

Figure 6.36 – Onboarding – General

For **Portal Name Type**, we can keep the **default domain**, which will provide a free subdomain for the gpcloudservice.com TLD. Alternatively, we can choose to use a **company domain**. The latter will require the SSL/TLS profile, as we saw in *Figure 6.36*, and will also require a public DNS record for your company domain hostname with a CNAME record pointing to the configured gpcloudservice.com subdomain.

Client authentication is configured in the GP configuration, similar to how this would be done in a normal deployment. **Internal Host Detection** can also be configured here and applied to all users, though it can also be configured in individual profiles in the gateway configuration. **Internal Host Detection** works by performing a reverse DNS lookup (from the IN_ADDR_ARPA record) against the local DNS server on the client machine. The IP must resolve to the exact hostname that was configured in **Internal Host Detection**.

A user at home may have the same local subnet as they have in their office, but the reverse lookup will resolve to a different hostname. Only when the user is in the office will the local DNS server be able to resolve the IP to the correct hostname. With **Internal Host Detection** enabled, GP will go into a disconnected state.

Enable Network Redundancy will connect each MU-SPN with a second SC-CAN. As you may recall from *Chapter 1*, each MU-SPN connects to a single SC-CAN for internal routing and user ID redistribution. Enabling this option will set up a secondary link to the next-nearest SC-CAN as a passive link. If the primary SC-CAN is disconnected or fails, the backup link will resume internal connectivity:

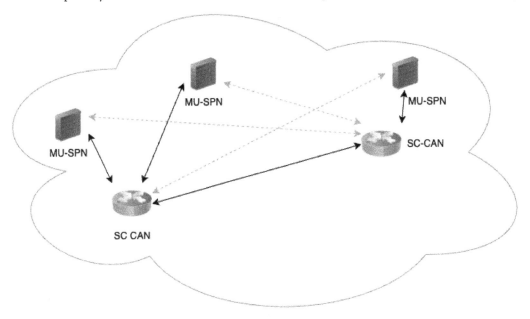

Figure 6.37 – MU-SPN network redundancy

If your organization has private SaaS applications that require an IP Allowlist containing allowed source IP addresses, enabling the IP Allowlist will prevent Prisma Access from activating IP addresses that have not been approved by you first. This does require monitoring on your part as new IP addresses will not be used, potentially blocking autoscaling, until they have been approved.

If this option is enabled, the main **Mobile User – GlobaProtect** page will show the following provisioning at the bottom. Manually approve all IP addresses per location to allow Prisma Access to use them for outbound traffic:

Figure 6.38 – IP Allowlist

Next, click the **Locations** tab to start selecting active locations. You can click a region to zoom in and select individual locations:

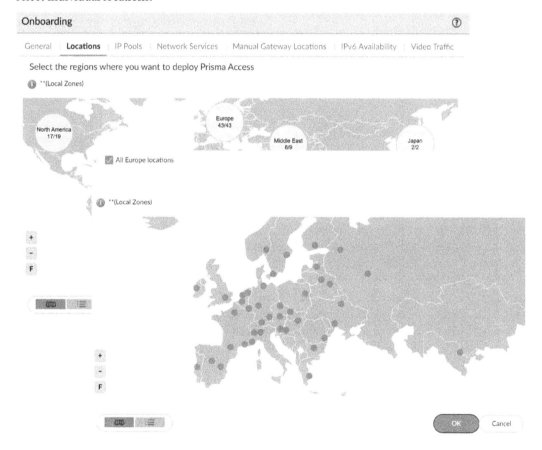

Figure 6.39 – The Locations tab

In the **IP Pools** tab, we can configure an IP pool per compute node, per region, and worldwide. The MU-SPNs will be assigned an initial /24 subnet from the most localized pool and can pull in additional /24 subnets if more users connect to a node. Once the local/regional pool is depleted, additional IP addresses can be obtained from the theater or worldwide pool. If IPv6 is enabled on the infrastructure, IPv6 pools can also be configured:

Figure 6.40 – The IP Pools tab

In the **Network Services** tab, we can configure DNS preferences. Each MU-SPN acts as a DNS proxy server for all its connected users, so DNS policies can be created to direct DNS lookups to specific DNS servers. Internal domains may need to be sent to a specific set of DNS servers, and there may also be hostnames that are served by different DNS servers with different DNS records, depending on the theater. These can be controlled by setting DNS rules worldwide or a theater (or compute node even) for the desired domain names pointing to the correct DNS server IP addresses. In the following screenshot, I am redirecting my internal domains to my internal DNS servers, while everything else is resolved by the default cloud DNS server. The public DNS servers can also be changed. If legacy NetBIOS name services are being used to reach internal resources, WINS configuration can be enabled and the appropriate servers set:

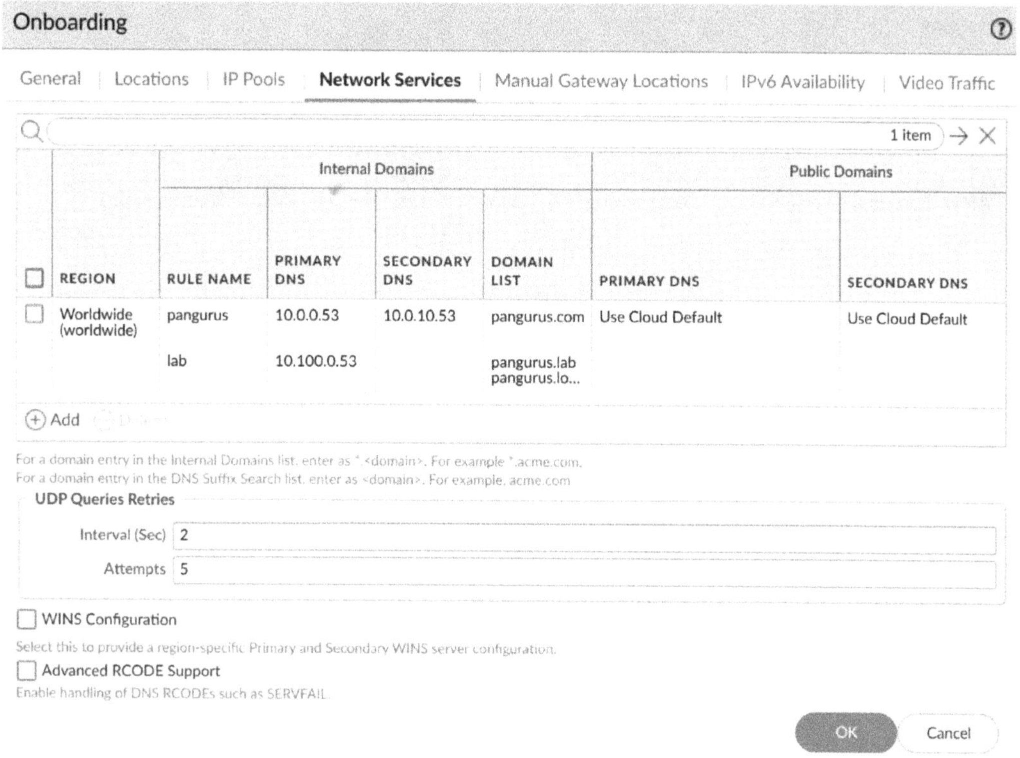

Figure 6.41 – The Network Services tab

In the **Manual Gateway Locations** tab, we can mark the gateways that will become available for manual selection in the GP agent. This will allow users to bypass the automatic gateway selection discussed at the start of this chapter, and instead choose a specific gateway to connect to:

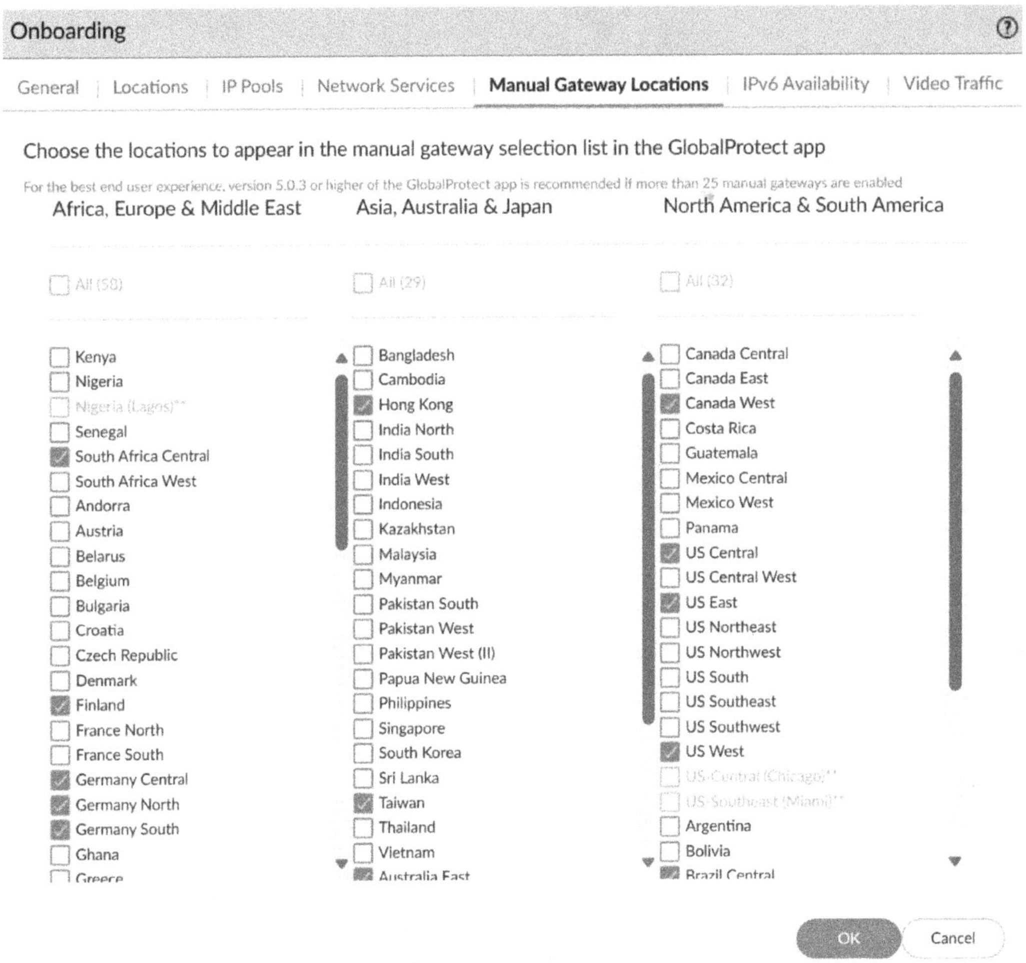

Figure 6.42 – The Manual Gateway Locations tab

Similar to manual gateway selection, if you have enabled IPv6 on the infrastructure, you can select which gateways will support IPv6 in the **IPv6 Availability** tab. Lastly, you can enable **Exclude video traffic from the tunnel** in the **Video Traffic** tab and then add the video streaming applications you want to exclude. This will cause them to break out locally on the client's ISP link. If you want to control these applications via a security policy or QoS, do not exclude them:

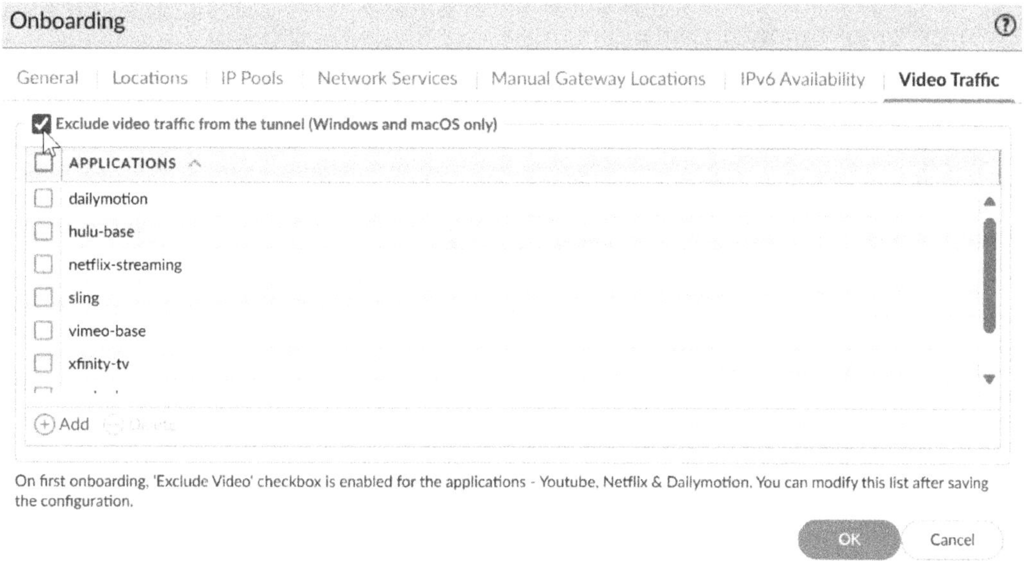

Onboarding   ⑦

General | Locations | IP Pools | Network Services | Manual Gateway Locations | IPv6 Availability | **Video Traffic**

☑ Exclude video traffic from the tunnel (Windows and macOS only)

☐ APPLICATIONS ∧

☐ dailymotion

☐ hulu-base

☐ netflix-streaming

☐ sling

☐ vimeo-base

☐ xfinity-tv

⊕ Add

On first onboarding, 'Exclude Video' checkbox is enabled for the applications - Youtube, Netflix & Dailymotion. You can modify this list after saving the configuration.

OK   Cancel

Figure 6.43 – Exclude video traffic

Click **OK** to conclude the onboarding configuration.

The last thing we need to do here is map the zones. To do this, need to create two zones minimum – one to represent the internet and one to represent everything internal. Go to **Templates** | **Network** | **Mobile_User_Template** | **Zones** and create these two zones. Then, go back to **Panorama** | **Cloud Services** | **Configuration** | **Mobile users – GlobalProtect** and open the **Zone Mapping** configuration.

Both zones will be listed in the **UNTRUSTED ZONES** column. Move the internal zone over to the **TRUSTED ZONES** side and click **OK**. As shown in the following screenshot, I created MU-Trust and MU-Untrust, and I moved MU-Trust into the **TRUSTED ZONES** area:

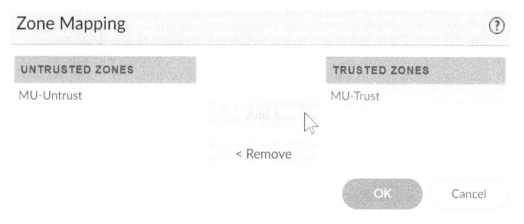

Figure 6.44 – Zone Mapping

We can now start configuring the portal.

GlobalProtect portal configuration

We'll start by preparing the authentication profile so that our users can log in. In this case, we'll use SAML (we can also configure LDAP, RADIUS, TACACS+, or Kerberos). Navigate to **Templates > Network > Mobile_User_Template > Device | Server Profiles | SAML** and **Import** the IdP meta file. This will automatically create the profile:

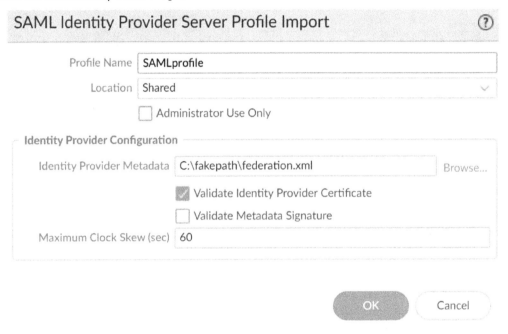

Figure 6.45 – Importing SAML metadata

Next, create an authentication profile by going to **Templates | Network | Mobile_User_Template | Device | Authentication Profile**. The certificate for signing requests should have been imported with the metadata. If not, you may need to download it from the IdP directly and upload it to **Templates | Network | Mobile_User_Template | Certificate management | Certificates**.

Don't forget to add `all` to the **Allow List** area in the **Advanced** tab to allow all users to authenticate:

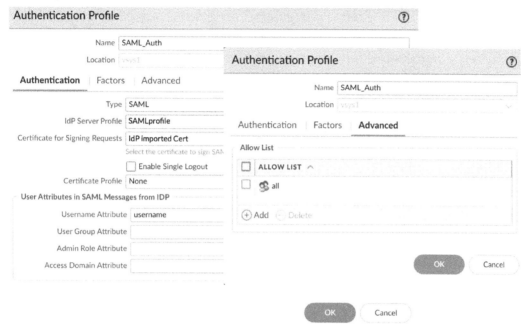

Figure 6.46 – Authentication Profile

We can now configure the portal by navigating to **Templates | Network | Mobile_User_Template | GlobalProtect | Portals | GlobalProtect_Portal**.

In the **Authentication** tab, we can create a new authentication rule that enables users to log in using the previously configured SAML authentication profile. Additionally, we can select a certificate profile that will enable client certificate authentication. You can combine SAML authentication and the client certificate by leaving **Allow Authentication with User Credentials OR Client Certificate** set to `no`. When the certificate profile is configured, it will require the user to have a certificate and produce login credentials for SAML.

Changing this setting to `yes` will allow a user to authenticate with just the certificate *or* by authenticating. The *yes* option can be useful in case pre-logon is used, in which case a user won't be able to authenticate:

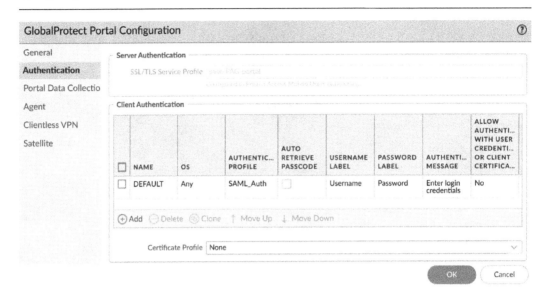

Figure 6.47 – Authentication

In the **Agent** tab, we can create agent profiles, which will control how the GP app will behave. A different profile can be created for groups of users or based on the operating system (or both).

We can also add trusted root certificates that will be installed on the client once they connect. This can be a useful means to distribute the SSL decryption certificate:

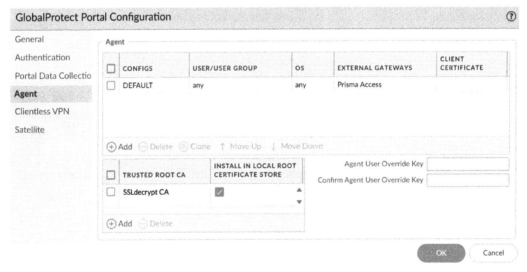

Figure 6.48 – Agent

In the agent **Authentication** tab, we can set the following options:

- **Client certificate**: Adding a client certificate here will automatically install the client certificate to the agent for increased connection security.

- **Save User Credentials**: This will allow or disallow saving the user credentials in GP. When a user logs back into their workspace with this option set to `yes`, they will immediately be able to log back on without typing their username and password (this does not apply to SAML, which uses a login page served by the IdP).

- **Authentication override**: This allows the use of an authentication cookie for an amount of time without the need to re-authenticate:

  - **Generate cookie for authentication override** creates the cookie. Depending on the **Certificate to Encrypt/Decrypt Cookie** option, this certificate can be shared between the portal and gateway.

  - **Accept cookie for authentication override** will allow the use of the cookie. Disabling this will require the user to authenticate, regardless of if there is a cookie or not.

  - **Cookie lifetime** determines how long the cookie will be accepted after it is generated.

  - **Components that require Dynamic Passwords**: When **one-time passwords** (**OTPs**) are to be used as opposed to **multi-factor authentication** (**MFA**), the appropriate components can be enabled so that the authentication mechanism is set to support OTP:

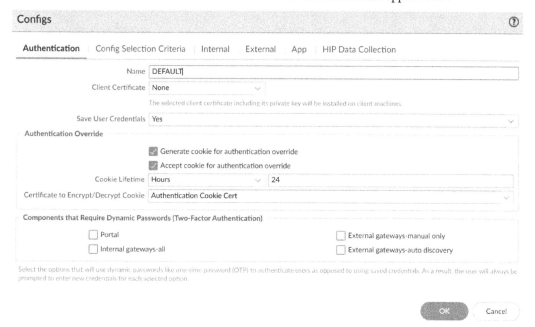

Figure 6.49 – The agent Authentication tab

In the **Internal** tab, we can configure **Internal Host Detection**. This mechanism will query the local DNS server on the network the client is connected to for the reverse record of an IP you configure. If the returned hostname is identical to the hostname configured in **Internal Host Protection**, the GP agent will know it's on the corporate network and go into a disconnected state.

If an internal gateway is configured, the GP agent will periodically check in to report its HIP status and register the logged-in username to user-IP mapping. If the internal gateway has a tunnel configuration, a secure connection will be established with the internal gateway:

Figure 6.50 – Internal Host Detection

In the **External** tab, the Prisma Access gateways are indicated with a single entry. We can add additional gateways here. If there are legacy gateways that still need to be reachable, they can be added here to become part of the available gateways. Any non-Prisma Access gateways that are added here need to be set as manual gateways as they will not be included in the automatic gateway selection process:

Figure 6.51 – External gateways

In the **App** tab, we can configure the behavior of the GP application:

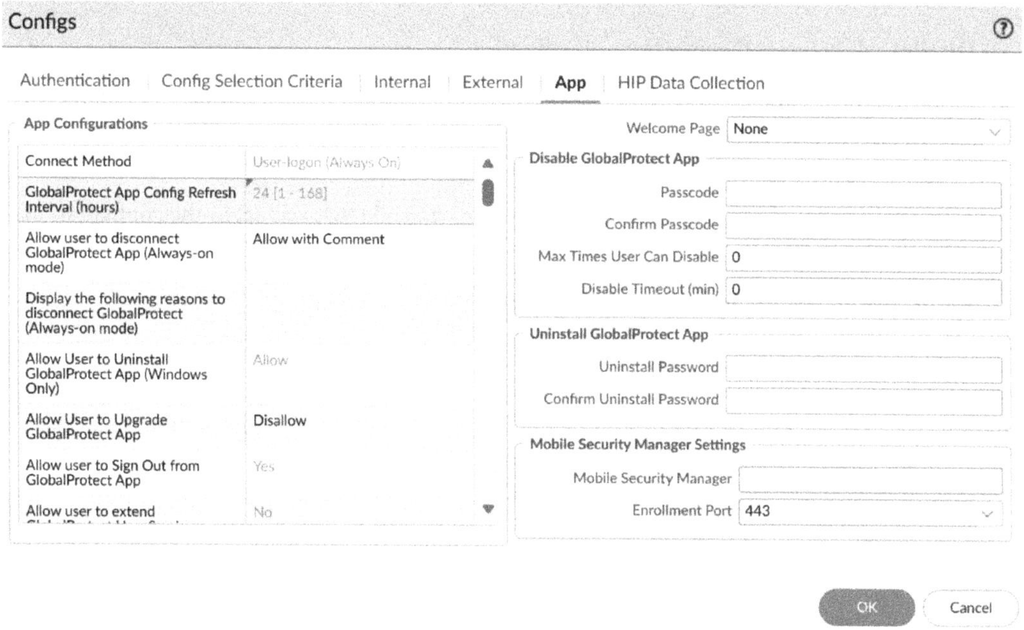

Figure 6.52 – App configuration

Connect Method contains four modes:

- **Always on**: Every time the user logs on, GP connects to Prisma Access.

- **Pre-logon**: A connection is established as soon as the endpoint is booted, even before the user is logged on.

- **On-Demand**: This allows the user to choose when to connect.

- **Pre-logon, then on-demand**: The connection is established before the user is logged on. Once the user logs on, the connection becomes on-demand.

GlobalProtect App Config Refresh Interval sets a refresh time for how often the GP agent needs to fetch a fresh configuration.

By default, all users are allowed to **disconnect** GP, which allows them to interrupt the always-on mode. This mode can be set to one of the following options:

- **Allow**: Allows the user to disable GP. This will grant them access to the internet without the need to use a VPN tunnel.

- **Disallowed**: Prevents the user from disabling GP.

- **Allow with comment**: The user must leave a comment about why they disabled GP. Preconfigured reasons can be provided in the **Display the following reasons to disconnect GlobalProtect (Always-on mode)** field. The reason is logged.

- **Allow with passcode**: The user needs to know the passcode that was set in the configuration to be able to disable GP.

- **Allow with ticket**: The user must reach out with a ticket number.

The maximum number of times the user is allowed to use the disable function can be controlled by setting a value in **Max Times User Can Disable**, with a maximum value of 25 (0 means the setting is disabled. The user will be able to disable GP as many times as they want). This number of disables is stored on the client machine registry key's **UserOverrides** under HKEY_CURRENT_USER\ Software\Palo AltoNetworks\GlobalProtect\Setting.

The time GlobalProtect remains disabled can also be controlled by setting **Disable Duration (min)** to a value of up to 65535 minutes, after which GP will automatically re-enable and connect if the connect method is set to always on.

Display the following reasons to disconnect GlobalProtect (Always-on mode) lets you set a few preconfigured options for the user to choose from when they want to disconnect GP.

User-initiated uninstall of the GP application can be **allowed**, **disallowed**, or **allowed with password**.

The GP application can be upgraded in the following ways:

- **Allow when the user accepts the upgrade prompt**: This is the default setting. When a new GP package is made available from the infrastructure, the user will be notified that a new version is available, at which point they can upgrade at their convenience.

- **Disallow**: Upgrades are not allowed. The software package is controlled through an external software management tool.

- **Allow manually**: Upgrades can be performed by the user.

- **Allow transparently**: When a new software package is made available, it is automatically and invisibly installed the next time the user logs on.

- **Allow when the user is in the corporate network**: The package will be upgraded when the GP agent detects it is internal via **Internal Host Detection**.

Enforce GlobalProtect Connection for Network Access prevents endpoints from accessing any resources until GP is connected.

Captive Portal Exception Timeout (sec) can be set for an amount of time to allow users to log on to a captive portal in a hotel, airport, or coffee shop before access is limited by connection enforcement.

Automatically Launch Webpage in Default Browser Upon Captive Portal Detection can be configured to load a specific web page as soon as GP detects a captive portal.

Allow User to Change Portal allows users to add additional portals or delete the current one. This can come in handy if a legacy or parallel portal exists, or if partners also offer GP connectivity.

Welcome Page allows you to load a small HTML page that displays when users connect. This can be handy to share the AUP/EULA or broadcast a MOTD.

In the **HIP Data Collection** tab, we can enable HIP data collection for use in matching HIP profiles in security rules.

Click **OK** to save the agent configuration.

Under **Clientless VPN**, we can add applications that are served from the portal web page. Users can log on to the portal page and will see a list of the available applications as tiles. Each tile can be clicked and a proxied web connection will be set up to the associated URL. This enables users to access intranet pages from any device without needing to install GP.

Enable **Clientless VPN** and select a **source zone** for the proxied connections, then create and select **Clientless Application**:

Figure 6.53 – Clientless VPN

In the **Crypto Settings** tab, we should make sure we set strong encryption ciphers for the clientless VPN connection:

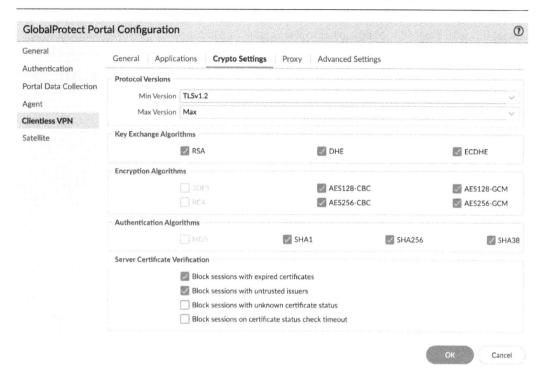

Figure 6.54 – The Crypto Settings tab

In the **Proxy** tab, we can add proxy configuration in case the clientless apps need to be routed via a proxy server.

We can go ahead and click **OK** to save the portal configuration. At this point, we can configure the gateway.

GlobalProtect gateway configuration

Navigate to **Templates | Network | Mobile_User_Template | GlobalProtect | Gateways | GlobalProtect_External_Gateways**.

In the **Authentication** tab, just like the portal configuration, we should create a new authentication rule that enables users to log in using the previously configured SAML authentication profile. Additionally, we can select a certificate profile, which will enable client certificate authentication. You can combine SAML authentication and the client certificate by leaving **Allow Authentication with User Credentials OR Client Certificate** set to no. When the certificate profile is configured, it will require the user to have a certificate and produce login credentials for SAML.

Changing this setting to yes will allow a user to authenticate with just the certificate *or* by authenticating. The yes option can be useful if pre-logon is used, in which case a user will not be able to authenticate:

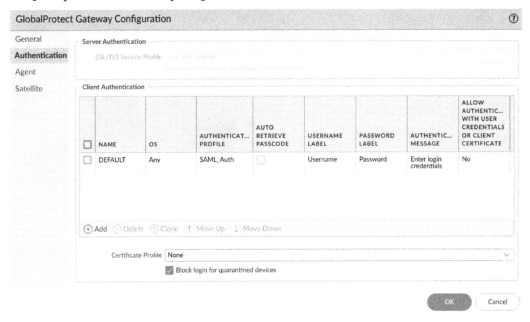

Figure 6.55 – Gateway authentication

In the **Agent** tab, under **Client Settings**, we can edit the default profile or create additional profiles with different selection criteria such as user ID, AD group membership, operating system, source region, or source IP address.

In the **Profile** tab, we can control the authentication override settings, where we can create authentication override cookies and choose to accept them as an authentication mechanism instead of regular authentication.

Let's look at some common ways of leveraging authentication cookies:

- **Generate and accept authentication cookies on the portal, accept cookies on the gateway**: When users log on to the portal to retrieve the configuration, the cookie is generated and then accepted so that the user can log into the gateway, skipping a second authentication to the gateway.

- **Generate but don't accept cookies on the gateway, accept cookies on the portal for an extended period**: Whenever a user connects to the gateway, a fresh cookie is generated. The portal never requires authentication and uses the cookie instead to retrieve the configuration:

Figure 6.56 – The Client Settings tab

The IP pool can't be configured here as it is configured in the plugin. **Split tunneling** lets us determine which traffic is routed into the tunnel and which networks are allowed outside of the tunnel.

Common configurations include the following:

- **0.0.0.0/0**: Present in the include list; routes all traffic into the tunnel.

- **Specific subnets in the exclude list**: This allows direct access outside of the tunnel. It's regularly used for Microsoft services such as Teams to conserve bandwidth and sometimes optimize performance.

- **Only corporate subnets in the include list**: This routes all internal traffic via the tunnel and allows all internet traffic to break out locally.

- **0.0.0.0/0 in the include list and corporate subnets in the exclude list**: This routes all internet traffic to Prisma Access but breaks out corporate subnets to the local network:

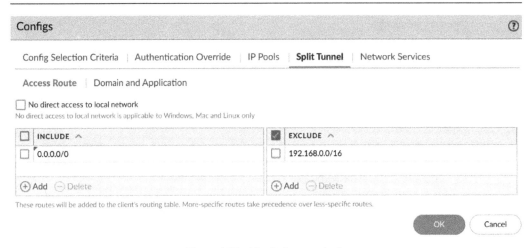

Figure 6.57 – The Split tunnel tab

Under **Network Services**, we can configure DNS servers instead of the MU-SPN proxy DNS service.

Click **OK** to save your settings.

Lastly, we can configure **Connection Settings** to change how long an agent is allowed to be idle before the connection is terminated, as well as the maximum lifetime a tunnel is allowed to remain connected without re-authentication (given that the user does not become idle for the duration).

We can also limit the usage of authentication cookies to reauthenticate timed-out tunnels:

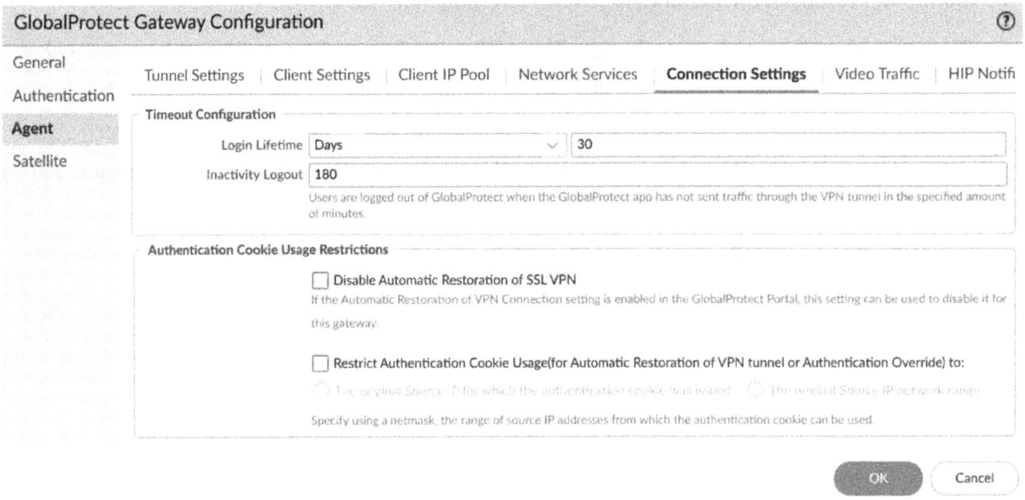

Figure 6.58 – The Connection Settings tab

Click **OK** to save the gateway configuration, and then commit the configuration by clicking **Commit** and then **Commit and Push**.

Summary

In this chapter, we've learned how to properly provision MU-SPN gateways and portals by selecting the appropriate locations and completing the onboarding configuration. We've learned how to configure the portal so it serves specific configuration to the GlobalProtect agent. In the next chapter, we'll learn how to configure a Secure Web Gateway, an alternative way of providing secure internet access to users.

7

Securing Web Gateway

Secure Web Gateway (**SWG**) provides an alternative means of connecting to the internet via a system or a browser's proxy configuration as opposed to building a VPN tunnel into the Prisma Access infrastructure. This can be a preferred connection method to provide secured internet access where a company is required to use proxies or for a company to transition over to **Secure Access Service Edge** (**SASE**) without impacting connectivity in the first phase.

In this chapter, we're going to cover the following main topics:

- Considerations when using the SWG
- Configuring the explicit proxy
- **Proxy Auto Configuration** (**PAC**) file and client configuration
- GlobalProtect in proxy mode

Technical requirements

This chapter will deal with proxy configuration. Some working experience with PAC files and proxies will help you understand the ramifications of using proxy configuration in your environment.

Considerations when using the SWG

While the `explicit proxy` SWG is an easy-to-deploy security enforcement solution, it does have some operational differences from MU-SPNs. Using the SWG will allow users and endpoints to connect from virtually anywhere via the TLS protocol, just like the MU-SPN. The connection uses TCP port `8080`, where SAML authentication is used, or TCP port `8081`, where Kerberos authentication is used. Consider that these ports need to be allowed from all locations that users are connecting from, and some networks may block these ports to prevent bypassing local security policies.

As you may have noticed in the previous paragraph, the SWG supports Kerberos and SAML authentication, whereas GlobalProtect can authenticate using many different protocols.

It is important to note that in contrast to its IPSec counterpart, GlobalProtect, the proxied method does not allow for network traffic other than HTTP/HTTPS and does not provide access to any other networks, resources, or private apps connected to the Prisma Access infrastructure. This includes other users, remote networks, private clouds, and data centers connected via an SC-CAN, and traffic steering cannot be applied to SWG sessions.

The SWG can only be used for secured internet access.

The explicit proxy can be used as a standalone solution or in conjunction with GlobalProtect. In the former scenario, SSL decryption must be enabled for all traffic: After an initial authentication, the user will receive an authentication cookie. This cookie will be included in the payload of every consecutive session and can only be verified by decrypting the session.

> **Important note**
> Access can be enabled by allowing the user's last known source IP to overcome needing to decrypt sensitive categories. However, this may pose a problem if multiple users are behind a gateway.

In the latter case, GlobalProtect, in proxy mode, can be used to provide authentication to the SWG.

To deploy GlobalProtect in proxy mode, agent version 6.2 or higher must be installed on the endpoint. In this operational mode, HIP checks and **Autonomous Digital Experience Manager** (**ADEM**) are not supported.

A common use case for the SWG is to enable IoT, industrial appliances, and other endpoints that do not support a VPN agent to have a secure internet connection via a proxy.

Configuring the explicit proxy

We'll start by taking a look at how the SWG can be deployed in Strata Cloud Manager, followed by how it can be configured via Panorama.

SWG in Prisma Cloud Manager

We first need to enable the explicit proxy In **Workflows** | **Prisma Access Setup** | **Mobile Users**. Click the **Enable** button next to **Explicit Proxy**. This will assign Mobile User licenses to the SWG and make the **Setup** menu available:

Figure 7.1 – Enabling the explicit proxy

You can navigate to the **Explicit Proxy Setup** by clicking the **Explicit Proxy Setup** button in **Workflows | Prisma Access Setup | Mobile Users**, or you can navigate to the newly appeared **Workflows** | **Prisma Access Setup** | **Explicit Proxy** navigation menu item.

We'll start by setting the Infrastructure configuration:

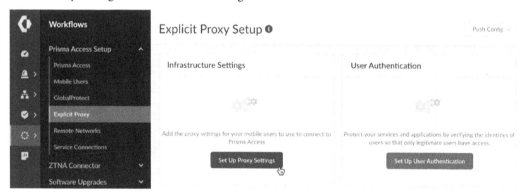

Figure 7.2 – Explicit Proxy Setup

Here, we can set the URL for the explicit proxy. We must first set a subdomain to the Palo Alto provided `<yourprefix>.proxy.prismaaccess.com`, which will be used to serve the explicit proxy on TCP port `8080` when using SAML authentication or TCP port `8081` when using Kerberos authentication.

A CNAME record can be added to your company's domain records to point towards the subdomain, e.g., `proxy.pangurus.com CNAME pangurus.proxy.prismaaccess.com`.

If you want to use GlobalProtect in proxy mode, check the **Enable Agent Proxy** box:

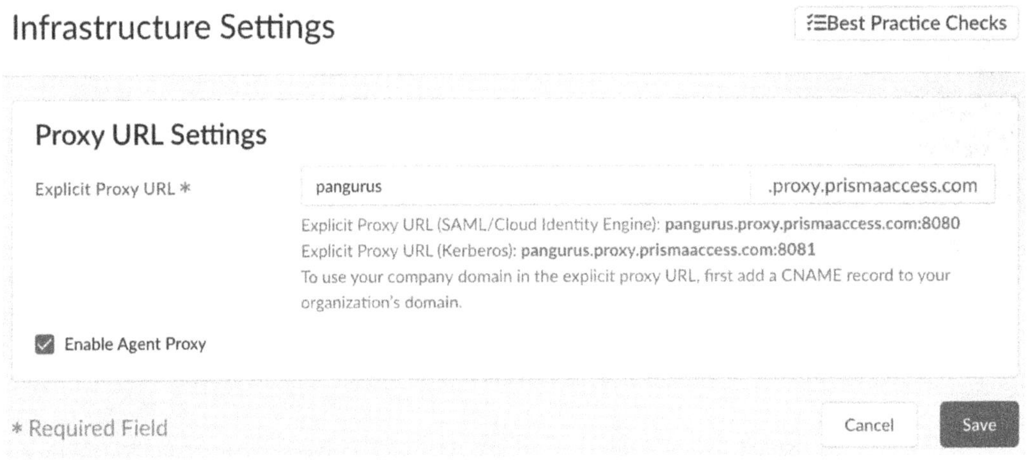

Infrastructure Settings

≡Best Practice Checks

Proxy URL Settings

Explicit Proxy URL *

pangurus   .proxy.prismaaccess.com

Explicit Proxy URL (SAML/Cloud Identity Engine): **pangurus.proxy.prismaaccess.com:8080**
Explicit Proxy URL (Kerberos): **pangurus.proxy.prismaaccess.com:8081**
To use your company domain in the explicit proxy URL, first add a CNAME record to your
organization's domain.

☑ Enable Agent Proxy

* Required Field   Cancel   Save

Figure 7.3 – Proxy URL Settings

Click **Save** to store the configuration, and you will be returned to the Explicit Proxy main page. Next, we will need to configure **User Authentication**.

Here, we can configure both SAML or the Cloud Identity Engine and Kerberos (we'll take a deeper look at the *Cloud Identity Engine* in *Chapter 9*):

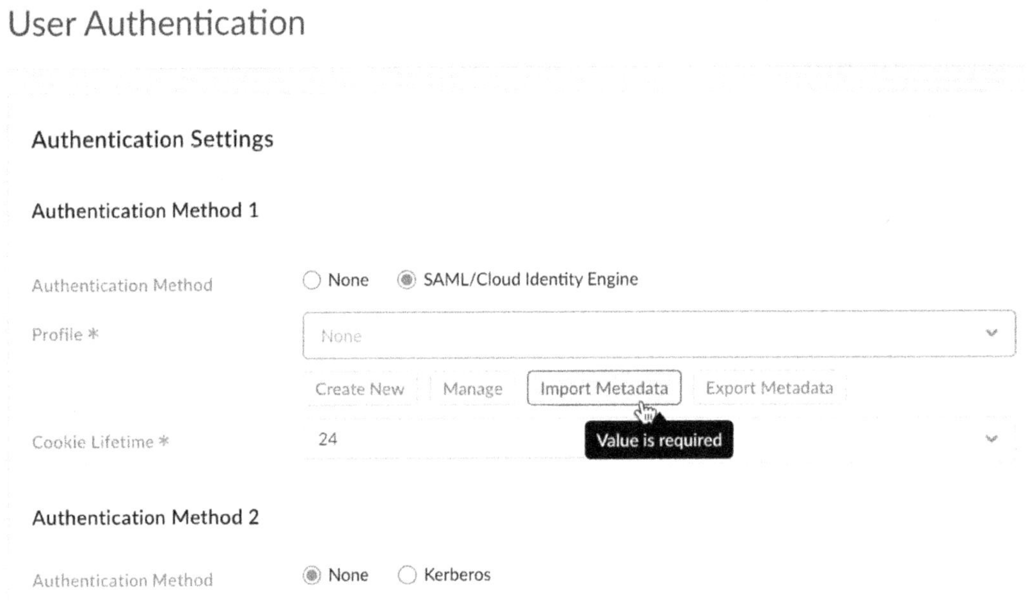

User Authentication

Authentication Settings

Authentication Method 1

Authentication Method   ○ None   ● SAML/Cloud Identity Engine

Profile *   None   ⌄

Create New   Manage   Import Metadata   Export Metadata

Cookie Lifetime *   24   Value is required   ⌄

Authentication Method 2

Authentication Method   ● None   ○ Kerberos

Figure 7.4 – User Authentication

To configure SAML, we can import the IdP metadata file or configure the profile manually. Once imported or manually configured, your page should look similar to the following screenshot:

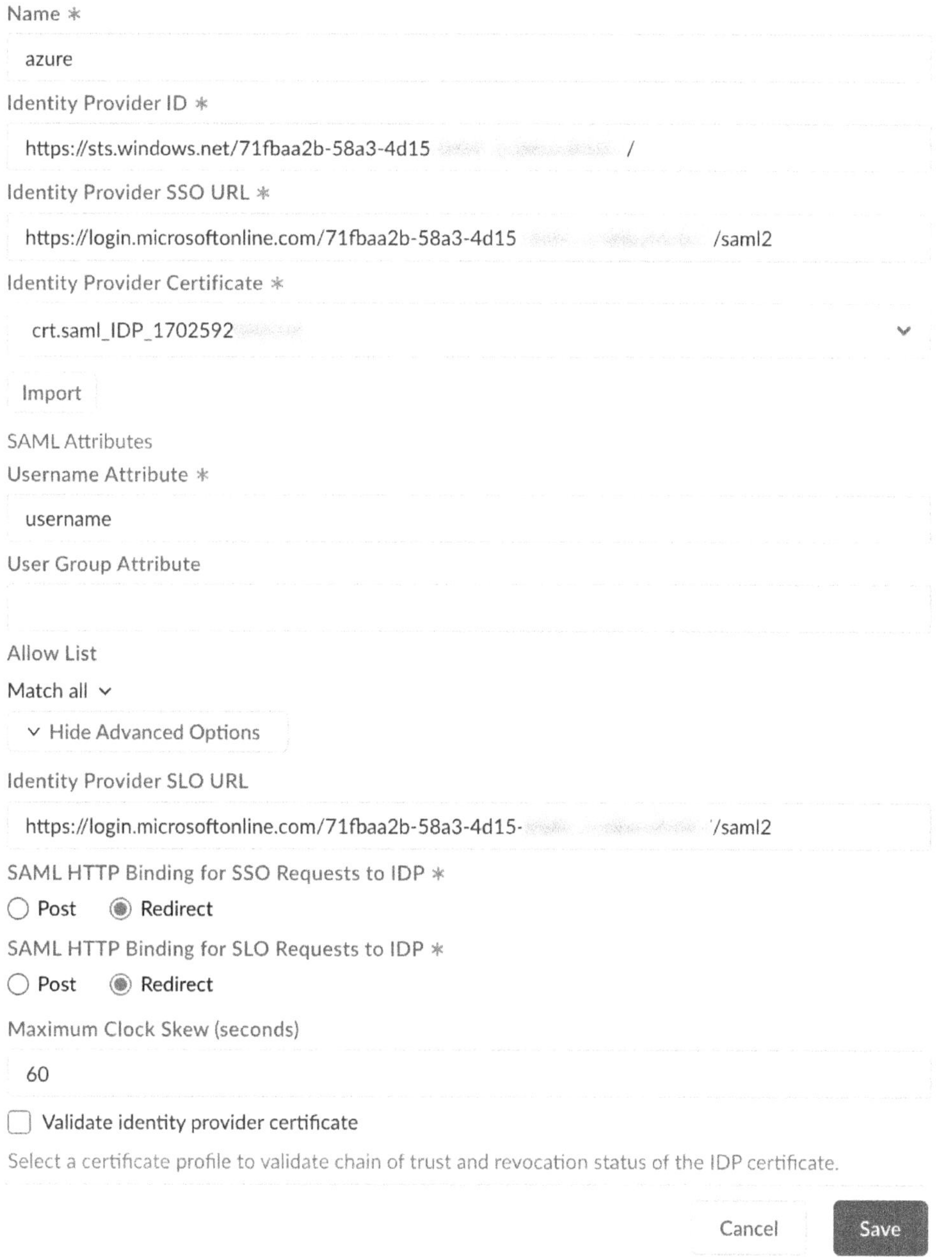

Name *

azure

Identity Provider ID *

https://sts.windows.net/71fbaa2b-58a3-4d15   /

Identity Provider SSO URL *

https://login.microsoftonline.com/71fbaa2b-58a3-4d15   /saml2

Identity Provider Certificate *

crt.saml_IDP_1702592   ⌄

Import

SAML Attributes
Username Attribute *

username

User Group Attribute

Allow List
Match all ⌄

⌄ Hide Advanced Options

Identity Provider SLO URL

https://login.microsoftonline.com/71fbaa2b-58a3-4d15-   /saml2

SAML HTTP Binding for SSO Requests to IDP *
○ Post   ◉ Redirect

SAML HTTP Binding for SLO Requests to IDP *
○ Post   ◉ Redirect

Maximum Clock Skew (seconds)

60

☐ Validate identity provider certificate

Select a certificate profile to validate chain of trust and revocation status of the IDP certificate.

Cancel   Save

Figure 7.5 – SAML profile

To add a Kerberos profile, we will need a keytab file (a keytab file contains a pair of Kerberos principals and encrypted keys derived from the Kerberos password; it is used in lieu of needing to input a password with each authentication):

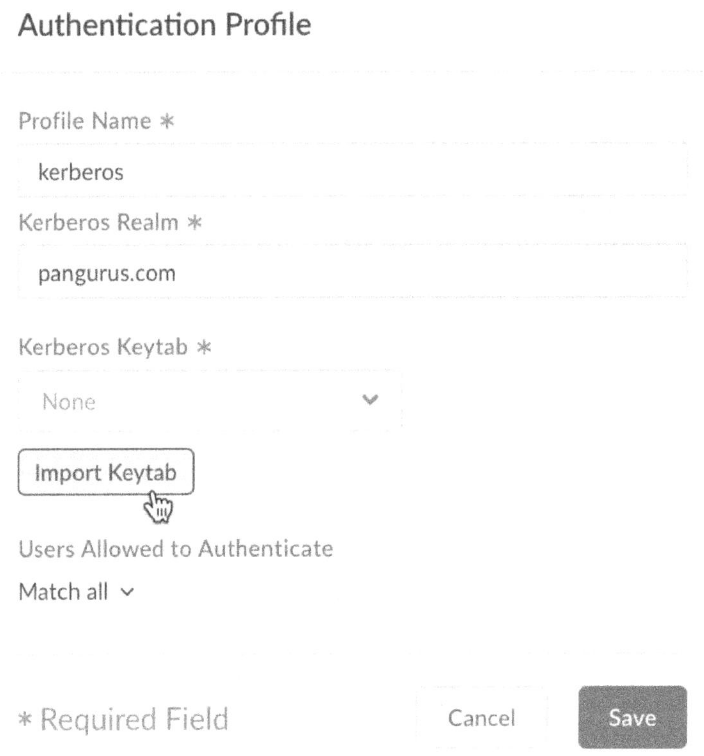

Authentication Profile

Profile Name *

kerberos

Kerberos Realm *

pangurus.com

Kerberos Keytab *

None   ⌄

Import Keytab

Users Allowed to Authenticate

Match all ⌄

* Required Field   Cancel   Save

Figure 7.6 – Kerberos profile

With at least one authentication profile configured, press **Save** to return to the Explicit Proxy main page. We are now able to add locations:

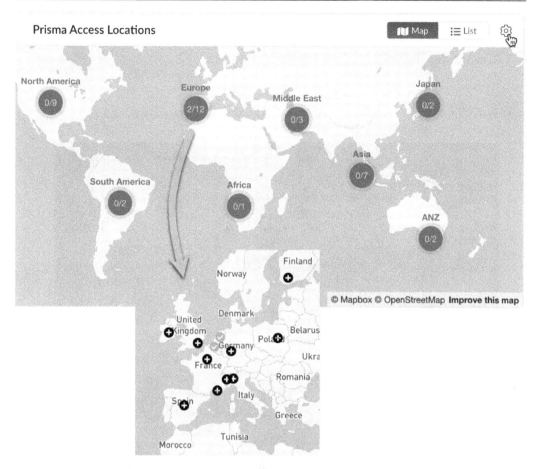

Figure 7.7 – Explicit proxy locations

You may have noticed there are fewer SWG locations than there are MU-SPN locations.

Below the SWG locations, you have two more settings to configure. Let's take a look at the **Forwarding Rules** first, as this is your cloud-hosted PAC file. You edit the PAC file directly from the web interface or use a rule-based configuration mode.

The default mode is the **PAC File Editor**:

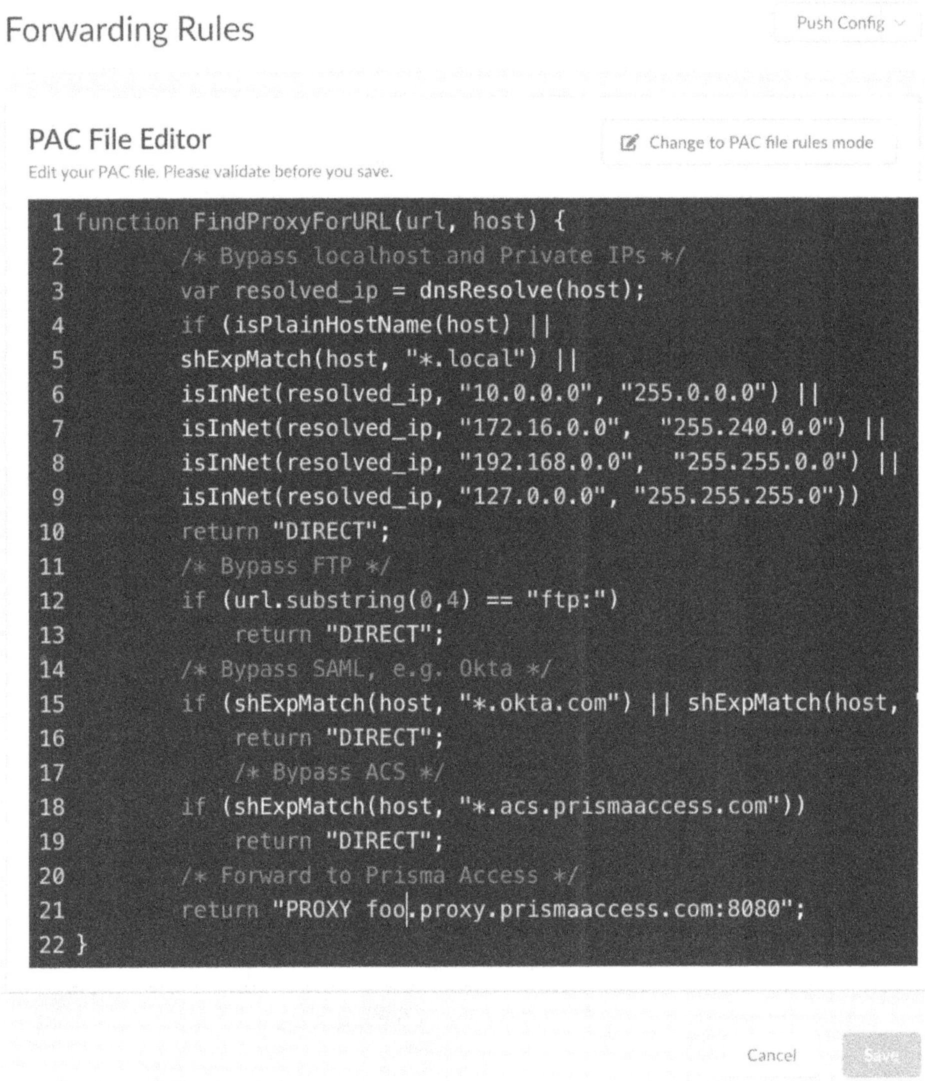

Forwarding Rules

Push Config ⌄

PAC File Editor

Edit your PAC file. Please validate before you save.

✎ Change to PAC file rules mode

```
 1 function FindProxyForURL(url, host) {
 2      /* Bypass localhost and Private IPs */
 3      var resolved_ip = dnsResolve(host);
 4      if (isPlainHostName(host) ||
 5      shExpMatch(host, "*.local") ||
 6      isInNet(resolved_ip, "10.0.0.0", "255.0.0.0") ||
 7      isInNet(resolved_ip, "172.16.0.0",  "255.240.0.0") ||
 8      isInNet(resolved_ip, "192.168.0.0",  "255.255.0.0") ||
 9      isInNet(resolved_ip, "127.0.0.0", "255.255.255.0"))
10      return "DIRECT";
11      /* Bypass FTP */
12      if (url.substring(0,4) == "ftp:")
13          return "DIRECT";
14      /* Bypass SAML, e.g. Okta */
15      if (shExpMatch(host, "*.okta.com") || shExpMatch(host,
16          return "DIRECT";
17          /* Bypass ACS */
18      if (shExpMatch(host, "*.acs.prismaaccess.com"))
19          return "DIRECT";
20      /* Forward to Prisma Access */
21      return "PROXY foo.proxy.prismaaccess.com:8080";
22 }
```

Cancel   Save

Figure 7.8 – PAC File Editor

Alternatively, you can switch to the PAC file rules mode:

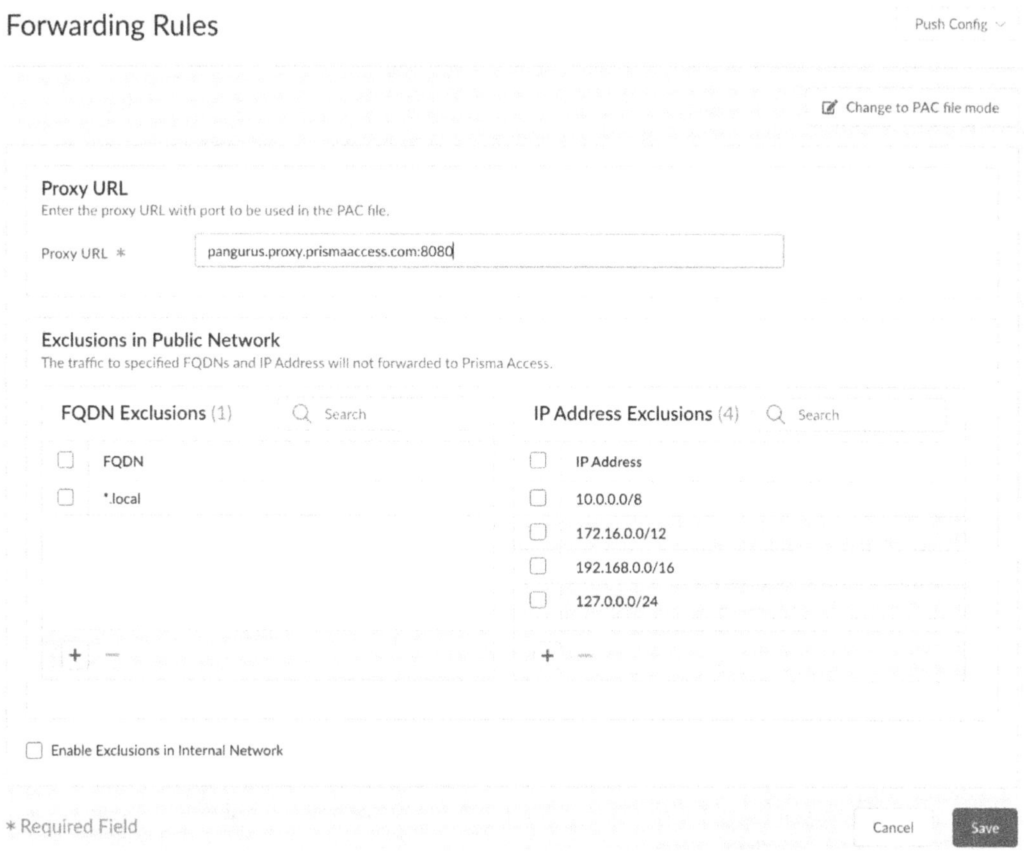

Forwarding Rules

Push Config ∨

☑ Change to PAC file mode

Proxy URL
Enter the proxy URL with port to be used in the PAC file.

Proxy URL ∗ | pangurus.proxy.prismaaccess.com:8080 |

Exclusions in Public Network
The traffic to specified FQDNs and IP Address will not forwarded to Prisma Access.

FQDN Exclusions (1)   🔍 Search   **IP Address Exclusions** (4)   🔍 Search

☐   FQDN   ☐   IP Address
☐   *.local   ☐   10.0.0.0/8
                                                        ☐   172.16.0.0/12
                                                        ☐   192.168.0.0/16
                                                        ☐   127.0.0.0/24

  ﹢ ﹣   ﹢ ﹣

☐ Enable Exclusions in Internal Network

∗ Required Field   Cancel   Save

Figure 7.9 – PAC File Rules editor

The PAC File Editor allows you to create a more comprehensive and complex PAC file. The rules editor allows you to keep it simple without needing to worry about JavaScript syntax errors. In both cases, you do need to **set the right URL and port number**.

Once you're happy with the PAC file configuration, press **Save**, and you'll be taken back to the Explicit Proxy main page. You will also gain access to the hosted URL, where all users can access your PAC file. This URL will be used on the endpoint's proxy configuration to retrieve the **Automatic Proxy Configuration (PAC)** file:

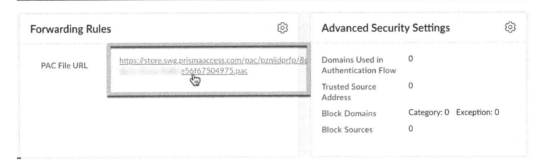

Figure 7.10 – Hosted PAC file

The last section is the **Advanced Security Settings**. Here, you can configure the following parameters:

- **Proxy mode for Remote Networks**: This needs to be enabled explicitly and will make explicit proxies available to remote networks. This setting also requires configuration in the remote networks section and can be set to explicitly trust the source addresses of remote networks to use the SWG without additional authentication.

- **Block Sources**: This comes with a default set of risky IP addresses that are not allowed to connect to the SWG. Additional regions (by country) or IP addresses can be added to block connections coming from these sources.

- **Block Domains**: This contains the URL categories that are not allowed and will be blocked for users connecting via the SWG. Exceptions can be added to the **Exception Lists**.

- **Authentication Settings**: Under this, domains used for authentication can be added to **Domains Used in Authentication Flow** to whitelist them. If any users connect from static IP addresses, these addresses can be added to **Trusted Source Address** to bypass authentication when the URL category is not decrypted.

- The following image is a screenshot of **Advanced Security Settings**:

Advanced Security Settings

Proxy mode for Remote Networks

Enable Proxy Mode

Block Sources

Traffic from these source addresses will be blocked.

	Blocked Source Address	Action
⌄	Predefined (4)	
☐	PA-SWG-bulletproof-ip-list	Add Exception
☐	PA-SWG-highrisk-ip-list	Add Exception
☐	PA-SWG-known-ip-list	Add Exception
☐	PA-SWG-torexit-ip-list	Add Exception

+   −

Block Domains

Blocked Domain Category Lists (2)

	Name
⌄	Predefined Category (2)
☐	malware
☐	command-and-control

Add ⌄   —

☐ Logs blocked domain requests

Exception Lists (0)

	Name

+   —

Authentication Settings

Domains Used in Authentication Flow

If authentication traffic is forwarded through Explicit Proxy, specify the domains used in the authentication flow.

	Name

+   −

☐ Any domain 🛈

Trusted Source Address

Specify IP addresses from which undecrypted HTTPS traffic and HTTP CORS should be allowed.   Delete   Add Address

	Name	Trusted Sour...	Skip authen...

☑ Use X-Authenticated-User (XAU) header on incoming HTTP/HTTPS requests for Identity

Required Field   Cancel   Save

Figure 7.11 – Advanced Security Settings

Push **Config** to activate the Explicit Proxy configuration. Once the commit is complete, you will be able to start using the proxy. The first time you commit an explicit proxy configuration, it may take some time to complete, as the selected locations may need to be provisioned, which can take up to 45 minutes.

Once the Push has completed, you will be able to start configuring your endpoints to start using the SWG. We'll learn about creating security rules for your users in *Chapter 8*.

In the following section, we'll take a look at how what we just did in Strata Cloud Manager can be achieved in Panorama.

SWG in Panorama

To activate the explicit proxy, we need to go to **Panorama** | **Cloud Services** | **Configuration** | **Mobile Users - Explicit Proxy**. We first need to complete the **Settings** portion before we can configure the connection parameters:

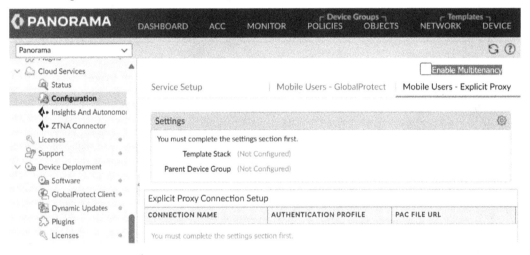

Figure 7.12 – Mobile Users – Explicit Proxy

On the main Settings page, we can see the **Explicit_Proxy_Template** Template and **Explicit_Proxy_Device_Group** Device Group configuration. Neither can be edited, moved, or replaced, but we can add additional subordinate templates to the **Explicit_Proxy_Template_Stack** template stack, and we can choose the parent Device Group for the **Explicit_Proxy_Device_Group**. We can also set the **User ID group mapping master device**, which is a physical or VM firewall configured to redistribute group information, or we can set Cloud Identity Engine (which we'll cover in more depth in *Chapter 9*):

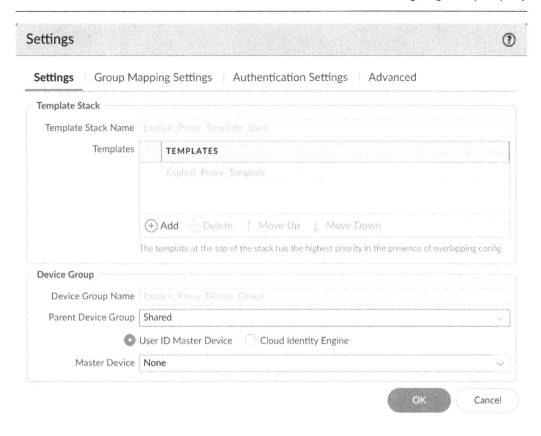

Figure 7.13 – The Settings tab

In the **Group Mapping Settings** tab, we can enable **Enable Directory Sync Integration**, which is a function inside Cloud Identity Engine that interfaces with a directory service and retrieves group memberships. When enabled, we can also control which attributes are collected for username matching. For example, if users log on using their User Principal Name, sAMAccountName, or email address, this should be reflected in the **Primary Username** or **E-Mail** fields. Alternate username attributes can also be added:

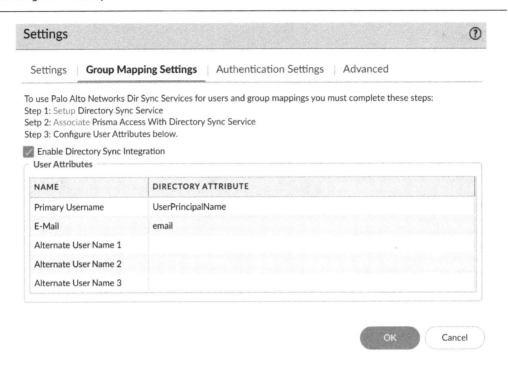

Figure 7.14 – The Group Mapping Settings tab

In the **Authentication Settings** tab, we can select how decryption is treated.

In the Explicit Proxy connection, the user is either authenticated by means of a cookie embedded in each HTTP session or via the GlobalProtect agent in proxy mode. In the former case, all web traffic should ideally be decrypted to be able to authenticate each user, but due to some rules, regulations, or laws (for example, **General Data Protection Regulation** (**GDPR**) in the European Union), this may not be permitted. You're able to choose two options for how to handle decryption:

- **Decrypt Traffic That Matches Existing Decryption Rules; For Undecrypted Traffic, Allow Traffic Only From Known IPs Registered By Authenticated Users**: In this case, the decryption policy will be used to decide what to decrypt. In case a site is not being decrypted, the user's last known source IP address is allowed to connect. This can cause some issues if a user boots up from a new IP address and immediately connects to a site that is not decrypted. They will first need to authenticate via a decrypted site before they are able to access unencrypted sites.

- **Decrypt All Traffic (Overrides Existing Decryption Rules)**: In this case, all Explicit Proxy traffic will be decrypted regardless of the decrypt policy.

- **If Authentication traffic is forwarded through Explicit Proxy, specify custom URL category with list of domains used in the authentication flow**: Here, you can select a custom URL category that contains all the **Identity Provider** (**IdP**) and **Access Control Service** (**ACS**) URLs that will be used to authenticate the user such that these will be decrypted by the explicit proxy.

Create the custom URL category in **Device Group | Objects | Custom Objects | URL Category**.

In **Trusted Source Address**, you can specify IP addresses that you explicitly trust and are not required to authenticate in order to be allowed to use the explicit proxy. If the downstream IP is a device (such as a web proxy) that is capable of injecting **X-Authenticated User** (**XAU**) headers, these can be accepted so that the user-ID can be applied to the incoming web request.

Enforce Authentication Only can be leveraged so that traffic that matches any of the security rules you select in the field below will be decrypted solely for the purpose of retrieving the authentication cookie, but no further inspection will occur, safeguarding the user's privacy in line with regulations:

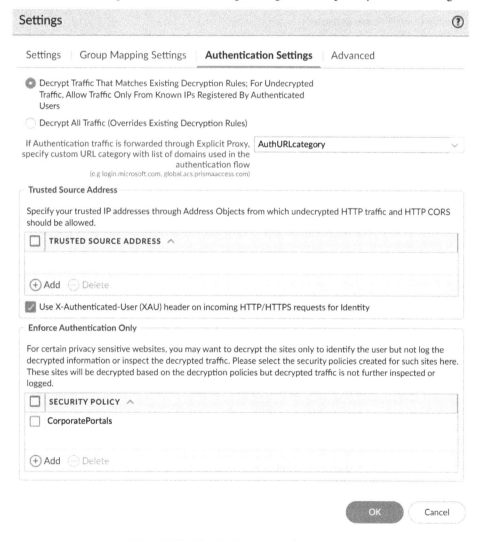

Figure 7.15 – The Authentication Settings tab

In the **Advanced** tab, we can enable **Forward Remote Network traffic to Explicit Proxy**, which, when enabled, will provision anycast IP addresses on the RN-SPNs that provide secure internet access to remote networks that do not have default routing set to the remote network connection:

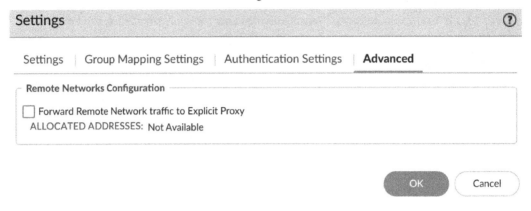

Figure 7.16 – The Advanced tab

Click **OK** to save the Settings. This will unlock the **Configure** button for the **Explicit Proxy Connection Setup**:

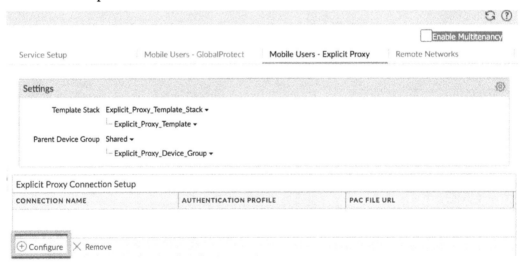

Figure 7.17 – Explicit Proxy Connection Setup

In **Explicit Proxy Connection Setup | Settings**, you can create the FQDN that will be used as the proxy server address and can only be a subdomain to `proxy.prismaaccess.com`.

You also need to define the authentication profile that will be used to authenticate users. This can be the same profile used for mobile users as long as it is a SAML profile. **LDAP**, **RADIUS**, **TACACS**, or local users are not supported for explicit proxy authentication. A Kerberos authentication profile can also be added.

When using SAML authentication, the proxy will be active on port 8080. In case Kerberos is used, the proxy can be accessed on port 8081.

If the PAC file needs to be hosted on Prisma Access so users can reach it from any location, we can upload it here. A sample PAC file can be downloaded so that you can get going immediately:

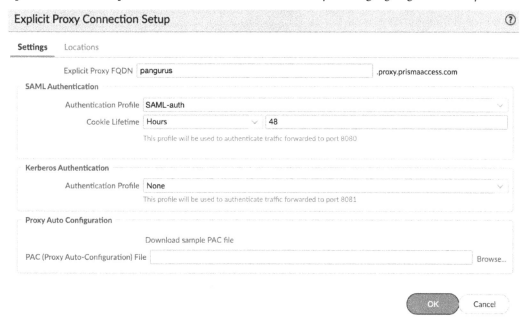

Figure 7.18 – Explicit Proxy Connection Setup Settings

On the **Locations** tab, we can enable all the locations where we need to have a proxy node available. They'll all respond to the same proxy FQDN, but clients will be routed to the nearest one:

Figure 7.19 – Proxy Locations

In the next section, we'll take a closer look at the contents of the PAC file.

Proxy Auto Configuration (PAC) file and client configuration

A PAC file is the configuration that dictates how a system or browser is supposed to reach certain resources. It can be used to redirect certain traffic to a proxy server while bypassing the proxy for other traffic. Different proxies can be defined for different destinations and so on. When configured properly, it can be a very powerful ally in controlling user's access to all kinds of resources.

The PAC file that contains the connection parameters for the browser to determine which connections should go to a proxy or should break out locally can be hosted on a local server. However, it can also be hosted on Prisma Access to allow remote users to download it from anywhere. When deciding where to host the PAC file, make sure users will be able to access it from anywhere they may need to.

The following is a template PAC file. It is set so that the RFC 1918 subnets and the local loopback subnet are not forwarded to the proxy. FTP sessions will also bypass the proxy, and authentication FQDNs for SAML authentication will also not be sent to the proxy.

A PAC file is essentially a JavaScript that contains a bunch of if statements followed by what exactly the browser or the system is supposed to do with the connection. The following is the default PAC file, as provided in the SWG:

```
function FindProxyForURL(url, host) {
    /* Bypass localhost and Private IPs */
    var resolved_ip = dnsResolve(host);
    if (isPlainHostName(host) ||
    shExpMatch(host, "*.local") ||
    isInNet(resolved_ip, "10.0.0.0", "255.0.0.0") ||
    isInNet(resolved_ip, "172.16.0.0", "255.240.0.0" ||
    isInNet(resolved_ip, "192.168.0.0", "255.255.0.0") ||
    isInNet(resolved_ip, "127.0.0.0",
"255.255.255.0"))                                    return "DIRECT";
    /* Bypass FTP */
    if (url.substring(0,4) == "ftp:")
        return "DIRECT";
    /* Bypass SAML, e.g. Okta */
    if (shExpMatch(host, "*.okta.com") || shExpMatch(host,
"*.oktacdn.com"))
        return "DIRECT";
    /* Bypass ACS */
    if (shExpMatch(host, "*.acs.prismaaccess.com"))
        return "DIRECT";
    /* Forward to Prisma Access */
    return "PROXY pangurus.proxy.prismaaccess.com:8080";
}
```

The first if statement contains all the things that should not be sent to the proxy, indicated by return "DIRECT" at the end:

- var resolved_ip = dnsResolve(host) introduces a variable that tells the system to first resolve the hostname to verify if it is in an IP subnet so the appropriate action can be applied based on the IP rather than the hostname.

- isPlainHostName(host) tells the system that hostnames without any dots should not be proxied in this instance.

- shExpMatch(host, "*.local") tells the system that internal hostnames (e.g., intranet.local) should not be sent to the proxy. Add or replace this statement if a different suffix is used internally.

- isInNet(resolved_ip, "10.0.0.0", "255.0.0.0") indicates an IP network and its subnet that should not be forwarded to the proxy in this case.

The second `if` statement ensures that the FTP connections initiated from inside a browser are also not sent to the proxy:

- `(url.substring(0,4) == "ftp:")` will tell the system to look at the first four characters (position 0 is the start of the string; position 4 is the fourth character) of the URL string, and if it matches `ftp:`, it will tell the system to take the action defined right after the `if` statement (http: would be `(0,5)` and https: would be `(0,6)`).

The third `if` statement looks for domain names that match the SAML authentication. In this example, we are using okta, but this will need to be updated to reflect your SAML IdP:

`(shExpMatch(host, "*.okta.com") || shExpMatch(host, "*.oktacdn.com"))`

The fourth `if` statement bypasses the proxy for the explicit proxy authentication hostnames:

`(shExpMatch(host, "*.acs.prismaaccess.com"))`

Finally, the last statement sends everything else to the proxy address provided in the statement:

`return "PROXY pangurus.proxy.prismaaccess.com:8080"`

With the above information, you will be able to build a customized PAC file to suit your needs. Read through the if statements carefully and add or remove what applies to your environment.

I touched on the possibility of setting GlobalProtect in the proxy mode earlier. In the next section, we'll take a quick look at how to configure this.

GlobalProtect in the proxy mode

In Prisma Access, GlobalProtect can be configured in three different connection modes:

- **Tunnel** mode Is the default setting in which GlobalProtect functions like a traditional VPN client and sends traffic via an IPSec tunnel based on its routing table. The MU-SPN takes care of routing internet and public SaaS apps out to the internet while routing private apps via the Prisma Access infrastructure.

- **Proxy** mode allows GlobalProtect to simply function as an authentication agent for the proxy connections so that there is no requirement to decrypt all traffic. All traffic is handled in accordance with the PAC file configuration.

- **Tunnel and Proxy** mode allows a user to combine both functions so that web traffic is sent via the explicit proxy and network access to the internal infrastructure and private apps are sent via an IPSec tunnel to the MU-SPN and then onto the infrastructure backbone.

In Panorama, this setting can be configured in **Templates | Network | GlobalProtect | Portal | GlobalProtect_Portal | Agent | Profile | App | Agent Mode for Prisma Access**, as seen in the following image. If **Proxy** mode is selected, the PAC file URL must be included in the configuration as well.

In hybrid mode, set **Set Up Tunnel Over Proxy** to No so that the IPSec tunnel does not traverse the proxy but is set up directly to the nearest MU-SPN.

Set **Detect Proxy for each connection** to Yes to ensure the proxy config is checked for each connection

It is recommended to set **Use Default browser for SAML authentication** to Yes for a smooth user experience:

Configs

Authentication	Config Selection Criteria	Internal	External

App Configurations

Servers Assigned by the Tunnel (Windows Only)	
Append Local Search Domains to Tunnel DNS Suffixes (Mac Only)	No
Update DNS Settings at Connect (Windows Only) (Deprecated)	No
Local Proxy Port	9999 [1024 - 65534]
Agent Mode for Prisma Access	Tunnel
Proxy Auto-Configuration (PAC) File URL	Proxy
Detect Proxy for Each Connection (Windows only)	Tunnel
	Tunnel and Proxy
Set Up Tunnel Over Proxy (Windows & Mac Only)	No
HIP Process Remediation Timeout (sec)	0 [0 - 300]

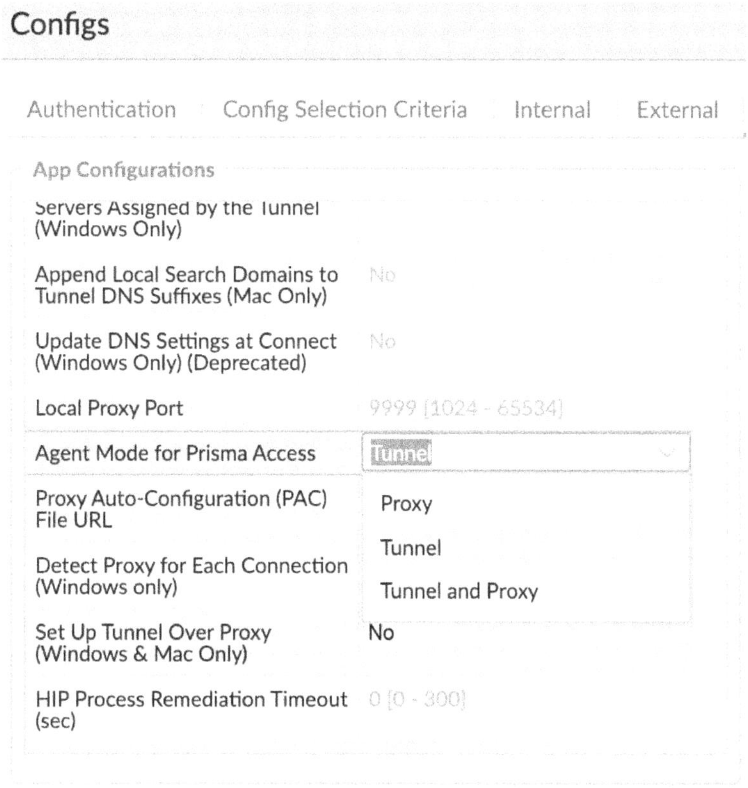

Figure 7.20 – GlobalProtect Agent Mode

In the Strata Cloud Manager, you can change the Agent Mode in **Workflows | Prisma Access Setup | GlobalProtect | App Settings | Advanced | Proxy**.

In hybrid mode, set **Set Up Tunnel Over Proxy** to No so that the IPSec tunnel does not traverse the proxy but is set up directly to the nearest MU-SPN.

Set **Detect Proxy for each connection** to Yes to ensure the proxy config is checked for each connection.

It is recommended to set **Use Default browser for SAML authentication** to Yes for a smooth user experience.

In Strata Cloud Manager, you can choose between using the regular PAC file or the Forwarding Profiles that can be configured in the Explicit Proxy config:

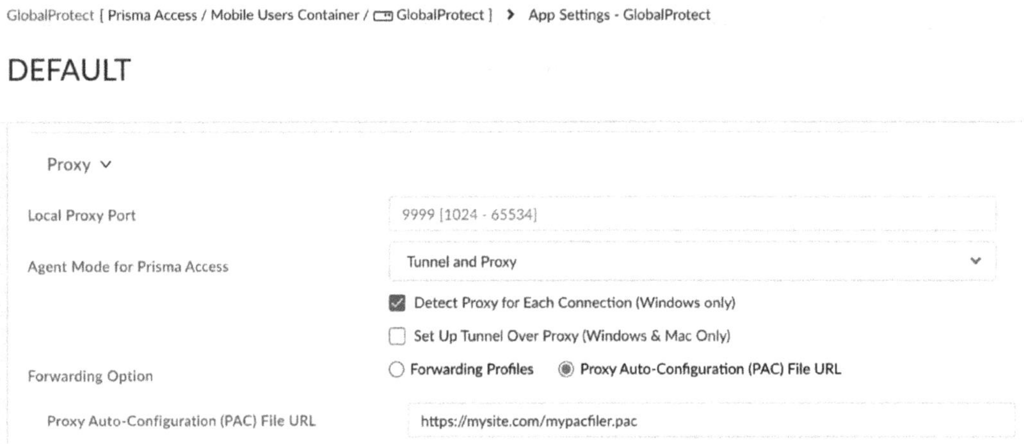

GlobalProtect [Prisma Access / Mobile Users Container / ▭ GlobalProtect] ❯ App Settings - GlobalProtect

DEFAULT

Proxy ⌄	
Local Proxy Port	9999 [1024 - 65534]
Agent Mode for Prisma Access	Tunnel and Proxy ⌄
	☑ Detect Proxy for Each Connection (Windows only)
	☐ Set Up Tunnel Over Proxy (Windows & Mac Only)
Forwarding Option	○ Forwarding Profiles ⦿ Proxy Auto-Configuration (PAC) File URL
Proxy Auto-Configuration (PAC) File URL	https://mysite.com/mypacfiler.pac

Figure 7.21 – GlobalProtect Agent Mode in Cloud Manager

You will now be able to set up the Secure Web Gateway, or Explicit Proxy, and leverage the proxy functionality to provide secure internet access without the need to tunnel everything.

Summary

In this chapter, you learned about the explicit proxy as an alternative means to connect mobile users and remote networks to the internet using a PAC file to control how traffic flows, as opposed to IPSec tunnels. This knowledge can be helpful in migrating a legacy network that relies on a proxy configuration into a SASE deployment.

In the next chapter, we'll take a look at how we can build security rules to control who is allowed to access which resources and how.

8

Setting Up Your Security Policy

In this chapter, we're going to learn about building security policies. These rules will ensure that users and remote networks are able to reach the resources they need but are prevented from accessing restricted resources. We'll learn how we can leverage user ID, HIP profiles, and tags to dynamically adjust access based on the user's access level and the device the user is connecting from. We'll also learn how to set up clientless VPN access to internal resources.

In this chapter, we're going to cover the following main topics:

- Why do we need security rules?
- Building security policies in Strata Cloud Manager
- Building security policies in Panorama
- Clientless VPN

Technical requirements

Readers should be familiar with Panorama and very familiar with PAN-OS, as the topics covered in this chapter are very basic but could prove challenging for new Strata Cloud Manager admins.

As such, we will be mostly covering Strata Cloud Manager and touching very briefly on Panorama.

Why do we need security rules?

In the previous chapters, we learned how we can establish different ways to connect to Prisma Access, the internet, service connections, and other security-processing nodes. To ensure access is controlled, we need to create security rules that match every scenario of access that is required. In general, there will be two large sets of access: access to the internet and access to internal resources or private applications.

As a rule of thumb, in Prisma Access, security rules are applied only to Inbound connections. This means that security rules are configured so the user or remote office is always the source of outbound connections. The only exception is when we create embargo rules (more about that later in this chapter), where we block certain countries from connecting to our infrastructure.

Policies are applied in the following way:

- **Enforced**: From mobile users or remote networks to the internet.

- **Enforced**: From mobile users or remote networks to service connections.

- **Partially enforced**: From mobile users to other mobile users or where remote network security rules are only applied to the MU-SPN the user is connected to.

- **Partially enforced**: From remote networks to other remote networks or where mobile user security rules are only applied to the RN-SPN that the remote network is connected to.

- **Not enforced**: From Service connections to mobile users or where remote network security is not enforced inside Prisma Access, a firewall in the data center or private cloud needs to control this inflow.

As illustrated in the following figure, policy is enforced on all the solid lines and not on the dotted lines:

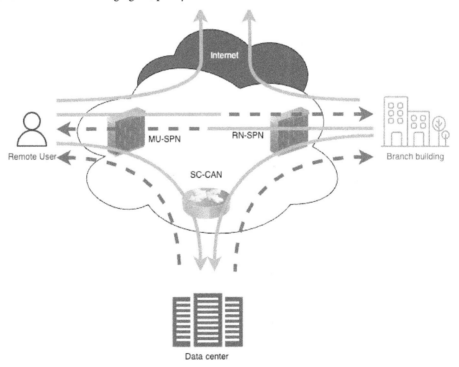

Figure 8.1 – Direction of security enforcement

> **Important note**
>
> Security rules are bi-directional, so no rules need to be created to account for return packets, regardless of what the preceding diagram displays.

As you may have noticed in the previous chapters, we have needed to prepare zone mapping for both mobile users and remote networks. With trust zones representing all internal resources, including mobile users and remote networks, and untrust zones representing the internet, many rules that allow users to access internal resources or private applications see to it that the security rule will be created as **Trust-to-Trust**.

> **Important note**
>
> Only the trust and untrust zones are used when creating security rules.

Let's take a look at the available rule bases in Strata Cloud Manager.

Building security policies in Strata Cloud Manager

When you're logged in to Strata Cloud Manager, which you can access via `https://apps.paloaltonetworks.com` or `https://stratacloudmanager.paloaltonetworks.com`, you can navigate to **Manage | Configuration | NGFW and Prisma Access** to access the security rule bases, which is split up into the following sections:

- **Security Services** constitute the security rules used to control which traffic is allowed and all of the deep packet (layer 7) inspection elements that can be applied to these sessions.

- **Network Policies** is where you can create application override policies. These are used to bypass App-ID for traffic flows that can't be identified, need to be identified as something else, or to prevent L7 inspection from happening on these flows.

- **Identity Services** is where you can configure and control user ID ingestion and redistribution.

- **Objects** is where all the user-created objects, such as address objects, groups, services, tags, and external dynamic lists, can be created or edited.

- **Global Settings** is where the SaaS application endpoints can be configured if the additional **Prisma Cloud** license was purchased.

To start configuring your first security policy, follow these steps, as illustrated in *Figure 8.2*:

1. Navigate to **Manage | Configuration | NGFW and Prisma Access**.
2. Select **Configuration Scope** to select in which hierarchical level a policy should be created:

   - *Global* means security policies that will be applied to all components and groups joined to the Strata Cloud Manager. This could include physical firewalls.

- Prisma Access will apply to all the Prisma Access components, which includes all MU-SPNs and all RN-SPNs.

- Mobile user container will apply to both GlobalProtect users and explicit proxy users.

- GlobalProtect uses security rules that only apply to GlobalProtect VPN users.

- Explicit proxy rules will only apply to users that connect using a proxy configuration instead of GlobalProtect.

- Remote networks only apply to remote RN-SPN connections.

- There are no security rules for service connections, as there is no enforcement on SC-CANs.

Let's start by selecting **GlobalProtect** in **Configuration Scope**.

3. Select **Security Services | Security Policy** to go to security rules:

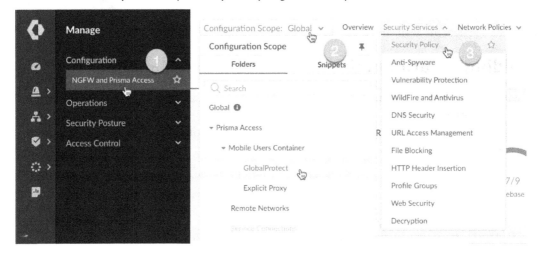

Figure 8.2 – Navigating the security services

Unlike Panorama, the security policy comes prepopulated with some best-practice security rules to help you on your way. There is also a helpful indicator of how many rules currently meet best practices, so once you start building security rules and forget to set them in accordance with best practices, this is reported at the top of the page. Let's take a closer look at the security rules.

Security rules

In *Figure 8.3*, you can see the predefined rules. The first five rules block inbound and outbound connections from known malicious and high-risk IP addresses. Rule number 6 blocks the Quic App-ID, which is capable of bypassing SSL decryption, and rule number 7 allows new App-IDs. This is to allow business continuity in case Palo Alto releases new App-IDs that could potentially cause existing rules to no longer be hit due to a new App-ID for a certain protocol.

Rules 8 through 11 are rules specific to Office 365 and have been disabled by default, so they can be enabled if Office 365 is used in a corporate environment or left disabled or deleted when not needed. The fact they are disabled already triggers a best practices check, as you might be able to see by the little orange exclamation mark in front of the rule in the following screenshot. Hovering your pointer over the exclamation point will pop up a clear explanation about the missed check:

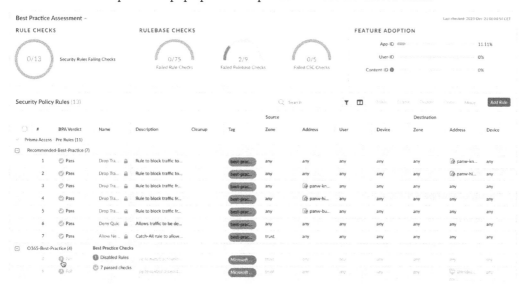

Figure 8.3 – Rule base landing page

We can add new rules by clicking **Add Rule** on the right-hand side.

In the new rule, there are three sections that need to be configured for the new rule to work: **General**, **Match Criteria**, and **Actions**.

In **General**, you can set a descriptive **Name** and a more verbose **Description**. If you uncheck the **Enable** box, the rule will be disabled and will not be used to match sessions. **Tag** can be added to classify and filter the rule, and **Schedule** can be added so that the rule is only active at certain times of the day or week:

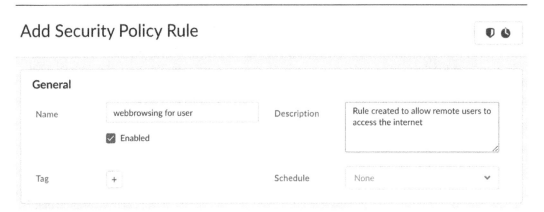

Figure 8.4 – General section

In **Match Criteria**, we define which traffic should be matched for this rule to be applied:

1. **Source** can be set to match a specific **Zone** or accept all source zones.

2. In **Address**, we can add single IP addresses or subnet objects to match specific networks.

3. Users can be set to **Any** to not match any users or **Select** to choose which specific user or AD user group this rule will apply to. **Pre Logon** only applies to devices that have connected to the pre-logon tunnel, which is applied before the user is logged on to their device. **Known User** applies to all users that have been identified, e.g., by connecting to an MU-SPN or being identified by any user ID mechanism. **Unknown** applies to any connections that have no user ID information.

4. The **Device** section applies to the source device being used. **Any** will apply to all possible source devices, whereas **Select** will require you to set a **host information profile** (**HIP**) profile so that the rule can be set to only apply to devices that match the selected profile. **No-hip** will only apply to devices that do not have a HIP match, whereas **Quarantined Devices** will only apply to devices that have been placed in quarantine due to a policy action:

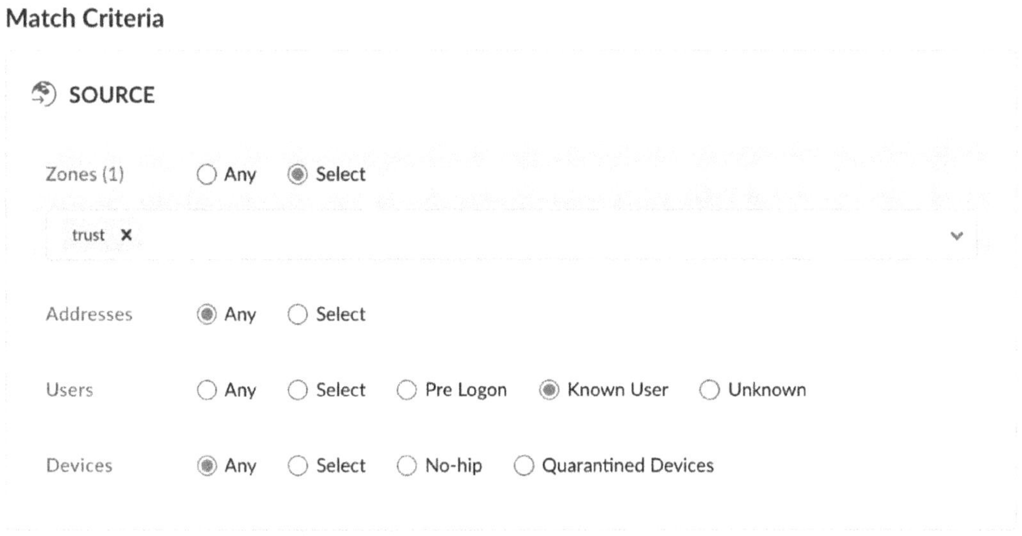

Match Criteria

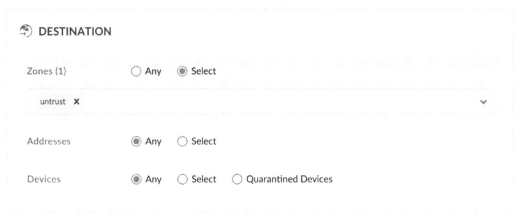

Figure 8.5 – Security rule source

5. **Destination** lets you set the destination **Zones**, which can be **Any** or **Select**, with these defining specific destination zones. In **Addresses**, you can pick **Any** for all destination IP addresses or **Select** whereby you can add single IP addresses or subnet objects. In **Destination**, we can't set **Users**, but we can set **Devices**. The options are slightly more limited than other sources, as we can set **Any** and **Select** to match a specific HIP profile or **Quarantined Devices**:

Figure 8.6 – Security rule destination

6.   In **Application/Services**, we can select the App-IDs and destination ports that this rule should match. In **Applications**, we can select **Any** for all App-IDs. We can use **Select** to choose which specific App-IDs, application filters, or application groups should be addressed in this rule. In **Service**, we can pick **Application Default**, which will restrict each App-ID to only use its default ports, preventing protocols from using unexpected ports (e.g., http on port 8000). We can also select **Any** for all ports or **Select**, whereby we can pick the exact ports that can be matched to this rule:

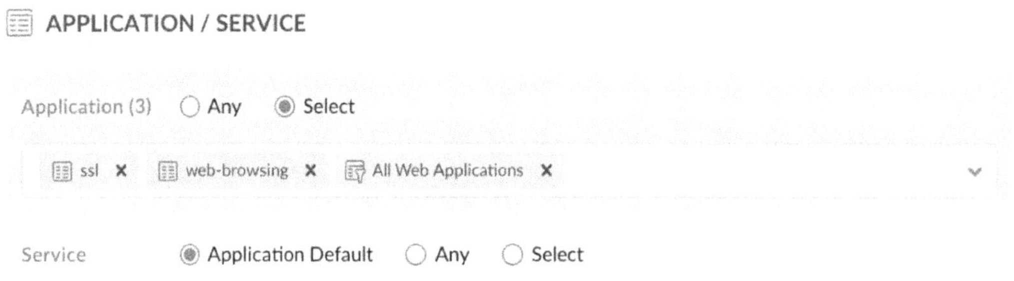

⊞ **APPLICATION / SERVICE**

Application (3)   ◯ Any   ◉ Select

⊞ ssl ✕   ⊞ web-browsing ✕   ⊡ All Web Applications ✕   ⌄

Service   ◉ Application Default   ◯ Any   ◯ Select

Figure 8.7 – Security rule application/service

7.   In **URL Category/Tenant Restriction**, we can set **URL Category** to one or several URL categories via **Select** or leave the default **Any** for all categories. Setting a URL category here will allow or block the traffic at **Layer 4**, as this is based on a URL category in the session (via SNI or HTTP GET, for example). The advantage here is that we don't need to apply a full URL filtering profile, which could inadvertently allow or block unintended URL categories; we can simply focus on the specific category at the security layer. **Tenant Restriction** can be used to target specific SaaS apps as matching criteria:

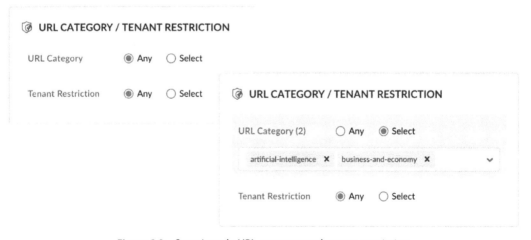

Figure 8.8 – Security rule URL category and tenant restriction

8. In **Actions**, we can set *what* the rule is supposed to do by setting **Action** to **Deny**, **Drop**, **Allow**, **Reset Client**, **Reset Server**, or **Reset Both Client and Server**. The **Deny** option will send RST packets or take appropriate deny actions based on the App-ID protocol, whereas **Drop** will silently discard packets and not notify the client or server. All three **Reset** options will send an RST packet to either the client, server, or both to signal the session was denied. You can select **Send ICMP Unreachable** to send an ICMP message when UDP traffic is dropped. In **Profile Groups**, we can set the security profiles that are used to inspect traffic hitting this rule. The default profile **best-practice** comes loaded with all profiles set according to the Palo Alto best practices. We'll cover creating custom profile groups later in this chapter:

Figure 8.9 – Security rule Actions

9. In the **Log Settings** tab, we can select if this rule should log at session start and/or session end. Session end is the default that triggers a log to be created when the session reaches its end, which can be due to a blocking action, hitting a vulnerability that terminates the session, or the natural end of the session after all data have been transferred. Logging at session end will also allow the log entry to contain all data pertaining to the session, such as the total length of the session, the bytes and packets transferred in either direction, and so on. Session start will immediately generate a log each time the session **starts** something new, such as a TCP handshake or a new App-ID. Log at session start should typically only be used for troubleshooting, as this setting will generate a larger log volume per session.

10. The **Others** tab allows us to enable **disable server response inspection** (DSRI), which will disable the inspection of server reply packets. This can be useful in case **server-to-client** (s2c) packets experience latency due to layer7 inspection or conserver resources. This setting will be flagged by best practice checks. We can also apply QoS marking, where the following options are available: Follow-c2s-flow, ip-dscp (af codepoints 001010 to 100110, cs codepoints 000000 to 111000, and ef codepoint 101110 expedited forwarding), and ip-precedence (cs codepoints 000 to 111):

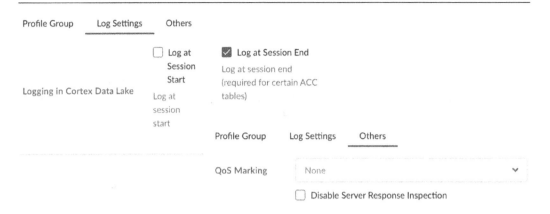

Figure 8.10 – Log Settings and Others

One of the most important components of a security rule is the security profile. These ensure deep packet inspection is applied to traffic flowing through a security rule and enforcement is performed as configured.

Custom security profiles

All security profiles come with a best practice profile that is set in accordance with the Palo Alto Networks recommendations, but we may need to create custom profiles to address specific requirements.

> **Important note**
>
> In the Strata Cloud Manager, there are some different default behaviors that we don't see in Panorama. In case the Prisma Access license is the **business** edition (instead of Business Premium or Enterprise) the anti-spyware or vulnerability protection profiles will not be available, whereas they will be displayed but not applied in Panorama.

If we navigate to **Manage | Configuration | NGFW and Prisma Access | Security Services | Anti-Spyware**, we first see the **Best Practice** profile checks to give us a quick view of how well our profiles are set for best practices, followed by the actual **Anti-Spyware** profiles. There are two predefined profiles: **web-security-default** and **best-practice**, which we can use in rules where we need them, but here, we can also add new anti-spyware profiles. At the bottom, we can add global overrides; these are applied across all profiles, so be careful when using these if an override is required. We can also add overrides in the individual profiles:

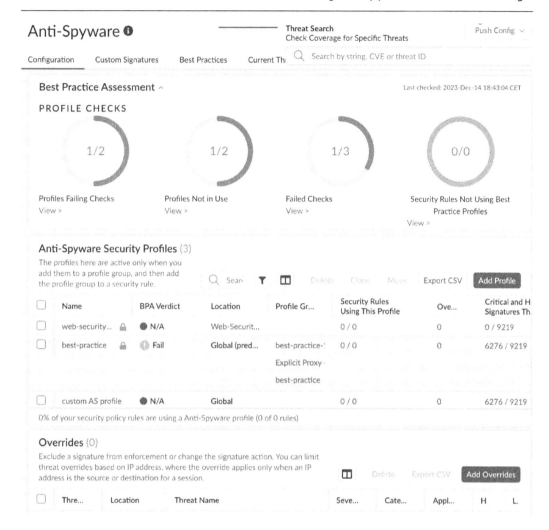

Figure 8.11 – Anti-Spyware profile

When creating a new custom profile, we can set very granular rules based on severity and category (e.g., cryptominer, backdoor, keylogger, and so on) and select which action should be taken (allow, alert, drop, reset client, reset server, reset both, or block IP for a certain amount of time).

We can also add **Overrides** to the profile itself, so they are only applied to security rules that have this profile set.

We can also enable **Inline Cloud Analysis** and select which machine learning models are enabled and the desired action for positive hits against each model (allow, alert, drop, reset client, reset server, or reset both).

Exceptions can be added in the form of an **external dynamic List** (**EDL**), URL, or IP addresses. These exceptions will exclude the EDL, URL, or IP address from hitting anti-spyware actions in this profile:

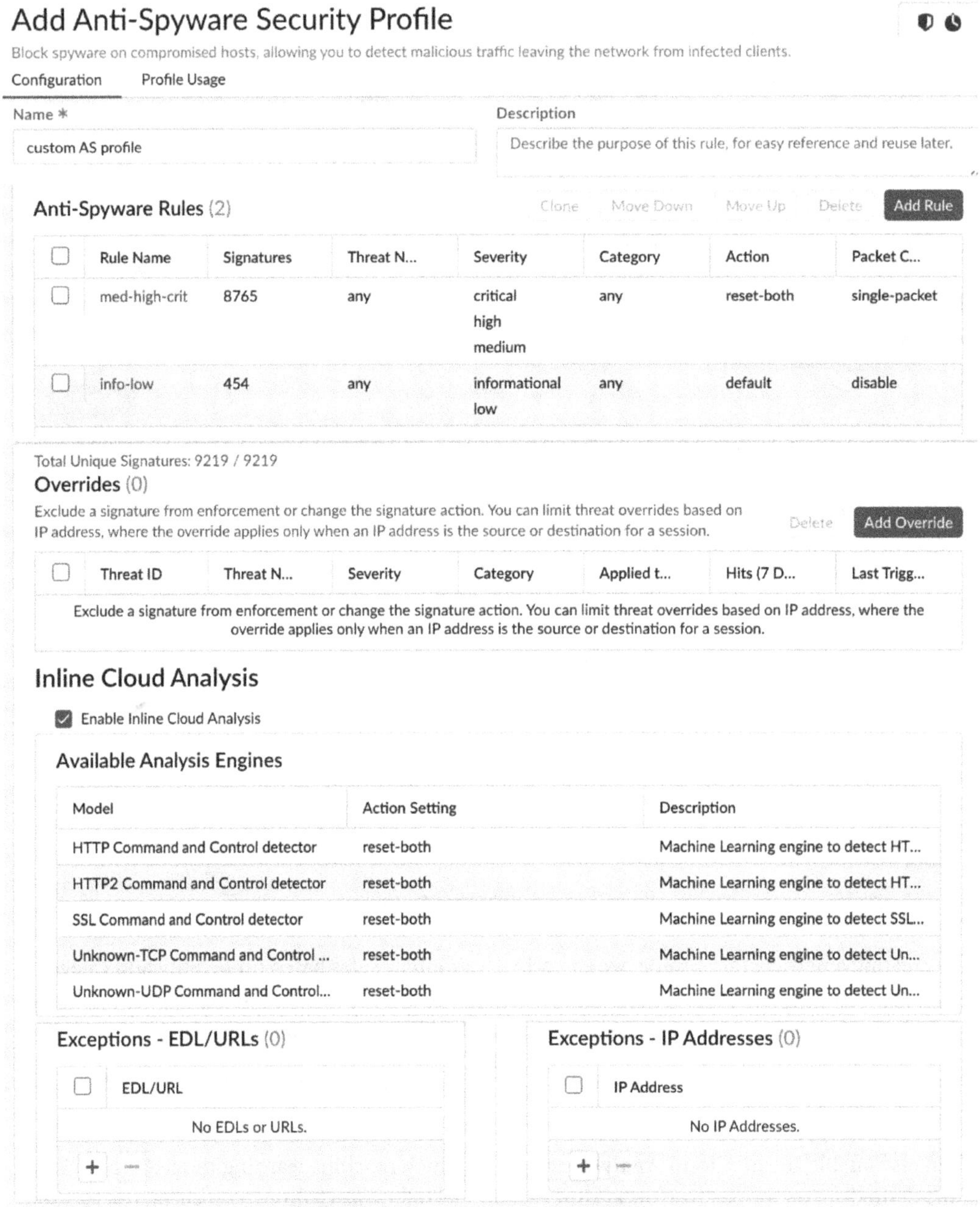

Add Anti-Spyware Security Profile

Block spyware on compromised hosts, allowing you to detect malicious traffic leaving the network from infected clients.

Configuration   Profile Usage

Name *

custom AS profile

Description

Describe the purpose of this rule, for easy reference and reuse later.

Anti-Spyware Rules (2)

Clone   Move Down   Move Up   Delete   Add Rule

	Rule Name	Signatures	Threat N...	Severity	Category	Action	Packet C...
	med-high-crit	8765	any	critical high medium	any	reset-both	single-packet
	info-low	454	any	informational low	any	default	disable

Total Unique Signatures: 9219 / 9219

Overrides (0)

Exclude a signature from enforcement or change the signature action. You can limit threat overrides based on IP address, where the override applies only when an IP address is the source or destination for a session.

Delete   Add Override

	Threat ID	Threat N...	Severity	Category	Applied t...	Hits (7 D...	Last Trigg...
	Exclude a signature from enforcement or change the signature action. You can limit threat overrides based on IP address, where the override applies only when an IP address is the source or destination for a session.						

Inline Cloud Analysis

☑ Enable Inline Cloud Analysis

Available Analysis Engines

Model	Action Setting	Description
HTTP Command and Control detector	reset-both	Machine Learning engine to detect HT...
HTTP2 Command and Control detector	reset-both	Machine Learning engine to detect HT...
SSL Command and Control detector	reset-both	Machine Learning engine to detect SSL...
Unknown-TCP Command and Control ...	reset-both	Machine Learning engine to detect Un...
Unknown-UDP Command and Control...	reset-both	Machine Learning engine to detect Un...

Exceptions - EDL/URLs (0)

	EDL/URL
	No EDLs or URLs.

+

Exceptions - IP Addresses (0)

	IP Address
	No IP Addresses.

+

Figure 8.12 – Anti-Spyware profile

If we navigate to **Manage | Configuration | NGFW and Prisma Access | Security Services | Vulnerability Protection**, we again see the **Best Practice** indicators followed by the profiles and global **Overrides**:

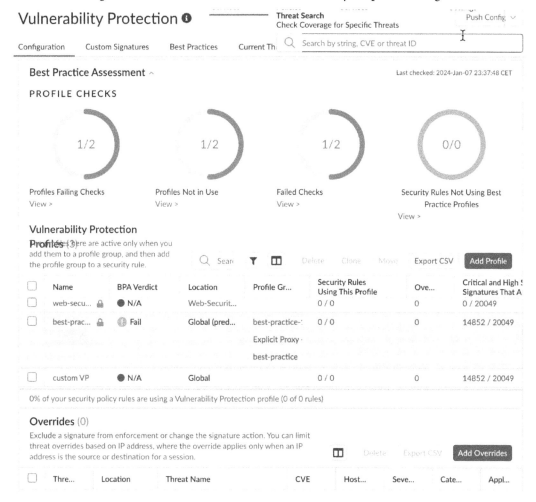

Figure 8.13 – Vulnerability profiles

When creating a new custom profile, we can set very granular rules based on severity, category (e.g., brute-force, code execution, overflow, and so on), and host type (client, server, or any) and select which action should be taken (allow, alert, drop, reset client, reset server, reset both, or block IP for a certain amount of time).

We can also add **Overrides** to the profile itself, so they are only applied to security rules that have this profile set:

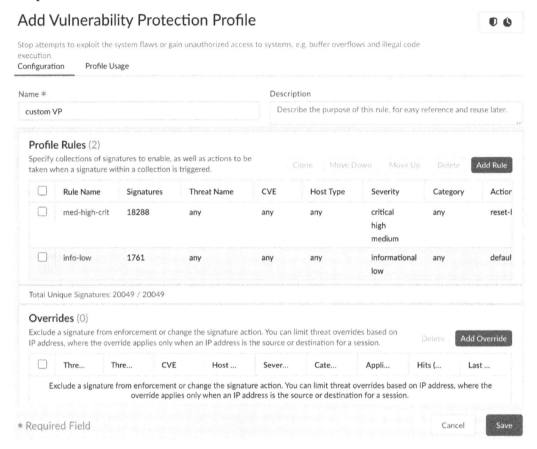

Add Vulnerability Protection Profile

Stop attempts to exploit the system flaws or gain unauthorized access to systems, e.g. buffer overflows and illegal code execution.

Configuration   Profile Usage

Name *

custom VP

Description

Describe the purpose of this rule, for easy reference and reuse later.

Profile Rules (2)

Specify collections of signatures to enable, as well as actions to be taken when a signature within a collection is triggered.

Clone   Move Down   Move Up   Delete   **Add Rule**

	Rule Name	Signatures	Threat Name	CVE	Host Type	Severity	Category	Actior
☐	med-high-crit	18288	any	any	any	critical high medium	any	reset-l
☐	info-low	1761	any	any	any	informational low	any	defaul

Total Unique Signatures: 20049 / 20049

Overrides (0)

Exclude a signature from enforcement or change the signature action. You can limit threat overrides based on IP address, where the override applies only when an IP address is the source or destination for a session.

Delete   **Add Override**

	Thre...	Thre...	CVE	Host ...	Sever...	Cate...	Appli...	Hits (...	Last ...

Exclude a signature from enforcement or change the signature action. You can limit threat overrides based on IP address, where the override applies only when an IP address is the source or destination for a session.

* Required Field

Cancel   Save

Figure 8.14 – Custom Vulnerability profile

If we navigate to **Manage** | **Configuration** | **NGFW and Prisma Access** | **Security Services** | **WildFire and Antivirus,** we see the **Best Practice** checks followed by the **WildFire** and **Antivirus** profiles. From here, we can only edit or create new profiles:

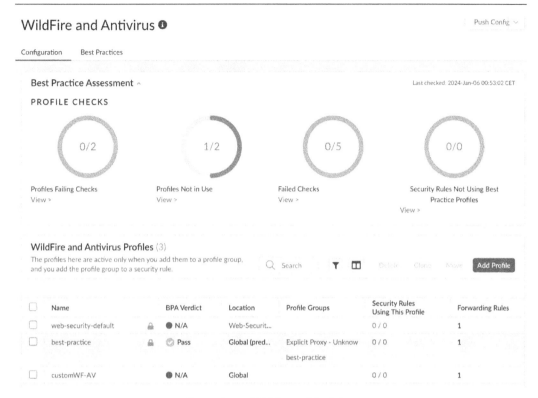

Figure 8.15 – WildFire and Antivirus

When creating a new profile, the available options should look very familiar.

We can set WildFire rules as needed. In the **customWF-AV** profile, I've set the WildFire action for downloads, the dropbox-downloading App-ID, and only **portable executable** (**PE**) filetypes, but you can, for example, set this profile to intercept and forward (to the cloud sandbox) both the upload and download direction and inspect all App-IDs for all supported file types.

I've also changed the smtp, imap, and pop3 default action of **alert** to **reset-both** and enabled all machine learning models:

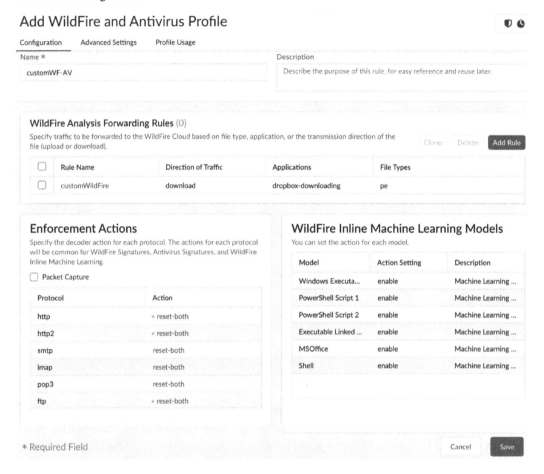

Figure 8.16 – Creating a new WF and AV profile

Next, let's check out DNS security profiles at **Manage | Configuration | NGFW and Prisma Access | Security Services | DNS Security**.

The landing page is similar to all the **Best Practice** checks at the top, followed by the profiles:

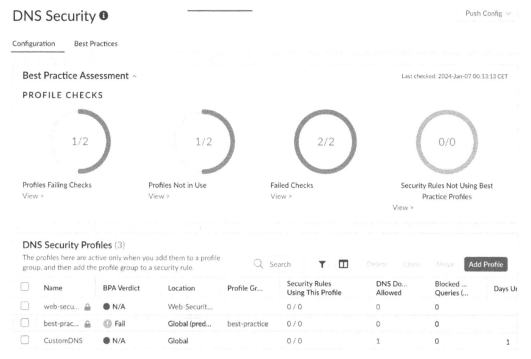

Figure 8.17 – DNS Security

Creating a new profile allows us to change some of the DNS Security actions, such as in the following example, where I set **Ad Tracking Domains** to **sinkhole** from the default **allow**, and I added my lab domain to the exceptions:

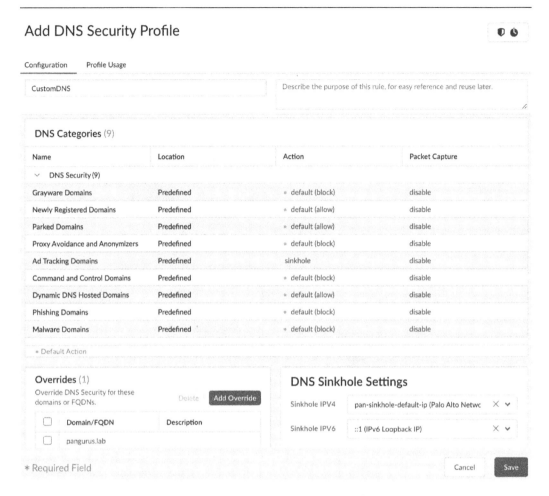

Figure 8.18 – Custom DNS Security Profile

URL Access Management will be the most impactful profile to most organizations, as it controls which URL categories can be reached by users. Navigate to **Manage | Configuration | NGFW and Prisma Access | Security Services | URL Access Management** to access the profiles. At the top, we see the **Best Practices** readouts again; in the middle, we have the URL filtering profiles that we can apply to security rules, and at the bottom, we have **Custom URL Categories**:

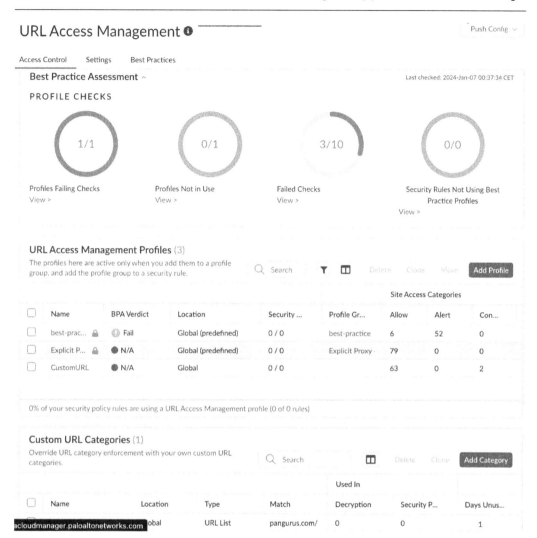

URL Access Management ⓘ

Push Config ⌄

Access Control   Settings   Best Practices

Best Practice Assessment ⌃

Last checked: 2024-Jan-07 00:37:34 CET

PROFILE CHECKS

1/1   0/1   3/10   0/0

Profiles Failing Checks   Profiles Not in Use   Failed Checks   Security Rules Not Using Best
View >   View >   View >   Practice Profiles
View >

URL Access Management Profiles (3)

The profiles here are active only when you add them to a profile group, and add the profile group to a security rule.

Search   Delete   Clone   Move   **Add Profile**

	Name	BPA Verdict	Location	Security ...	Profile Gr...	Site Access Categories		
						Allow	Alert	Con...
☐	best-prac... 🔒	ⓘ Fail	Global (predefined)	0 / 0	best-practice	6	52	0
☐	Explicit P... 🔒	● N/A	Global (predefined)	0 / 0	Explicit Proxy ⌄	79	0	0
☐	CustomURL	● N/A	Global	0 / 0		63	0	2

0% of your security policy rules are using a URL Access Management profile (0 of 0 rules)

Custom URL Categories (1)

Override URL category enforcement with your own custom URL categories.

Search   Delete   Clone   **Add Category**

	Name	Location	Type	Match	Used In		Days Unus...
					Decryption	Security P...	
☐	acloudmanager.paloaltonetworks.com	obal	URL List	pangurus.com/	0	0	1

Figure 8.19 – URL Access Management

We can add **Custom URL Categories** at the bottom by clicking **Add Category** to serve as a whitelist, blacklist, or as exceptions for machine learning:

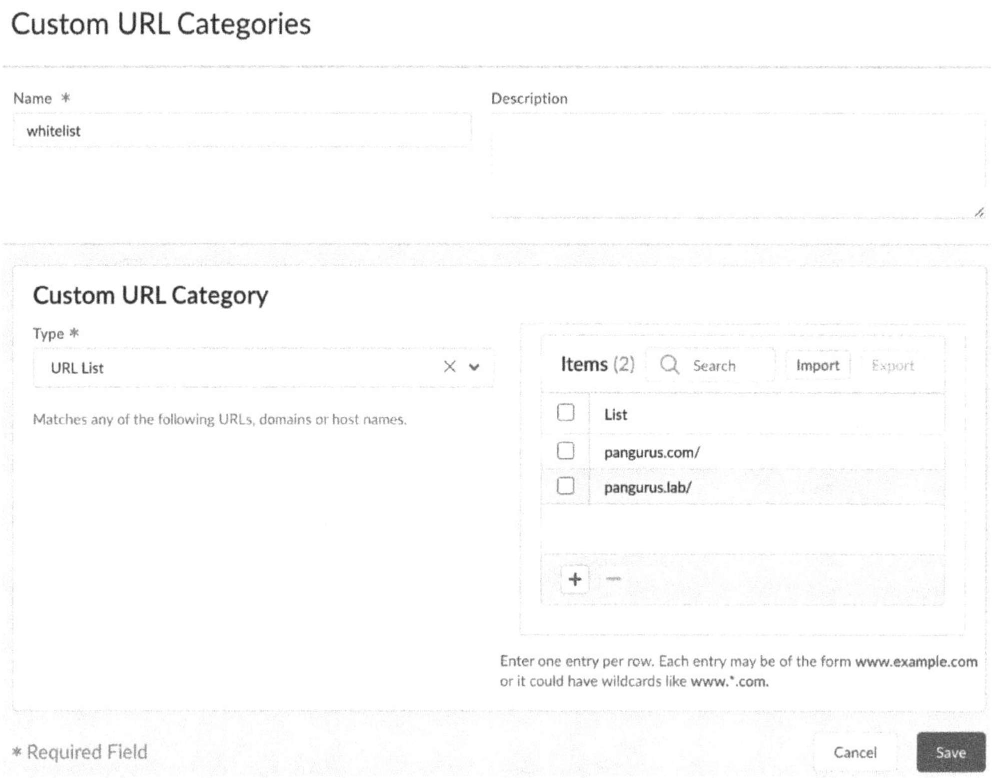

Custom URL Categories

Name *

whitelist

Description

Custom URL Category

Type *

URL List   ✕ ⌄

Matches any of the following URLs, domains or host names.

Items (2)   🔍 Search   Import   Export

☐   List

☐   pangurus.com/

☐   pangurus.lab/

\+   —

Enter one entry per row. Each entry may be of the form www.example.com or it could have wildcards like www.*.com.

* Required Field

Cancel   Save

Figure 8.20 – Custom URL Category

Once Custom URL categories are created, they will appear in URL profiles so that we can assign a `Site Access` action to them. Click **Add Profile** to create a fresh profile and configure all **Custom URL Categories** and **Pre-Defined Categories** to reflect the access users are permitted to use while browsing the internet (or internal resources). On the right side, we can also configure **User Credential Detection** and enable inline machine learning to improve URL categorization. In **Settings**, we can select some privacy options, such as **Log Container Page Only**, which will prevent the logging of the full path of the URL that a user is accessing. **Safe Search Enforcement** will block users from using search engines without the safe search option being enabled. Additional logging can be enabled by checking the **User Agent**, **Referrer**, and **X-Forward-For** boxes to log these session attributes.

In **Site Access**, the following options are available:

- **Allow** will allow access to a URL category without logging
- **Alert** will allow access to a URL category and create a log entry

- **Block** will block access to the URL category

- **Continue** will serve the user with a configurable response page that requires them to read the notification and press a button labeled **Continue** before being allowed access to the URL category

- **Override** will serve a response page that requires a password before access is granted

Figure 8.21 – URL filtering profile

From the main page, you can also access the **Settings** tab, which contains some additional URL filtering configurations. In the **General Settings**, some timeouts can be configured, indicating how long a user can keep using a URL category after having clicked continue or provided the password in the override option. The passwords for the override option can also be configured here.

At the bottom, all the response pages can be customized. You can download the default page for each category of the response page, make changes, and upload to replace the default page:

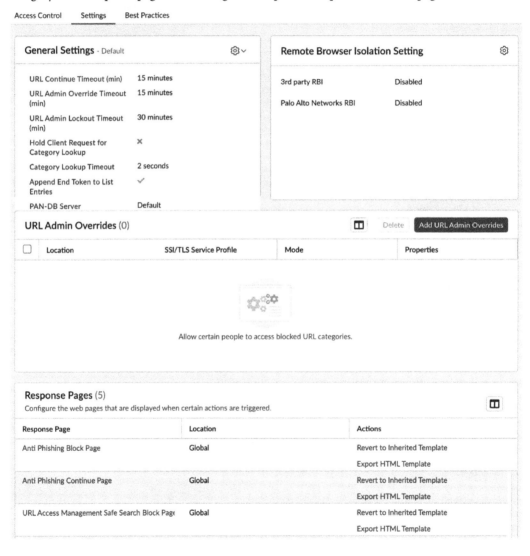

Figure 8.22 – The Settings tab

On the right-hand side, you'll notice there is an option to enable **Remote Browser Isolation** (**RBI**). At this time, you can set up Palo Alto Networks (Prisma Access Browser/Talon) RBI or select from four supported third-party RBI vendors: Ericom, Authentic8, Menlo Security, or Proofpoint.

If you have a license for Prisma Access BrowserTalon or one of the supported third-party vendors, you can enable RBI integration, which will unlock an additional **Site Access** option called `Isolate with <RBI vendor>`. Setting this action in the URL filtering profile will forward sessions matching the category to the RBI integration instead of taking direct action, and the RBI will take care of securing the content:

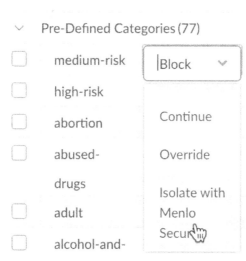

Figure 8.23 – RBI integration

Next, we can take a look at file blocking in **Manage** | **Configuration** | **NGFW and Prisma Access** | **Security Services** | **File Blocking**. On the main page, we have the **Best Practices** indicators and the **File Blocking** profiles in the middle. Near the bottom, we have the **Response** pages that can be customized to indicate why certain filetypes have been blocked or allow the user to choose to go ahead with the download via the continue action:

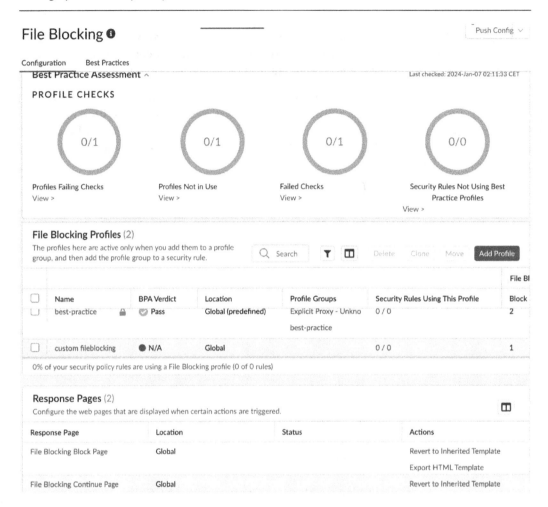

File Blocking ❶

Configuration   Best Practices

Best Practice Assessment ∧   Last checked: 2024-Jan-07 02:11:33 CET

PROFILE CHECKS

| 0/1 | 0/1 | 0/1 | 0/0 |

Profiles Failing Checks   Profiles Not in Use   Failed Checks   Security Rules Not Using Best
View >   View >   View >   Practice Profiles
                                                                  View >

File Blocking Profiles (2)

The profiles here are active only when you add them to a profile group, and then add the profile group to a security rule.

🔍 Search   ▼ ⊞   Delete   Clone   Move   **Add Profile**

	Name	BPA Verdict	Location	Profile Groups	Security Rules Using This Profile	Block
☐	best-practice 🔒	✅ Pass	Global (predefined)	Explicit Proxy - Unkno best-practice	0 / 0	2
☐	custom fileblocking	● N/A	Global		0 / 0	1

0% of your security policy rules are using a File Blocking profile (0 of 0 rules)

Response Pages (2)

Configure the web pages that are displayed when certain actions are triggered.   ⊞

Response Page	Location	Status	Actions
File Blocking Block Page	Global		Revert to Inherited Template Export HTML Template
File Blocking Continue Page	Global		Revert to Inherited Template

Figure 8.24 – File Blocking

In a custom profile, there are three types of rules you can set: **Block**, **Continue**, and **Alert**. In these rules, you can determine in which direction (upload, download, or both), specific App-ID (or any), and filetype should be blocked, presented a response page, or allowed, and this generates a log.

> **Important note**
> Any file types added to the alert rules will be allowed but generate a log, and any filetypes not covered by any of the rules will be allowed and not logged.

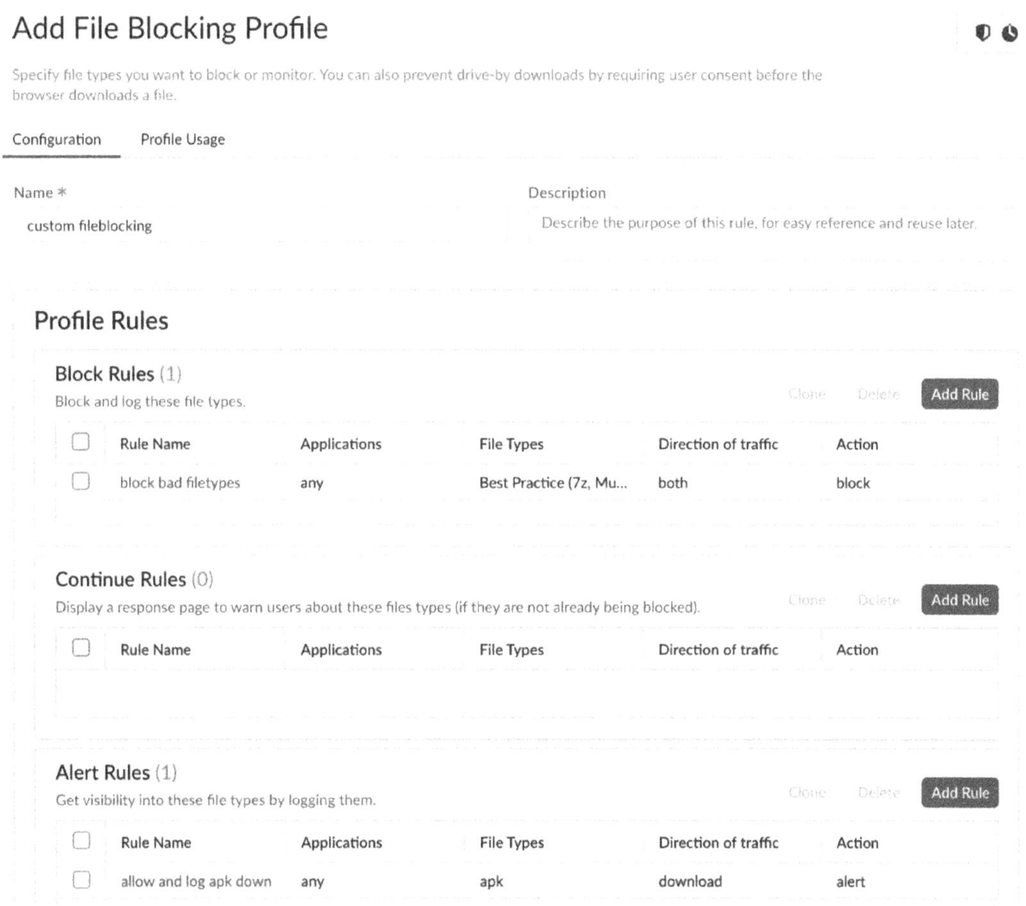

Add File Blocking Profile

Specify file types you want to block or monitor. You can also prevent drive-by downloads by requiring user consent before the browser downloads a file.

Configuration   Profile Usage

Name *
custom fileblocking

Description
Describe the purpose of this rule, for easy reference and reuse later.

Profile Rules

Block Rules (1)
Block and log these file types.   Clone   Delete   Add Rule

	Rule Name	Applications	File Types	Direction of traffic	Action
☐	block bad filetypes	any	Best Practice (7z, Mu...	both	block

Continue Rules (0)
Display a response page to warn users about these files types (if they are not already being blocked).   Clone   Delete   Add Rule

	Rule Name	Applications	File Types	Direction of traffic	Action

Alert Rules (1)
Get visibility into these file types by logging them.   Clone   Delete   Add Rule

	Rule Name	Applications	File Types	Direction of traffic	Action
☐	allow and log apk down	any	apk	download	alert

Figure 8.25 – Custom File Blocking Profile

We can also rewrite certain URLs with **HTTP Header Insertion**, which you can access via **Manage | Configuration | NGFW and Prisma Access | Security Services | HTTP Header Insertion**. This is especially useful to restrict users to the corporate tenant of SaaS applications, such as Office 365, Dropbox, and Google apps, by replacing any connection attempt for an external tenant with your own.

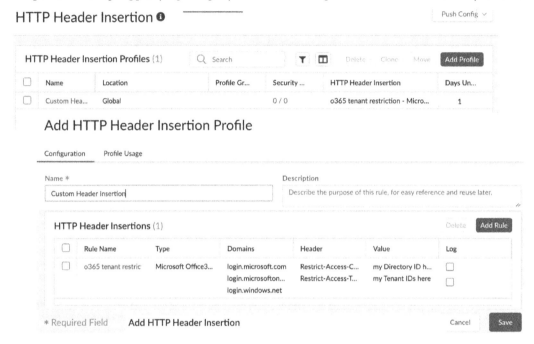

Figure 8.26 – HTTP Header Insertion

To create an Office 365 header insertion profile, select **o365vtenant restriction** from the dropdown, which will automatically populate the domains used for logging onto 0ffice 365. Next, add the **tenant ID** and **Directory ID** so any other ID can be replaced with the appropriate corporate IDs:

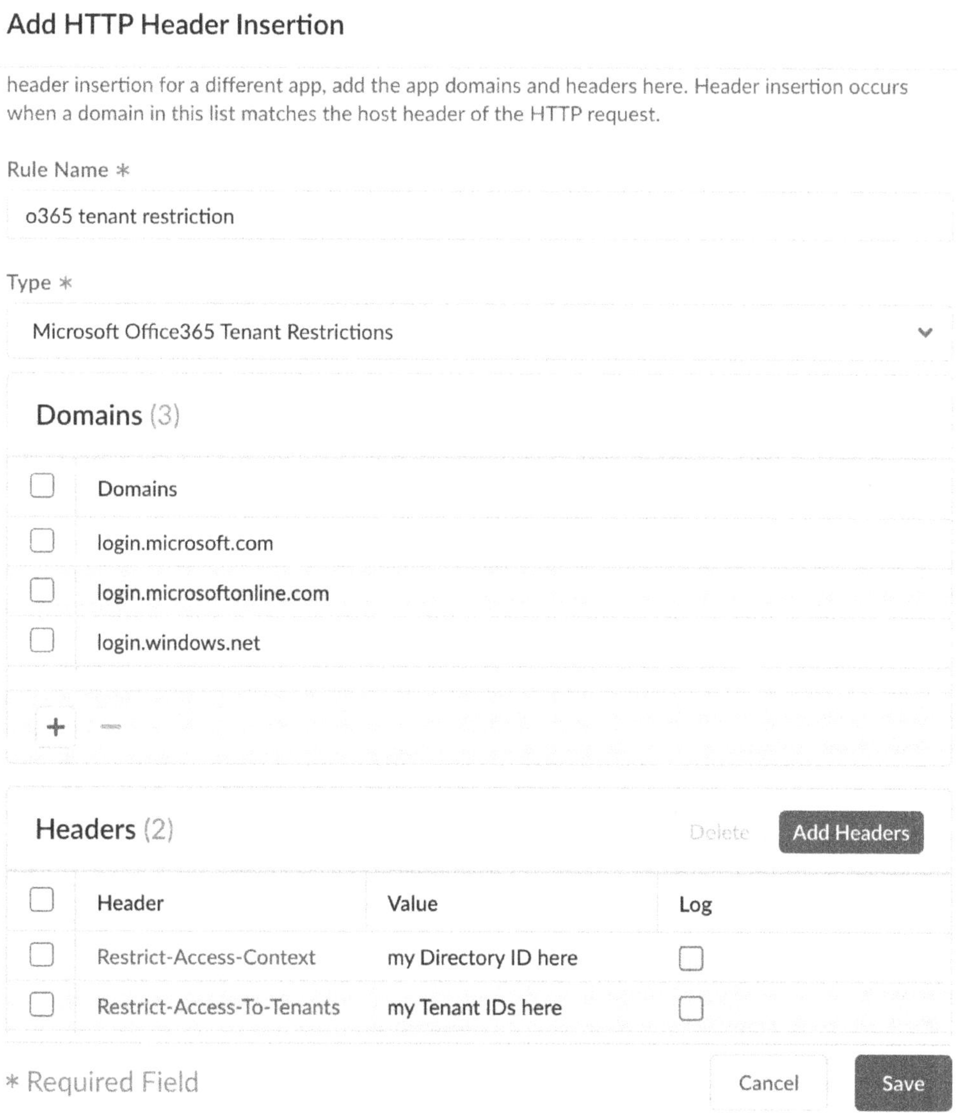

Add HTTP Header Insertion

header insertion for a different app, add the app domains and headers here. Header insertion occurs when a domain in this list matches the host header of the HTTP request.

Rule Name *

o365 tenant restriction

Type *

Microsoft Office365 Tenant Restrictions

Domains (3)

	Domains
☐	login.microsoft.com
☐	login.microsoftonline.com
☐	login.windows.net

\+

Headers (2)   Delete   **Add Headers**

	Header	Value	Log
☐	Restrict-Access-Context	my Directory ID here	☐
☐	Restrict-Access-To-Tenants	my Tenant IDs here	☐

* Required Field   Cancel   **Save**

Figure 8.27 – Configuring the Tenant Header Insertion IDs

After having created all the above profiles, we can put them in a profile group so we can easily add them to security rules as a package vs. needing to select each individual profile each time we create a rule. We can create as many profile groups as needed. When dealing with a lot of exceptions, it may be a good idea to have a group for internet-bound and one for data center-bound traffic, for example. In **Manage | Configuration | NGFW and Prisma Access | Security Services | Profile Groups**, we can see the pre-configured **best-practice** and **Explicit Proxy – Unknown Users** profiles we saw earlier in the security rule:

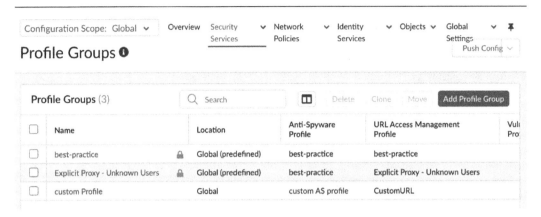

Figure 8.28 – Profile Groups

When creating a custom profile, simply select each profile that needs to be used by this profile group (e.g., internet profiles into the internet profile group, private app profiles into a private apps profile group, and so on):

Add Profile Group

Configuration

Profile Group

Name *	custom Profile
Anti-Spyware Profile	custom AS profile
Vulnerability Protection Profile	custom VP
URL Access Management Profile	CustomURL
File Blocking Profile	custom fileblocking
HTTP Header Insertion Profile	Custom Header Insertion
WildFire and Antivirus Profile	customWF-AV
DNS Security Profile	CustomDNS
Data Loss Prevention Profile	None

* Required Field   Cancel   Save

Figure 8.29 – Custom Profile Group

Before we move forward, we need to revisit the **Configuration Scope** hierarchy.

Configuration scope hierarchy

You may have noticed each profile and the profile group has a `location` column. This column indicates where this profile `lives` in the hierarchy we saw in *Figure 8.2*.

Any profiles created in **Global** can be used in all branches and `child` nodes.

If a profile should only be used in, for example, the GlobalProtect node, we can choose to move or clone the profile. Moving the profile will make it unique to the GlobalProtect node and unusable by other nodes.

> **Important note**
> Make sure a profile is not being used in any rules or profile groups that belong to Global before trying to move it elsewhere because this will prevent you from moving the profile.

Cloning **Profile** will make a copy of it in the desired node, so the original is retained, and changes can be made to the newly created profile in the GlobalProtect (or other) node.

To move or clone a profile into a node, do the following:

1. First, navigate to the node by selecting it from **Configuration Scope**.

2. Then, select the desired profile.

3. Click **Clone** or **Move** (notice that **Move** is greyed out because the donor profile is used in two profile groups).

4. A new profile is created in the GlobalProtect Node:

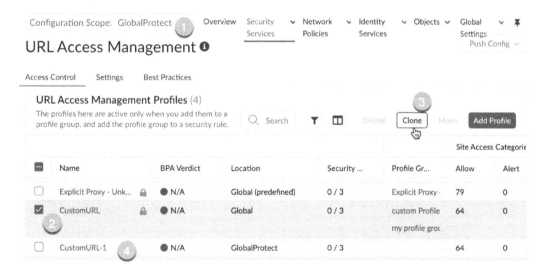

Figure 8.30 – Cloning profiles

> **Important note**
> This hierarchy also applies to security rules, decryption rules, objects, and so on.

Next, we will take a look at another set of important security-related rules: decryption rules.

Decryption

SSL decryption is the cornerstone of applying actual security and being able to perform deep packet inspection. Since nearly all web traffic is encrypted, having security profiles in place does very little if the traffic is not decrypted.

We can access the decryption profiles via **Manage | Configuration | NGFW and Prisma Access | Security Services | Decryption**.

At the top, we again see the **Best Practice** gauges followed by the **Decryption** policies. Two sets of two rules each have been predefined but are disabled. Disabled rules cause the best practice indicator to show a fail; so, consider enabling the rules if you intend to use them or delete them if you don't need them to clear up the **Best Practice** fail condition.

The first set is the recommended best practice set that, if enabled, will decrypt the following URL filtering categories: parked, questionable, unknown, web-based email, and web-hosting. And not-decrypt sensitive URL categories like financial services, government, health and medicine, and shopping.

The second set addresses O365 best practices so as not to decrypt the Microsoft recommended IP lists "*Worldwide Any Optimize IPv4*" and "*Worldwide Any Optimize IPv6*". These are external dynamic list (EDL) objects that contain a dynamically updated set of IP addresses, as recommended by Microsoft.

In most cases, I'd recommend deleting both sets and creating your own, as the decrypted/non-decrypted URLS will vary depending on your company and local law, and the Microsoft EDLs may need to be set according to your particular region or country.

You can find all the hosted EDL URLs at the following location: `https://docs.paloaltonetworks.com/resources/edl-hosting-service`.

At the bottom of the screen, we can find **Decryption Profiles**, **Global Decryption exclusions**, and **Decryption Settings**.

Decryption exclusions allows us to add URLs that we want to exclude from decryption; this can be due to privacy reasons or because, for example, the site or app uses an unsupported cipher, client certificates, or pined certificates, which we need to allow through, even though the decryption profile would block this URL normally. At this time, 300 URLs have also been added that are known to be decryptable due to the use of pinned certificates or mutual authentication.

> **Important note**
>
> A pinned certificate has an attribute that dictates which certificate authority must be in the certificate chain as the signing authority. Since decryption replaces this certificate, the handshake will fail.

In **Decryption Settings**, we can see the certificate that will be used for decryption, as this operation requires a **certificate authority** (**CA**) certificate that will perform a **man-in-the-middle** by proxying the client's session and terminating the outbound TLS connection locally and setting up a new session towards the server, allowing the firewall to inspect traffic passing through the tunnel. The default certificate used by Prisma Access is automatically deployed to clients connecting via GlobalProtect, but this certificate can be replaced by a CA certificate from the enterprise PKI infrastructure.

The **forward-trust-CA** certificate is used for **good** decryption and should be trusted by the client as a **trusted root certificate**.

The **forward-untrust-CA** certificate is used when the server returns an abnormal certificate such that the certificate error is relayed to the client's browser. This certificate should not be trusted by the client, so the browser can show a certificate error page. This type of interaction will only happen in the case where **Decryption Profile** is set to allow certain faulty certificates in the first place:

Decryption ⓘ   Push Config ∨

Rulebase   Best Practices

Best Practice Assessment ∧   Last checked: 2024-Jan-08 23:56:02 CET

CHECKS   RULEBASE CHECKS   PROFILES

        4/4   1/2   0/0   0/2   1/1   1/1
                      Failed CSC Checks Failed Rulebase Checks Policy Rules Not In Us   Profiles Not In Us

Decryption Rules Failing Checks   Profiles Failing Checks
                                                             View Failing Profiles >

Decryption Policies (4)
Decrypt SSL traffic, including SSL encapsulated   🔍 Search   ▼ ▥   Delete Enable Disable Clone Move ∨   **Add Rule**
protocols, for visibility, control, and granular security.

☐	#	Name	BPA ...	Source A...	Source U...	Destinati...	Destinati...	URL Cate...	Acti...
∨	Prisma Access - Pre Rules								
⊟	Recommended-Best-Practice (2)								
	1	best-practice-decry... 🔒	ⓘ Fail	any	any	untrust	any	parked questionable unknown web-based-e... web-hosting	decrypt
	2	best-practice-no-de... 🔒	ⓘ Fail	any	any	untrust	any	financial-serv... government health-and-... shopping	no-decr...
⊞	O365-Best-Practice (2)								

Decryption
Profiles control
specific SSL and SSH
traffic
you have specified for   ▼ ▥   Delete Clone **Add Profile**
decryption.

Name	BPA Verdict	Number of ...	Days Unused
web-security-d... 🔒	ⓘ Fail	0	
best-practice 🔒	● N/A	5	

Global Decryption Exclusions
Exclude traffic for technical, business, regulatory, personal, or other reasons.

Non-Decryptable Sites   300 of 300 predefined exclusions are enabled
(Predefined)   This list is based on the latest content version:
                          8793-8478

Custom Exclusions   saasedl.paloaltonetworks.com ···

                          *.dem.prismaaccess.com ···   +

Decryption Settings   ⚙

Best Practice Check ✓
Certificate Settings
* Certificate When Proxying for Trusted Sites

RSA	Forward-Trust-CA	◔ **Valid** until Sep 9 22:50:12 2025 GMT
ECDSA	Forward-Trust-CA-ECDSA	◔ **Valid** until Sep 9 22:50:12 2025 GMT

Certificate When Proxying for Untrusted Sites

RSA	Forward-UnTrust-CA	◔ **Valid** until Sep 9 22:50:13 2025 GMT
ECDSA	Forward-UnTrust-CA-ECDSA	◔ **Valid** until Sep 9 22:50:14 2025 GMT

Inspection Settings

Present   Enabled
response
pages
even
while not
decrypti...
URLs

Inspect   Disabled
TLS
handsha...

Figure 8.31 – SSL decryption

Let's first take a look at the best practice, **Decryption Profile**.

In **Handshake Settings**, we can configure which TLS protocols and cipher suites are accepted. In best practices, the minimum TLS version is set to TLS1.2. This means if a TLS1.1 handshake is received, the firewall will force the use of TLS1.2. If case this is not respected, the session will be blocked to prevent weak ciphers. The same holds true for the **Key Exchange**, **Encryption**, and **Authentication** algorithms. This allows us to ensure only strong encryption is used in TLS sessions.

In the **SSL Forward Proxy** section, we can block sessions that do not meet the handshake setting in the **Unsupported Mode Checks**; unchecking these options will allow sessions that do not meet the above requirements.

Additionally, we can block certificates that have expired or are not from trusted issuers in **Server Certificate Verification**. If a certificate is blocked due to the unknown issuer, the root certificate can be downloaded from the certificate authority and set as a trusted root certificate so that the firewall can trust the issuer going forward.

In the **SSL Inbound Inspection** section, we can also block sessions based on the **Handshake Settings**. In **Failure Checks**, we can additionally block inbound SSL decryption if the firewall runs out of resources or if the private key is stored on an HSM that is unavailable.

Lastly, in the **No Decryption** section, we can block sessions with an expired or untrusted certificate, even while we're not applying decryption to the session:

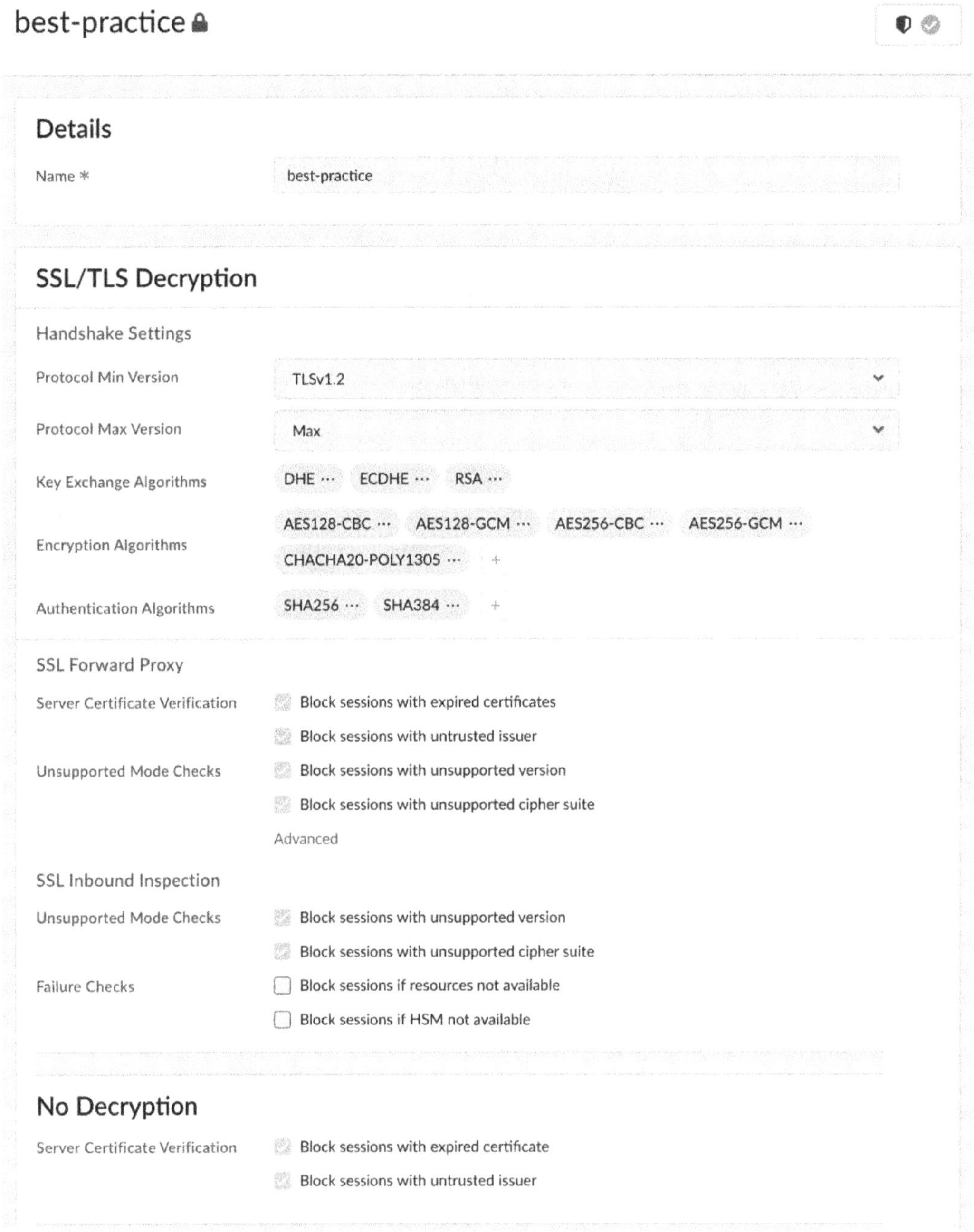

best-practice 🔒

Details

Name *   best-practice

SSL/TLS Decryption

Handshake Settings

Protocol Min Version	TLSv1.2
Protocol Max Version	Max

Key Exchange Algorithms   DHE ⋯   ECDHE ⋯   RSA ⋯

Encryption Algorithms   AES128-CBC ⋯   AES128-GCM ⋯   AES256-CBC ⋯   AES256-GCM ⋯
CHACHA20-POLY1305 ⋯   +

Authentication Algorithms   SHA256 ⋯   SHA384 ⋯   +

SSL Forward Proxy

Server Certificate Verification   ☑ Block sessions with expired certificates

☑ Block sessions with untrusted issuer

Unsupported Mode Checks   ☑ Block sessions with unsupported version

☑ Block sessions with unsupported cipher suite

Advanced

SSL Inbound Inspection

Unsupported Mode Checks   ☑ Block sessions with unsupported version

☑ Block sessions with unsupported cipher suite

Failure Checks   ☐ Block sessions if resources not available

☐ Block sessions if HSM not available

No Decryption

Server Certificate Verification   ☑ Block sessions with expired certificate

☑ Block sessions with untrusted issuer

Figure 8.32 – Decryption profile

Next, let's take a look at creating decryption rules. I'm first going to create a no-decrypt rule that lists all the categories I **don't** want to decrypt.

The first section of the rule looks nearly identical to a regular security rule.

In the **Source** section, we determine where the traffic is coming from by means of the source zone, source addresses, or address groups. We can even set EDLs and regions.

We can also add specific users or user groups to be affected by this rule and, lastly, determine the source devices by means of the HIP profile.

I have only set the source zone to trust and users to **match known user**, so all identified users will use this no-decrypt rule.

In the **Destination** section, you can select the destination zone, destination addresses, address groups, EDL, region, SaaS application endpoints (requires a Prisma Cloud subscription for your private apps), and device profile via HIP.

I have only selected the untrust zone in the destination to apply this rule to all traffic outbound to the internet:

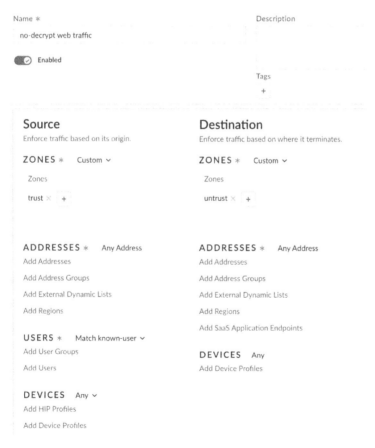

Figure 8.33 – Decryption rule source and destination

The bottom half of the security rule contains **Services and URLS**, which allows us to set which ports, if any, should be applied to this security rule, followed by the URL categories this rule should apply to.

I have kept the default **Service Entities** setting of **Any Service**, as I want this rule to apply to all outbound traffic regardless of the port being used in the case where a browsing session is somehow set up to a non-default port.

In the URC category entities, I set a handful of categories that are not supposed to be decrypted for privacy reasons. As an example, I have selected the following categories: `financial-services`, `government`, `religion`, `health-and-medicine`, and `abortion`. Do review your local laws, regulations, and corporate privacy practices when setting your n-decrypt rule, if any.

You can also add custom categories and EDLs with excluded websites.

In **Actions and Advanced Inspection**, we first select if we want this rule to encrypt or decrypt. In this particular case, we don't want to decrypt so, I have selected **Do Not Decrypt**.

In **Type**, we can select if this is an **SSL Forward Proxy** or an **SSL Inbound Inspection** rule. All outbound traffic towards the **internet** should be set as **SSL Forward Proxy**. If SSL decryption is intended for an **internally hosted private app**, we can set the **SSL Inbound Inspection**, but in this case, we do need to upload the server certificate with the private key.

Decryption profile will determine if untrusted or expired certificates will expire. Since this is a no-decrypt rule, there will not be any protocol enforcement.

In **Log Settings**, the **Log Unsuccessful TLS handshakes** setting is enabled by default and allows for troubleshooting in case sessions are failing.

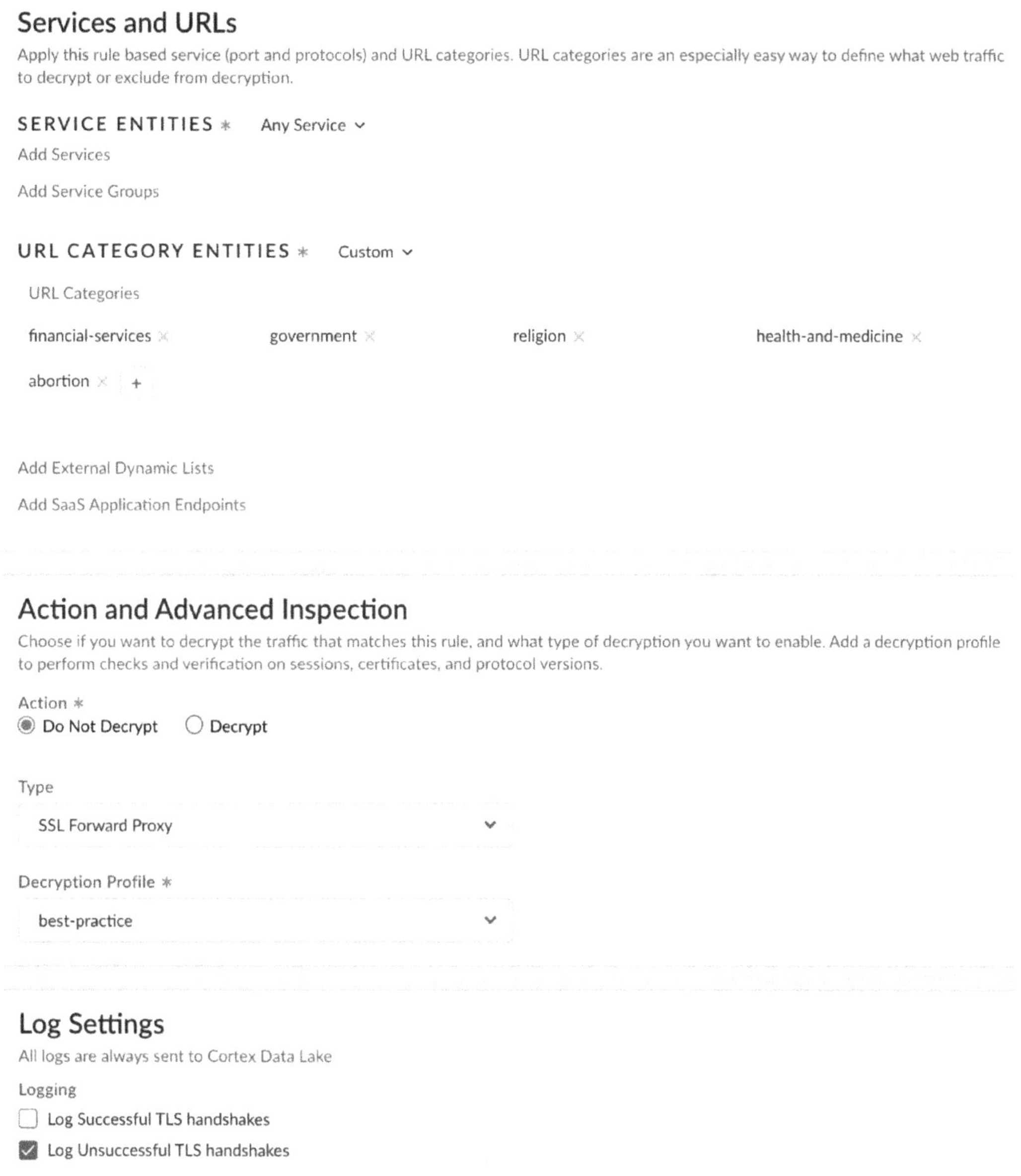

Services and URLs

Apply this rule based service (port and protocols) and URL categories. URL categories are an especially easy way to define what web traffic to decrypt or exclude from decryption.

SERVICE ENTITIES *   Any Service ∨

Add Services

Add Service Groups

URL CATEGORY ENTITIES *   Custom ∨

URL Categories

financial-services ×   government ×   religion ×   health-and-medicine ×

abortion ×   +

Add External Dynamic Lists

Add SaaS Application Endpoints

Action and Advanced Inspection

Choose if you want to decrypt the traffic that matches this rule, and what type of decryption you want to enable. Add a decryption profile to perform checks and verification on sessions, certificates, and protocol versions.

Action *
◉ Do Not Decrypt   ○ Decrypt

Type

| SSL Forward Proxy | ∨ |

Decryption Profile *

| best-practice | ∨ |

Log Settings

All logs are always sent to Cortex Data Lake

Logging

☐ Log Successful TLS handshakes

☑ Log Unsuccessful TLS handshakes

Figure 8.34 – Decryption rule Services and URLs

As a quick reference, these are the categories the EU **General Data Privacy Regulation** (**GDPR**) considers sensitive and special categories:

- Racial or ethnic origin

- Political opinions

- Religious or philosophical beliefs

- Trade union membership

- Genetic data

- Biometric data (where processed to uniquely identify someone).

Another important section is **Objects**. The objects make up the building blocks used to represent source and destination IPs or regions and applications in security rules.

Objects

The **Objects** menu contains all the configuration elements we will be using in the rules:

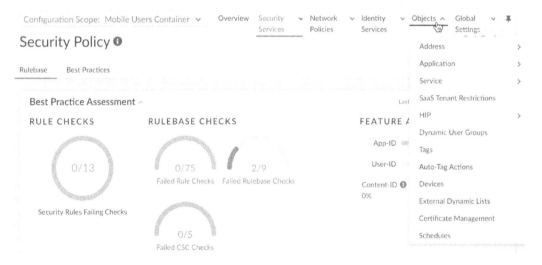

Figure 8.35 – Objects

We can add the following objects:

- **Address**

  - **Addresses** represent single IP or subnet objects.

  - **Address Groups** allow us to bundle address objects into a group.

  - **Regions** come pre-configured with country codes for each country, but we can create custom regions containing IP subnets or IP ranges as well.

- **Applications**

  - **Applications** contains all the predefined App-IDs, but we can also create custom applications to match privately hosted applications.

  - **Application groups** can be used to bundle App-IDs that are frequently used together.

  - **Application Filters** can be created to represent all applications that match a certain category, technology, risk factor, characteristic, or predefined tag. The advantage of Application filters is that it incorporates new App-IDs that match the behavior automatically, so admins don't need to worry about reviewing rules that allow or block a certain type of application each time new App-IDs are released by Palo Alto Networks:

Figure 8.36 – Application Filter

- **Service**

  - **Services** contain port and protocol (TCP or UDP)-based objects that can be used in security rules to specify which port will be allowed or blocked.

  - **Service Groups** allow us to bundle service objects that are frequently used together.

- **SaaS Tenant Restrictions** is where we can configure the SaaS tenant restrictions that we saw in URL filtering in *Figure 8.8*.

- **HIP**

  - **HIP Objects** represent individual HIP checks that are used to identify source devices. Currently, 27 **HIP Objects** are pre-configured, which range from identifying the operating system on the client machine and if it is patched to verifying if the anti-virus is running and up to date or if the firewall is enabled. Custom objects can be created to identify specific system attributes or security vendor software.

  - **HIP Profiles** group **HIP Objects** together in a profile that can be used in security and decryption rules to identify source devices.

- **Dynamic User Groups** are objects that, instead of relying on IP addresses or usernames, group objects by tag. Security rules can be applied to every object that is tagged with a specific tag. Tags can be added to nearly every object manually by using **Auto-Tag Actions** or by using the XML API.

- **Tags** is where we can configure all the tags that will be used throughout the configuration. Rules can be tagged to easily sort them by use case, and objects can be tagged to indicate their usage.

- **Auto-Tag Actions** lets us create an automatic tagging rule that is triggered by a log event. A `source address`, `destination address`, `x-forwarded-for address`, or a `user` can be tagged by setting a filter to be matched in a certain log type. In the following screenshot, I have created a filter to match any logs that carry a severity of `critical` in the `Threat` log. This will automatically tag the source address with the bad tag for 24 hours (configurable 0 to 4,320 minutes). I can then use a **Dynamic User Group** object to match the bad tag and use it in a blocking security rule:

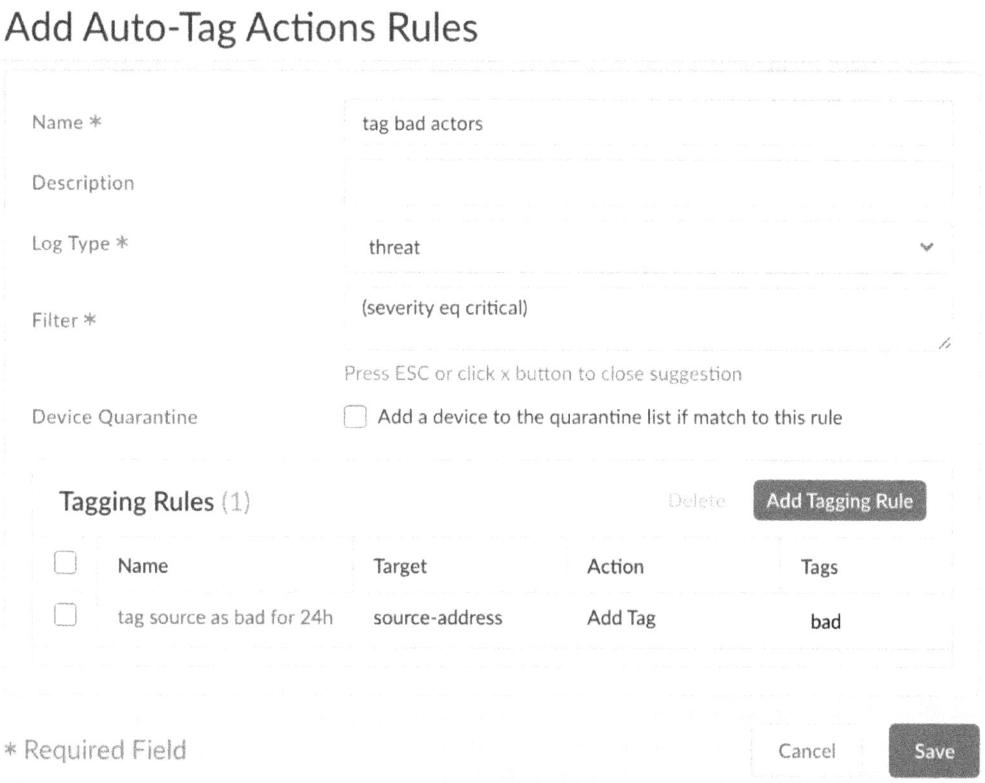

Add Auto-Tag Actions Rules

Name *	tag bad actors
Description	
Log Type *	threat ⌄
Filter *	(severity eq critical)
	Press ESC or click x button to close suggestion
Device Quarantine	☐ Add a device to the quarantine list if match to this rule

Tagging Rules (1)   ~~Delete~~   **Add Tagging Rule**

	Name	Target	Action	Tags
☐	tag source as bad for 24h	source-address	Add Tag	bad

* Required Field   Cancel   **Save**

Figure 8.37 – Auto-Tag Actions

- **Devices** are used to create IoT device objects, and this requires the IoT add-on license.

- **External Dynamic Lists** (**EDL**) is an object feting its content from a remote webpage. It can be used for IP lists, URL lists, or domain lists. The IP list can be used in security rules as source or destination objects, the URL lists can be used in URL filtering as a white or blacklist or in security rules as a URL category match, and the domain lists can be used in anti-spyware DNS security. Some EDL URLs for common services (Azure, AWS, Office 365, and so on) can be found here: `https://docs.paloaltonetworks.com/resources/edl-hosting-service`.

- **Certificate Management** is where all the certificates used for SSL decryption, SSL/TLS profiles, certificate authorities, trusted root certificates, and GlobalProtect client certificates are stored. From here, new certificates can be imported, existing certificates can be exported, and self-signed certificates can be generated.

- **Schedules** are objects that indicate when a rule can be active. If, for example, users are allowed to use social media before and after hours and during lunch, a schedule can be set to match those times and then added to a security rule so that the rule will only become active during the times set in the schedule

Let's take a look at how we can build a security policy in Panorama.

Building security policies in Panorama

When building rule bases in Panorama, there is also a hierarchy that allows us to create rules in a parent group so that they apply to all `children`. You may recall from previous chapters that we could choose a parent device group in the mobile users and remote networks settings. Depending on the number of device groups and firewalls managed in Panorama, you can place all the device groups in **Shared** (or one level down, as I did in the following screenshot) by creating a parent device group called **Prisma** that contains all the Prisma access device groups:

Figure 8.38 – Parent Device Group

In this way, any rule created in `Prisma` will apply to all nodes in remote networks, mobile users, and explicit proxies. If you want to have another parent available for shared policies between the explicit proxy and GlobalProtect (mobile users), you can add another layer via **Panorama | Device Groups**.

As you can see in the following screenshot, security rules for the Prisma access nodes are exactly the same as those for other Panorama-managed device groups. The yellowy-orange-colored rules are from a parent, and the white background rules belong to the local container. Pre- and post-rules apply in the same way as regular device groups, except that there is no notion of local rules for Prisma access nodes:

Figure 8.39 – Security rules in Panorama

SSL decryption also follows the same principle as all the other device groups. Make sure to add a no-decrypt rule for sensitive categories:

Figure 8.40 – SSL decryption

Let's take a look at how we can offer connectivity to applications without requiring special configurations:

Clientless VPN

Clientless VPN is a setting that enables the Prisma access portal to serve applications via a web interface. On the frontend, the users will be served a set of clickable tiles that represent web applications they can access without the need for a GlobalProtect agent or proxy configuration. In the backend the portal will serve as a client to communicate with the destination server and collect the web content to display this information to the user as a reverse proxy.

Let's take a look at setting up clientless VPN in Strata Cloud Manager:

To configure clientless VPN, navigate to **Workflows | Prisma Access Setup | GlobalProtect | Clientless VPN**. From here, we need to create new applications to represent the page we want to be made available through the portal:

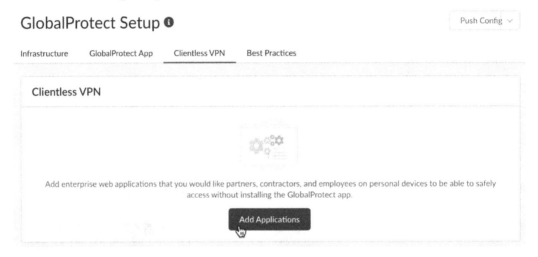

Figure 8.41 – Clientless VPN

When you click **Add Application** for the first time, you are taken to the **Clientless VPN** configuration page, where we can activate the clientless VPN feature.

New applications can be created by clicking **Add Rule**.

Timeout Settings can be tuned to allow users more or less time to be connected to the portal to browse published applications.

In **Crypto Settings**, we see settings similar to SSL decryption, where we can control which TLS versions and cipher suites the clientless VPN reverse proxy will support when connecting to published apps.

On the bottom of the **Settings** page, we can add a proxy configuration if the portals' connections need to go through a proxy before they can reach resources, and we can add **Rewrite Exclude Domain List**.

Because the clientless VPN is a reverse proxy, it rewrites URLs for the published applications served on the portal page as the user navigates the pages therein. The REDL comes in handy when, for example, an internal page calls on a resource that does not need to be rewritten (otherwise, it could break the page); those domains can be added to the REDL so they are not rewritten:

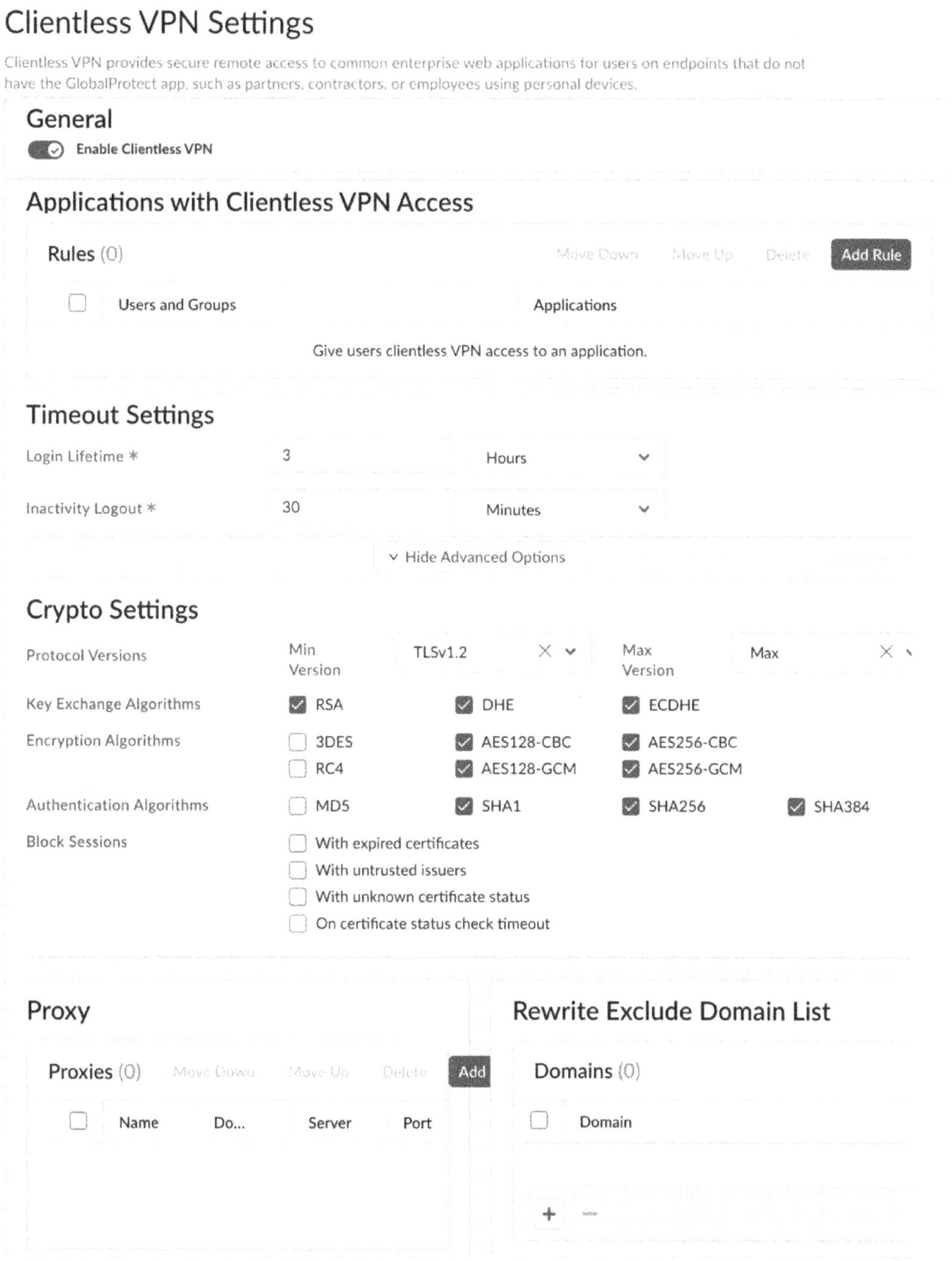

Clientless VPN Settings

Clientless VPN provides secure remote access to common enterprise web applications for users on endpoints that do not have the GlobalProtect app, such as partners, contractors, or employees using personal devices.

General

🔘✓ Enable Clientless VPN

Applications with Clientless VPN Access

	Rules (0)	Move Down	Move Up	Delete	Add Rule

	Users and Groups	Applications

Give users clientless VPN access to an application.

Timeout Settings

Login Lifetime *	3	Hours	⌄
Inactivity Logout *	30	Minutes	⌄

⌄ Hide Advanced Options

Crypto Settings

Protocol Versions	Min Version	TLSv1.2	✕ ⌄	Max Version	Max	✕ ⌄
Key Exchange Algorithms	☑ RSA	☑ DHE		☑ ECDHE		
Encryption Algorithms	☐ 3DES	☑ AES128-CBC		☑ AES256-CBC		
	☐ RC4	☑ AES128-GCM		☑ AES256-GCM		
Authentication Algorithms	☐ MD5	☑ SHA1		☑ SHA256		☑ SHA384
Block Sessions	☐ With expired certificates					
	☐ With untrusted issuers					
	☐ With unknown certificate status					
	☐ On certificate status check timeout					

Proxy

	Proxies (0)	Move Down	Move Up	Delete	Add

	Name	Do...	Server	Port

Rewrite Exclude Domain List

Domains (0)

	Domain

+ ▬

Figure 8.42 – Clientless VPN Settings

From here, we get in a little bit of a chicken and egg situation, as we do not have any applications yet, but we need to start creating a rule before we can create apps. When you click the **Add Rule** button, you see the rule creation screen with **Manage Applications** and **Manage Application Groups** at the bottom. From there, you first need to go into **Manage Applications** and click **Add** to create a new application.

Follow the steps listed here (and also shown in the screenshot that follows):

1. Click **Add Rule**
2. Click **Manage Applications**
3. Click **Add** to create a new app
4. Provide an easy-to-identify **Name**
5. Add the application URL
6. Provide a short description
7. Optionally upload an icon for the tile
8. Click **Save**
9. Click the **return** button to go back to the rule
10. Click the + sign to add a new app to the rule and select the application you just created
11. Select a username or user group if the application is intended for only a specific group of users
12. Click **Save**:

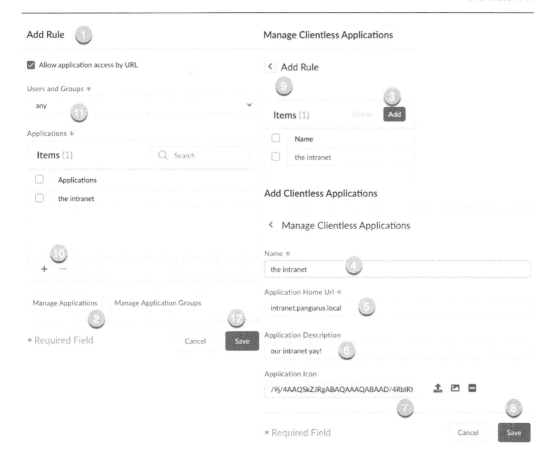

Figure 8.43 – Creating a clientless app

After creating the Clientless VPN rule, make sure to push the configuration to the infrastructure. Now, when a user logs on to the portal (your FQDN or your `host.gpcloudservice.com`) they will see the tiles matching the clientless VPN rule. Clicking the tile will take the user to the intranet without leaving the portal in their own browser:

Figure 8.44 – Clientless VPN portal

When configuring clientless VPN in Panorama, we can first navigate to **Templates | Network | GlobalProtect | Clientless Apps** and create the applications we want to make available to our users. If we need to have different groups of users, each with their own set of apps, we can also create **Clientless App Groups**:

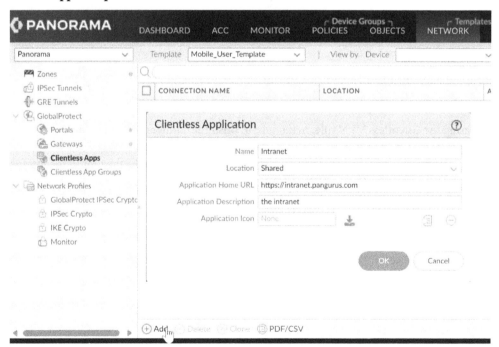

Figure 8.45 – Creating Clientless Apps

Once the required apps are created, we can navigate to **Templates | Network | GlobalProtect | Portals** and edit the Prisma Access **GlobalProtect_Portal**.

Navigate to the **Clientless VPN** tab and ensure the **Clientless VPN** checkbox is selected. In **Security Zones**, set the zone that will be used to match the source of the connections established by the reverse proxy. In the following example, I set the **Trust** zone as the source:

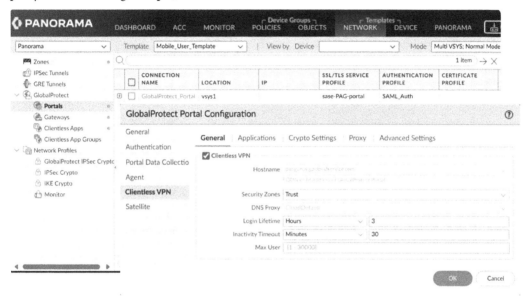

Figure 8.46 – Enabling Clientless Apps

In the **Applications** tab, you can add a configuration for individual users, user groups, or all users. Assign the clientless apps we created in *Figure 8.45* to a rule to make it available for users connecting to the portal:

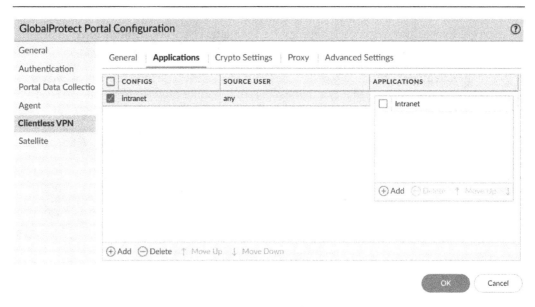

Figure 8.47 – Creating application rules

In **Crypto Settings**, we can set which minimum protocol version and cipher suites should be supported by the egressing reverse proxy connection to ensure security:

Figure 8.48 – Crypto Settings

In the **Proxy** tab, we can add a proxy configuration in case our egress proxy needs to relay sessions via a proxy:

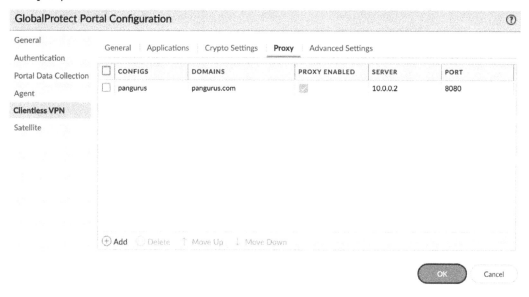

Figure 8.49 – Proxy settings

In **Advanced Settings**, we can add **Rewrite Excludes** for domains that should not be rewritten by the reverse proxy: When a remote user accesses a URL, the request goes through the GlobalProtect portal. In some cases, the website may have content that does not need to be accessed via the portal. Add the domains that should be excluded from the rewrite.

Wildcards are only allowed at the beginning of the FQDN, and paths cannot be used in the rewrite exclusion:

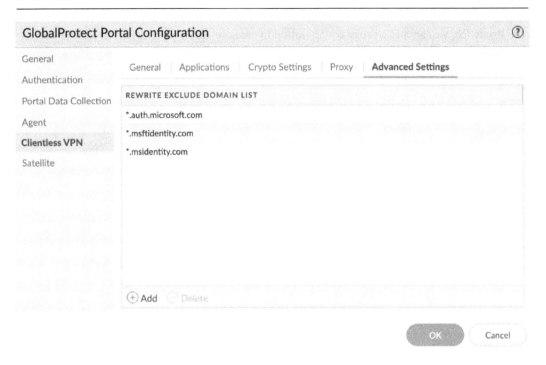

Figure 8.50 – Advanced Settings

With this configuration, you are now able to serve applications to users that do not have GlobalProtect installed, which can come in handy if certain users only need to be able to access the intranet pages while not in the office or if you have a handy IT team that can set up a Guacamole server and serves additional applications and protocols over ssl.

Summary

In this chapter, you learned a great deal about how to create rules in the Strata Cloud Manager and where to find all the objects and profiles needed to build comprehensive rules.

In the next chapter, we're going to take a closer look at user IDs, redistribution, group mapping, and integration with Cloud Identity Engine.

Part 3: Advanced Configuration and Best Practices

In this part, advanced topics are covered to improve the security stance of the deployment and gain a deeper understanding of how routing is performed inside Prisma Access. This part has the following chapters:

- *Chapter 9, User Identification and Cloud Identity Engine*

- *Chapter 10, Advanced Configurations and Insights*

- *Chapter 11, ZTNA Connector*

User Identification and Cloud Identity Engine

In this chapter, we will learn about user identification and leveraging Cloud Identity Engine to interface with on-premises or cloud active directory to retrieve group information. User identification is one of the major pillars of zero trust as it allows you to grant or deny access to resources based not just on a user's source IP address but on the identity. Cloud Identity Engine allows you to aggregate different sources of group membership.

We're going to cover the following main topics so you can build a solid security policy to control who has access to what:

- User identification and group mapping
- Cloud Identity Engine
- User ID redistribution

Technical requirements

Users will gain the most from this chapter if they're already familiar with User-ID to IP mapping, as used on Palo Alto Networks firewalls.

User identification and group mapping

User identification (**user ID**) is an integral part of Palo Alto Networks SASE technology, and together with Prisma Access, it forms a very important cornerstone of building security policies. As we've seen in previous chapters, all mobile users receive IP addresses from regional or global IP pools. The IP pools are split into 24 subnets and distributed randomly across deployed MU-SPNs, so IP-based policies are difficult to maintain. Deploying security rules based on usernames or AD group membership is much easier and allows users to roam freely between countries while maintaining the same access without needing to maintain complex IP address management.

User ID works by mapping the username associated with a session to the IP address that was assigned from the IP pool. This information can also be shared with other firewalls outside of Prisma Access so that the IP address assigned to a user logging in from the Netherlands, associated with their username, can be learned by a datacenter firewall in the US. When connections originating from that IP address arrive via the Service Connection into the datacenter, the on-premises firewall can also apply security policy and log the activity, including the username, for the inbound connections. For user ID to work, nothing needs to be configured; this is achieved by having users log on via GlobalProtect.

Group mapping retrieves security groups from the directory service. These security groups will contain *members* in the form of usernames. These usernames can be matched against logged-on users in Prisma Access. The security groups can be used in security rules to enforce policies based on the users' membership to a security group.

Group mapping may require some tweaking depending on the username format (for example, User Principal Name or sAMAccountName) used to log into GlobalProtect versus the username attribute retrieved from the directory service. For example, if users log on to GlobalProtect using SAML, their username will most likely be UPN and look like `user1@domain.com`, and the `username` attribute in a security group may be set to the user's username without domain `user1`. In this case, the group mapping configuration needs to be set so the UPN attribute is retrieved, or the username and group mapping membership won't match. We'll see how to do that later in this chapter.

One of the easiest ways to integrate group mapping is by using the **Cloud Identity Engine** (**CIE**)

Cloud Identity Engine

The CIE is a free service that you can activate from the Palo Alto HUB at `https://apps.paloaltonetworks.com`. In this section, we'll be using two portals at the same time, one for CIE and one for Azure, so to make things easy on yourself, I recommend you keep two browser windows open so you can easily copy information from one window to the next.

To get started with the CIE, log into the HUB and click **Activate** in the Cloud Identity box in **Explore Apps from Palo Alto Networks**:

Figure 9.1 – Activating Cloud Identity Engine

Next, you will need to associate the CIE to the appropriate `Customer Support Account` instance in case your account has been linked to multiple customer accounts and `Region` for where the CIE will be active. You will be offered the region(s) available for CIE to be deployed that are closest to your Prisma Access tenant:

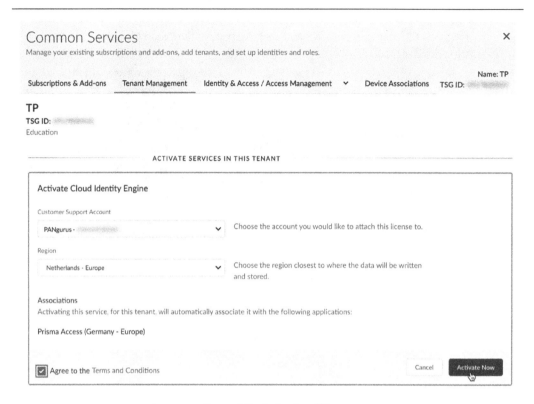

Figure 9.2 – Activating CIE

Once the CSP and region are set, click **Activate Now** to spin up the CIE. Once the process is completed, you will have a new tile available in the CIE hub:

Figure 9.3 – HUB view with CIE

When you click the **Cloud Identity Engine** tile, you will be taken to `https://directory-sync.<countrycode>.apps.paloaltonetworks.com`, and the `<country code>` part represents the region where you deployed the CIE. You should land on the **Directories** tab, which, right now, is still empty except for the blue **Add New Directory** button at the top right. Click this to be taken to the **Set Up Directory** menu, as illustrated in the following screenshot. You can choose to deploy an agent if you have an on-premises active directory to interface with the directory server, or you can choose from Azure, Okta, Google, or SCIM for cloud directories:

Figure 9.4 – Setting up a directory

We'll start with setting up directory sync in Azure. Start by selecting Azure from the **Cloud Directory** dropdown.

Setting up a directory sync in Azure

When you configure directory sync for Azure, you will be presented with the following connection flow options:

Client Credential Flow: This option will require you to provide a Directory ID, Client ID, and a Client Secret, which you'll need to retrieve from the **Microsoft Entra ID** (formerly Azure Active Directory) tenant:

1. **Auth Code Flow** skips the preceding steps, but the user can use it to make the connection if they have at least the following permissions:

   - `Directory.Read.All`

   - `Organization.Read.All`

2. If you have Azure AD Identity Protection deployed in your Entra ID, you can select the **Collect User Risk Information** button to ingest this information into CIE. This allows you to create cloud dynamic user groups.

3. **Collect enterprise applications** will collect enterprise application data and display this information in the Directory Data. This setting may increase sync time, so consider leaving it off in large Entra ID environments.

4.   Proceed by clicking **Sign in with Azure** if you want to proceed with Auth Code Flow:

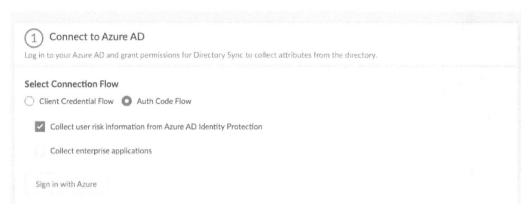

Configure Directory Sync for Azure Active Directory

Grant permissions for Directory Sync to access your Azure Active Directory (Azure AD) and collect user, group, and device attributes. Click here to learn how to configure Azure AD for Directory Sync.

(1)   **Connect to Azure AD**

Log in to your Azure AD and grant permissions for Directory Sync to collect attributes from the directory.

Select Connection Flow

◯ Client Credential Flow   ⦿ Auth Code Flow

☑ Collect user risk information from Azure AD Identity Protection

☐ Collect enterprise applications

Sign in with Azure

Figure 9.5 – Configuring directory Sync for Azure

Once you click **Sign in With Azure**, you'll see the typical Azure login page where you need to provide your credentials and MFA authentication.

Once you are authenticated, the **Sign in** button will change to a green **Signed In** button; in step 2, the **Check Connection Status** the **Test Connection** buttons will now become available. Click **Test Connection** to connect to the AAD and verify if the account you selected has the appropriate privileges. You may be asked to reconfirm the username used during this connection:

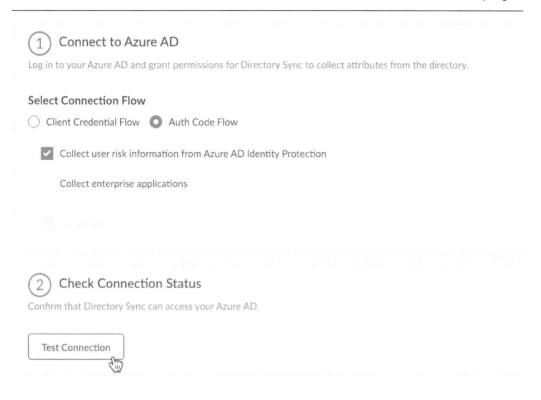

① **Connect to Azure AD**

Log in to your Azure AD and grant permissions for Directory Sync to collect attributes from the directory.

Select Connection Flow

◯ Client Credential Flow   ⦿ Auth Code Flow

☑ Collect user risk information from Azure AD Identity Protection

Collect enterprise applications

② **Check Connection Status**

Confirm that Directory Sync can access your Azure AD.

Test Connection

Figure 9.6 – Test Connection

If the connection succeeds, the CIE will now be able to fetch your directory ID and Primary Domain name from the Entra ID.

In step 3, you can use **Customize Directory Name** to change the display name that will be used to represent this directory connection. Once that is done, you can click **Submit** at the bottom right to finalize the configuration:

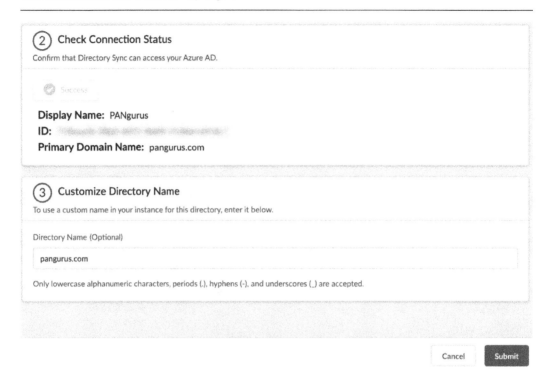

Figure 9.7 – Successful connection

After you click **Submit**, you will be taken back to **Directories**, and the new directory will start the sync process. Depending on the number of objects in the Entra ID, this may take a while. With very large environments, this initial sync can take several hours. In extremely large environments, SCIM may be an alternative to consider to decrease sync time. Sync time depends heavily on the size of the directory and the amount of group nesting.

In the following screenshot, you can see what this process will look like. The new connection will take a while to sync, and when it is completed, it will list the number of users and groups that were retrieved:

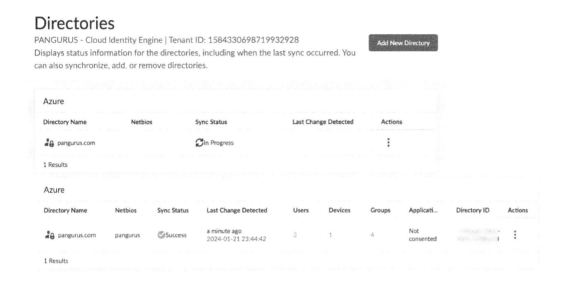

Figure 9.8 – Directory sync

Once the directory is synced, it can be used for group mapping. There are a few actions we can run manually:

> **Important note**
> CIE automatically updates partial changes every 5 minutes and performs a full sync weekly.

As illustrated in the following screenshot, the following manual actions are available once a directory sync has been established:

Reconnect is used in case the connection to Entra ID is severed:

- **Sync Changes** can be run manually when changes are made (users added; group members changed). Only changes since the last sync are updated.
- **Full Sync** retrieves the entire directory and can be used in case you're experiencing issues.

- **Remove** is used to remove this directory connection:

Figure 9.9 – Directory actions

Let's take a look at how we would add a SCIM connector.

Setting up a SCIM connector

Before we start configuring the SCIM connector, we first need to collect the Entra ID tenant ID. From the Azure portal, navigate to your active directory (Microsoft Entra ID). The easiest way is to use the search bar at the top of the portal and search for `entra`:

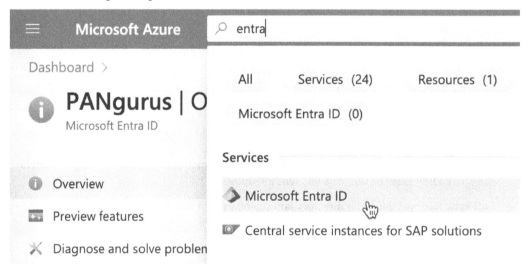

Figure 9.10 – Microsoft Entra ID

When you select your Entra instance, you should immediately see the **Tenant ID** on the **Overview** page. Copy the tenant ID and store it in a notepad, as we will need it in the next steps:

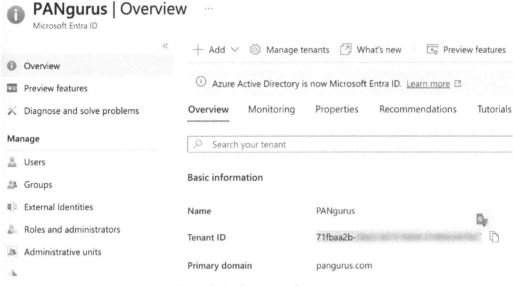

Figure 9.11 – Entra overview page

Next, we need to prepare the SCIM connection on the CIE side by selecting SCIM in **Set Up Directory**, as we saw in *Figure 9.4*.

We will need to do the following things in preparation for what we'll need to do in Azure:

1. Paste the **Tenant ID** we copied earlier.
2. Click **Generate Token** at the bottom of the page.
3. Copy the **Bearer Token** by clicking the copy button. Save the token somewhere safe for now.
4. Copy the **Base URL** by clicking the copy button. Save the URL somewhere for now.
5. Click **Submit**.

6. The SCIM setup page should look similar to the following screenshot:

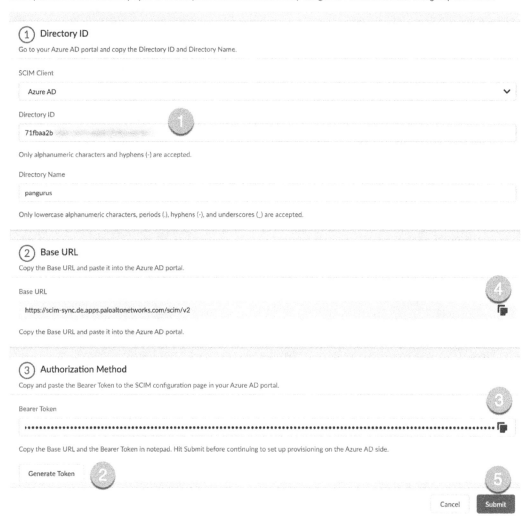

Configure Directory Sync for SCIM

Grant permissions for Directory Sync to access your Azure Active Directory using SCIM and collect user and group attributes.

① Directory ID

Go to your Azure AD portal and copy the Directory ID and Directory Name.

SCIM Client

Azure AD

Directory ID

71fbaa2b

Only alphanumeric characters and hyphens (-) are accepted.

Directory Name

pangurus

Only lowercase alphanumeric characters, periods (.), hyphens (-), and underscores (_) are accepted.

② Base URL

Copy the Base URL and paste it into the Azure AD portal.

Base URL

https://scim-sync.de.apps.paloaltonetworks.com/scim/v2

Copy the Base URL and paste it into the Azure AD portal.

③ Authorization Method

Copy and paste the Bearer Token to the SCIM configuration page in your Azure AD portal.

Bearer Token

••

Copy the Base URL and the Bearer Token in notepad. Hit Submit before continuing to set up provisioning on the Azure AD side.

Generate Token

Cancel   Submit

Figure 9.12 – Configuring Directory Sync for SCIM

Next, we will set up the SCIM connector Enterprise Application via the Azure portal.

In Azure, navigate to the Enterprise Applications and then do the following:

1. Click **New application**
2. Search for `palo alto scim connector`

3. Click the **Palo Alto SCIM Connector** tile

4. Click **Create** to deploy the new application

Once done, you should be able to see something similar to the following screenshot:

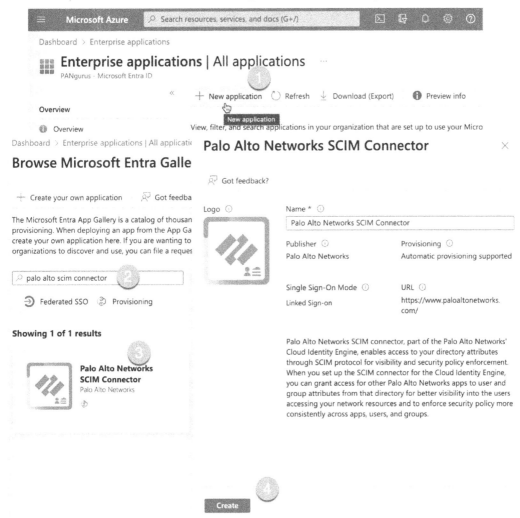

Figure 9.13 – New SCIM enterprise application

From the SCIM overview page, click **Provisioning** to start the provisioning configuration:

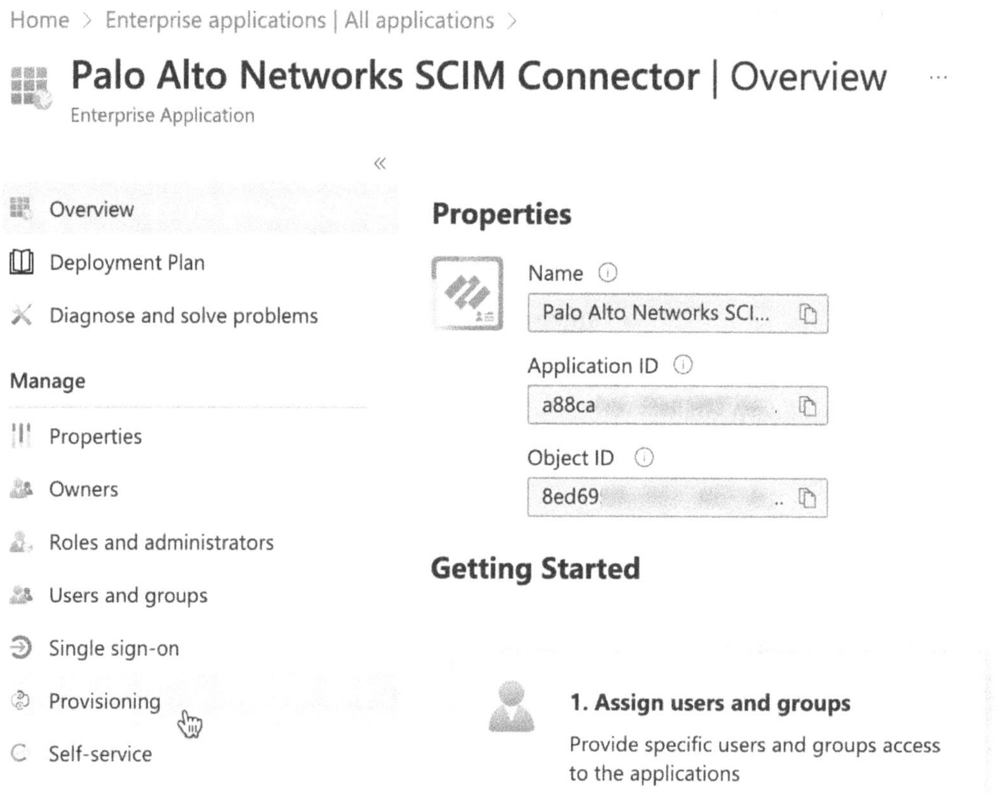

Home > Enterprise applications | All applications >

Palo Alto Networks SCIM Connector | Overview   ···
Enterprise Application

«

- Overview
- Deployment Plan
- Diagnose and solve problems

Manage

- Properties
- Owners
- Roles and administrators
- Users and groups
- Single sign-on
- Provisioning
- Self-service

Properties

Name ⓘ

Palo Alto Networks SCI... ⧉

Application ID ⓘ

a88ca ⧉

Object ID ⓘ

8ed69 ⧉

Getting Started

1. Assign users and groups

Provide specific users and groups access to the applications

Figure 9.14 – SCIM overview

You may end up on an initial landing page; click **Get Started** to go on to the actual provisioning. In the next screen, set provisioning to `Automatic` and paste the base URL and Bearer token that we collected in *Figure 9.12*. Then, click **Test Connection**.

If the test succeeds, click **Save**.

In case the test does not succeed, make sure to check if you clicked **Submit** in the CIE SCIM configuration that we saw in *Figure 9.12* and that it was completed successfully. Otherwise, repeat the steps by creating a new SCIM connection in CIE, pasting the new Bearer token in *Figure 9.15*, and testing again:

Provisioning …

🖫 Save   ✕ Discard

Provisioning Mode

Automatic	⌄

Use Microsoft Entra to manage the creation and synchronization of user accounts in Palo Alto Networks SCIM Connector based on user and group assignment.

⌃ Admin Credentials

Admin Credentials

Microsoft Entra needs the following information to connect to Palo Alto Networks SCIM Connector's API and synchronize user data.

Tenant URL * ⓘ

https://scim-sync.de.apps.paloaltonetworks.com/scim/v2	✓

Secret Token

•• …

Test Connection

Test Connection

Figure 9.15 – SCIM provisioning

Next, go back to the **Provisioning** page and click **Edit Provisioning** to select the groups you want to provision. These groups will be synchronized to the CIE:

Home > Enterprise applications | All applications > Palo Alto Networks SCIM Connector | Provisioning >

ⓘ Palo Alto Networks SCIM Connector | Overview …

« ▷ Start provisioning ☐ Stop provisioning ↻ Restart provisioning ✐ Edit provisioning ⧉ Provisio

Edit provisioning

ⓘ Overview	**Current cycle status**	**Statistics to date**
⧉ Provision on demand		
Manage	Incremental cycle completed.	⌄ View provisioning details
⧉ Provisioning	_____ 100% complete	
⧉ Users and groups		⌄ View technical information

Figure 9.16 – Edit provisioning

Once the desired groups have been added, save to go back to the **Provisioning** page, and click **Start Provisioning**:

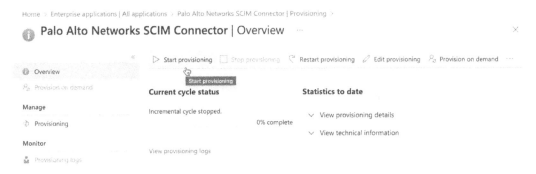

Figure 9.17 – Start provisioning

The next step is to add CIE to your Prisma Access deployment.

Adding CIE to Prisma Access

To add the CIE to the Strata Cloud Manager, navigate to **Manage | Configuration | NGFW and Prisma Access | Identity Services | Cloud Identity Engine**. Click the **Cloud Identity Engine Settings** to start the configuration:

Figure 9.18 – Adding the Cloud Identity Engine

Next, you can pick which User Attributes should be collected. The user attribute should match the username used by mobile users to log on to the MU-SPN, so if authentication is set to sAMAccountName for the authentication of mobile users, make sure to select sAMAccountName here as well. Since we set up SAML for authentication, we'll set **User Principal Name** as the **Primary User Name**. Please note that the **Primary User Name** attribute must match the authentication profile username format:

Figure 9.19 – User Attributes

Once you click **Save**, you'll see an overview of the selected **User Attributes** and the **Directories** being synced:

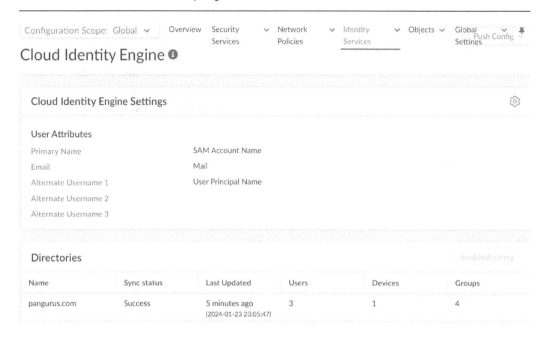

Figure 9.20 – Cloud Identity Engine overview

Don't forget to click **Push Config** in the upper-right corner to save your changes.

Once the commit is completed, you can now start using users or groups in security rules or, for example, GlobalProtect configuration profiles.

If we look at a security rule as an example, go to **Manage | Configuration | NGFW and Prisma Access | Security Services | Security Policy** and open or create a security rule. In the **source users**, we can perform the following steps to add groups:

1. Set **Users** to **Select**.

2. Use the dropdown arrow to open the selection window.

3. You'll first see the usernames of the known users.

4. Click **User Groups** to get a list of Entra ID groups. Select the ones you want to use in this security rule.

5. Once you've added the appropriate user groups, save the rule and click **Push Commit**:

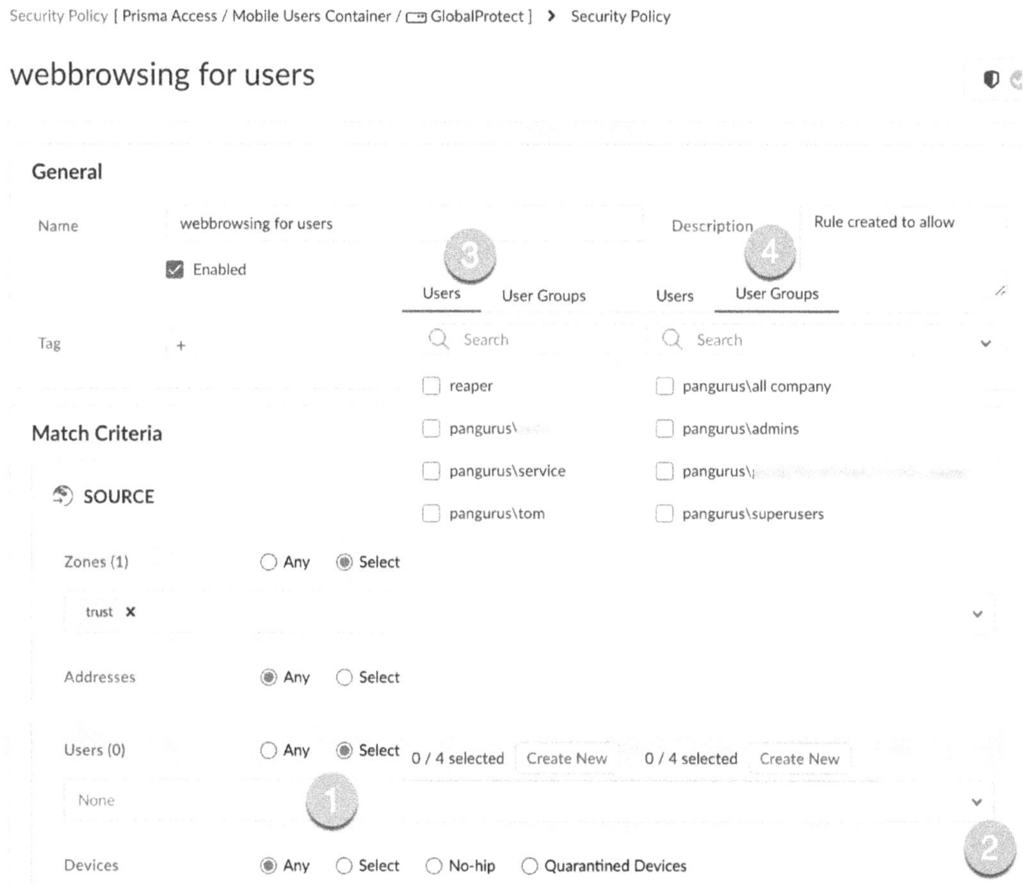

Security Policy [Prisma Access / Mobile Users Container / ▭ GlobalProtect] ❯ Security Policy

webbrowsing for users

General

Name: webbrowsing for users

☑ Enabled

Tag: +

Description: Rule created to allow

3 Users | User Groups

🔍 Search

☐ reaper
☐ pangurus\
☐ pangurus\service
☐ pangurus\tom

4 Users | User Groups

🔍 Search

☐ pangurus\all company
☐ pangurus\admins
☐ pangurus\
☐ pangurus\superusers

Match Criteria

🕓 **SOURCE**

Zones (1)   ○ Any   ◉ Select

trust ✕

Addresses   ◉ Any   ○ Select

Users (0)   ○ Any   ◉ Select   0 / 4 selected   Create New   0 / 4 selected   Create New

None   **1**

2

Devices   ◉ Any   ○ Select   ○ No-hip   ○ Quarantined Devices

Figure 9.21 – Adding a user group to a security rule

In Panorama, we can attach the Cloud Identity Engine by navigating to **Templates | Device | Mobile_User_Template | Device | User Identification | Cloud Identity Engine** and adding a new CIE profile:

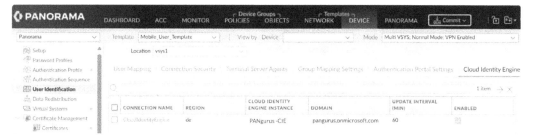

Figure 9.22 – CIE profile

We must select the appropriate region in which our CIE is hosted, so select **Engine Instance**. This should automatically populate. If no instance appears in the dropdown, review the region that the CIE was deployed in. Select the domain for which the groups need to be collected. In a multi-domain environment, create multiple profiles so each domain has a profile.

In **User Attributes**, select the appropriate username attribute (`sAMAccountName` for LDAP, `UserPrincipalName` for SAML, and so on) and also set the appropriate **Group Attribute** option. Azure uses **Common Name** by default, but this may differ if group attributes were adjusted in Azure:

Figure 9.23 – Configuring CIE attributes

Now that we are able to collect group information, let's take a look at redistributing user mapping.

User ID redistribution

When users log on to a MU-SPN via GlobalProtect, they receive an IP address from the pool used by the SPN. Their username is also mapped against that IP address to form a user ID. These User-IDs can be used to grant users access to specific resources via security rules, provide them with a specific GlobalProtect agent configuration, or simply log what they are doing in terms of traffic, URLs, and threat logs.

This user ID can also be shared with other Palo Alto NGFW so that policies can be applied to down range. This can be useful when a user is connecting to a datacenter resource that is behind a service connection. Security is only enforced on the SPN in Prisma Access, so the datacenter must have its own security enforcement, and any subsequent connected networks may also be equipped with their own NGFW. Without user ID redistribution, these firewalls outside Prisma Access will only be able to apply security based on the source address.

There is already some user ID redistribution set up in Prisma Access. All MU-SPNs share their user ID information with the SC-CAN they're connected to (remember that each MU-SPN connects to one SC-CAN). This SC-CAN can then, in turn, be set as a **collector** for other devices to collect user ID information from them:

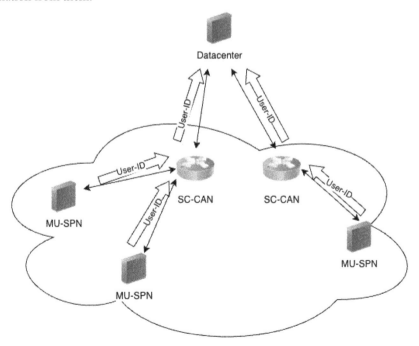

Figure 9.24 – User ID redistribution in Prisma Access

After setting the SC-CANs to redistribution agents, redistribution to external firewalls can be achieved in two ways:

- Panorama can be configured to collect user ID information from all the SC-CANs and then be configured as a collector for managed firewalls to receive user ID information.

- External firewalls can fetch the user ID information directly from the SC-CAN

Let's start by setting an SC-CAN as a collector.

User ID collector in Strata Cloud Manager

First, set **Configuration Scope** to **Service Connections** and then navigate to **Manage | Configuration | NGFW and Prisma Access | Identity Services | Identity Redistribution**. At the bottom, you will find the IP addresses of the SC-CAN user ID redistribution nodes:

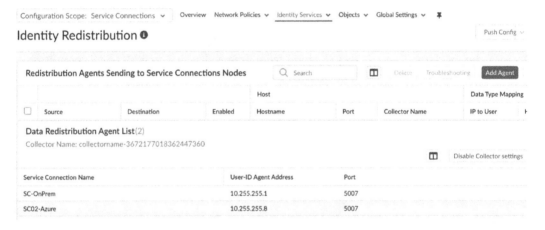

Figure 9.25 – Identity Redistribution

By changing **Configuration Scope** to **Prisma Access**, we can configure which information is made available for redistribution.

Identity data types that you can redistribute include the following:

- HIP data

- IP-address-to-tag mappings

- IP-address-to-user mappings

- User-to-tag mappings

- Quarantined devices

The interactive **Identity Redistribution** page will look like the following screenshot. You can edit each information flow and control which information is shared in each direction and towards each component:

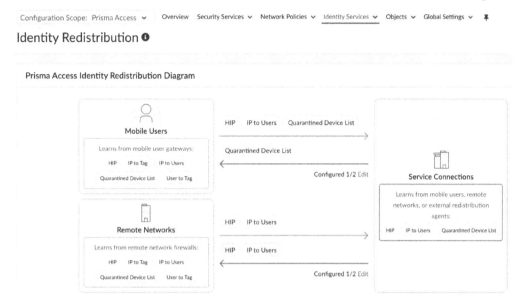

Figure 9.26 – Redistribution diagram

User ID collector in Panorama

In Panorama, the collector needs to be created via **Service_Conn_Template** in **Template | Device | Data Redistribution | Collector Settings**. Here, we will configure the collector or **Redistribution Agent** name and shared key, which other systems will use as remote agents to retrieve data from Panorama:

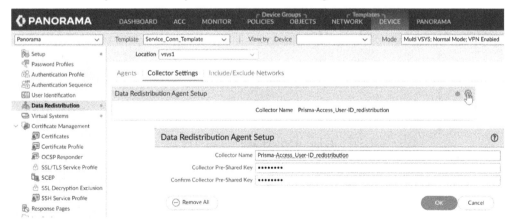

Figure 9.27 – Data Redistribution Agent Setup

The associated IP addresses for each service connection can then be collected via **Panorama | Cloud Services | Status | Network Details | Service Connections**:

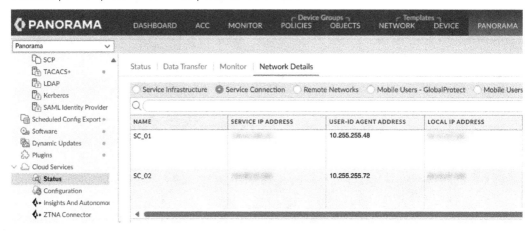

Figure 9.28 – SC-CAN User ID agent IP

We can now add the collectors to regular firewalls so they can start receiving user ID information:

User ID agents on firewalls

Any firewall that has access to a service connection (appropriate routing towards the infrastructure subnet and security policies allowing access to port 5007 and or App-ID `paloalto-userid`-agent) can then be configured to connect to each SC-CAN to receive User ID information:

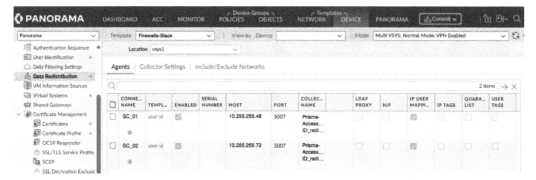

Figure 9.29 – User ID agent

You can add each service connection individually by using its service IP; **Collector Name** will be identical for all SC-CANs, and it needs to match **Collector Name** in **Service_Conn_Template**:

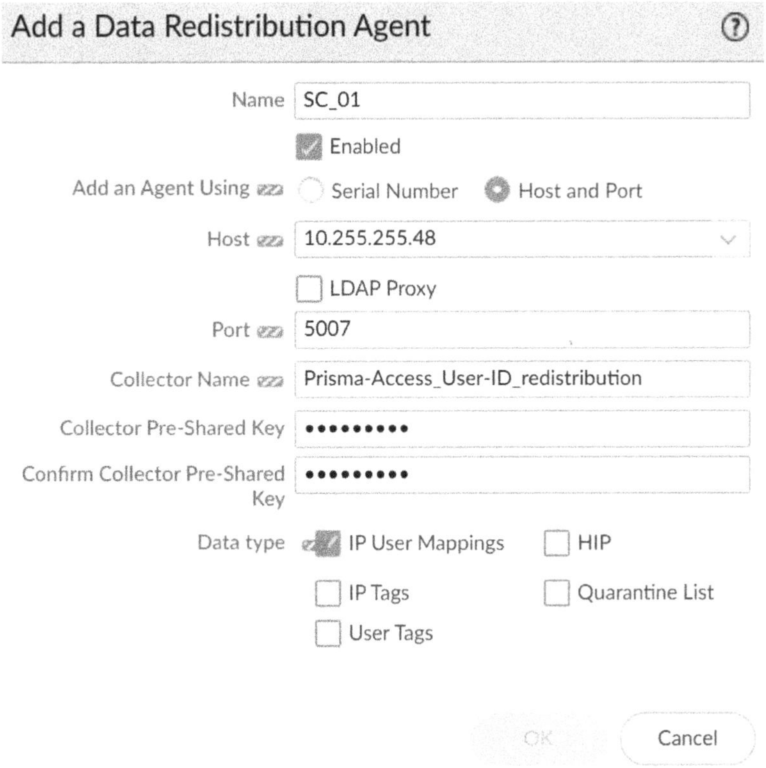

Figure 9.30 – Adding a data redistribution agent

Once these changes are committed to both Prisma Access and the firewall, the firewalls will start receiving user-to-IP mapping.

Summary

In this chapter, we learned how to deploy Cloud Identity Engine and how to connect it to a directory service such as Microsoft Entra ID. You are now able to use group membership as a parameter in Prisma Access for Security rules and GlobalProtect profiles.

We also learned about user ID redistribution so that on-premises and cloud NGFWs are also able to leverage user ID information in their respective policies.

In the next chapter, we will be learning about insights, configuring Cortex Data Lake, and advanced configuration.

10

Advanced Configurations and Insights

In this chapter, we'll learn how to configure Cortex Data Lake quotas and log forwarding. We'll take a closer look at how Prisma Access is licensed and a few important consequences of choosing a particular license model.

In this chapter, we're going to cover the following topics:

- Licensing
- Cortex Data Lake
- Insights

Licensing

Prisma Access is a cloud tenant that has three different licensing editions. Depending on the edition that is applied to your tenant, some limitations will apply, as not all features will be available in all editions:

- **Business** is the basic package that provides secure web connectivity
- **Business Premium** adds some advanced protection capabilities to the Business edition
- **Enterprise** combines the full set of secure internet connectivity of the Business Premium edition with service connections and private app access

Furthermore, each edition comes in two flavors that limit the number of locations that can be provisioned:

- **Local** allows up to five locations to be provisioned
- **Worldwide** allows all locations to be provisioned

Let's take a look at the features for each edition:

	Business	Business Premium	Enterprise
Internet Security Explicit Proxy	+	+	+
Private App Access	-	-	+
Number of Service Connections	-	-	2 with Local edition 5 with a Worldwide edition
Advanced Threat Prevention	-	+	+
Advanced URL Filtering	+	+	+
DNS Security	+	+	+
Advanced WildFire	-	+	+

Table 10.1 – Features included in license flavors

There are also a handful of add-on licenses that enable additional features not included in the base license:

	Business	Business Premium	Enterprise
Next-Gen CASB	+	+	+
Enterprise DLP	+	+	+
Inline SaaS Security	+	+	+
IoT Security	+	+	+
Additional Service Connections	+	+	+
Net Interconnect	-	-	+
ADEM	+	+	+
AI-Powered ADEM	+	+	+
ZTNA Connector	+	+	+
Traffic Replication	+	+	+
Colo Connect	+	+	+
RBI	+	+	+
App Acceleration	+	+	+

Table 10.2 – Features included in license flavors, continued

As you can see from the previous table, all add-on licenses can be applied to any edition, except the Net Interconnect license. Let's review what all the add-on licenses do:

- **Next-Gen CASB** enables a **Cloud Access Security Broker** (CASB), which is a security enforcement point that sits between a cloud service provider and its users.

- **Enterprise DLP** is an advanced machine learning-powered **Data Loss Prevention** (DLP) add-on that can help prevent sensitive data exfiltration.

- **Inline SaaS Security** enables inline visibility into SaaS app usage and can be integrated with sanctioned applications to provide additional security.

- **IoT Security** enables insights and mapping of the IoT landscape and will provide recommended security rules to allow IoT devices to be connected via Prisma Access securely. This feature can only be used on RN-SPN.

- **Additional Service Connections** are what the name suggests, additional SC-CANs on top of the included number of service connections.

- **Net Interconnect** is a license that enables routing to allow mobile users to establish sessions to remote networks, and remote networks to connect to other remote networks.

- **Autonomous Digital Experience Management** (ADEM) is a monitoring and testing plugin that can be added to GlobalProtect. It runs tests to different parameters regarding the user's connectivity ranging from the devices' resource usage, Wi-Fi signal strength, upstream ISP connectivity, and so on, all the way down to the applications users need for their daily work, allowing quick troubleshooting.

- **AI-Powered ADEM** adds machine learning and ingests additional sources of information to measure user experience.

- **ZTNA Connector** allows additional ZTNA Connector connections for private app access.

- **Traffic Replication** enables complete packet capturing for forensic analysis.

- **Colo Connect** allows for a very high bandwidth uplink of up to 20 Gbps using a dedicated or partner-enabled interconnect into the Google Cloud Platform.

- **RBI** or **Remote Browser Isolation** can be added so URL filtering can be enhanced and certain URL categories be made available to users via a virtual browser without disrupting their user experience.

- **App Acceleration** improves application throughput and user experience in loading applications.

This should help you decide which edition, flavor, and (potentially) any additional add-on licenses you may need.

Remember that on top of the Prisma Access tenant licenses, you will also need a Cortex Data Lake license, as this will be the only option available to store traffic, threat, and system logs.

Cortex Data Lake

At the beginning of this book, we learned that we need to activate a **Cortex Data Lake (CDL)** instance to be used to receive logs from Prisma Access, but we still need to configure CDL for the log volume stored for each log type and retention period.

You can access CDL from the Palo Alto hub (`https://apps.paloaltonetworks.com`) and click the **Cortex Data Lake** tile:

Figure 10.1 – Palo Alto networks hub

On the **Dashboard** tab, you will see some general information regarding your CDL instance including the storage used and the number of connected firewalls. For a Prisma Access-only deployment, there will be no firewalls (**0**) listed; this number only reflects the number of physical or VM firewalls also connected to CDL.

Navigate to the **Configuration** tab to configure the **Storage** parameters:

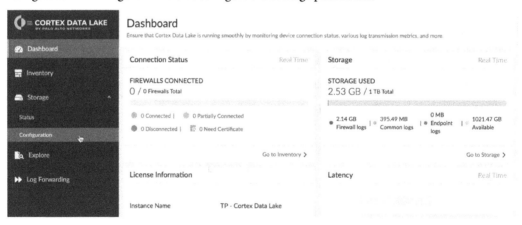

Figure 10.2 – CDL dashboard

The default configuration will indicate that **0.00 MB** of your available storage has been assigned, and all the log types will have empty **QUOTA (%)** and **MAX RETENTION DAYS** values:

Configuration

Configure granular storage and retention for every log type within Cortex Data Lake to meet your data retention requirements.

STORAGE USED
0.00 MB / 1 TB Total

● 0 MB Firewall logs | ◉ 0 MB Common logs | ● 0 MB Endpoint logs | ○ 1 TB Unallocated

LOG TYPE	QUOTA (%)	ALLOCATED SIZE	MAX RETENTION DAYS	ACTUAL RETENTION DAYS
Endpoint		-		
ztna_agent	Empty or [0-100]	-	Empty or [0-2000]	1
Firewall Logs		-		
auth	Empty or [0-100]	-	Empty or [0-2000]	1
decryption	Empty or [0-100]	-	Empty or [0-2000]	1
dns_security	Empty or [0-100]	-	Empty or [0-2000]	1

Figure 10.3 – Unconfigured CDL

To determine the right quota for each log type, we will first need to estimate how much log storage we will need for our environment for the desired log retention period.

This can be achieved by calculating the average logs received per second, taking into account that each log is about 2,500 bytes in size. If the expected average log rate is not known yet, Palo Alto has a very helpful estimator tool, which can be accessed via `https://apps.paloaltonetworks.com/cortex-sizing-estimator`.

If we know the number of users and the minimum log retention period, we can calculate how much storage needs to be provided. As an example, in the following screenshot, you can see that for 100 users and a minimum log retention of 30 days, Palo Alto recommends 31 GB of storage:

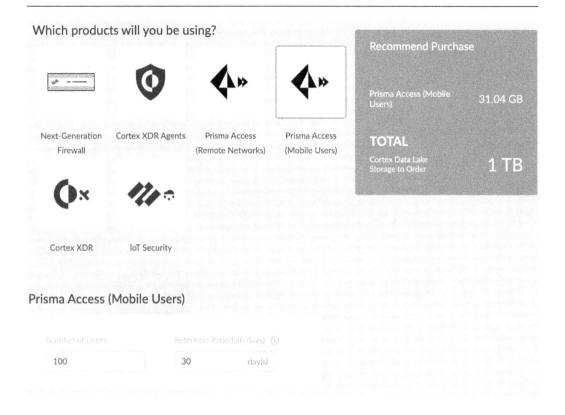

Figure 10.4 – Cortex sizing estimation

This can come in handy beforehand when deciding how much total storage will be needed, but can also help give an indication of how to set our quotas.

If we leave the **QUOTA** field empty, it will use any unassigned storage as a pool. All log types that are left empty will share the same pool of unallocated storage. Once the unallocated pool is depleted, CDL will delete old logs on a **First In, First Out** (**FIFO**) basis, which could impact retention periods for logs that need to be retained for a minimum period due to regulations (for example, PCI DSS 1 year, ISO 27001 3 years, and NIST 3 years).

If Prisma Access has already been set up and users are actively using the infrastructure, we can take a look at the current log consumption to gain an insight into how much quota we'd need for each log type. On the **Dashboard** page, scroll all the way down to see how much log capacity is currently being used by each log type:

Incoming Logs	Forwarding Logs				Q
Log Type	Actual Retention	Target Retention	Avg Incoming Log Rate	↓	Storage Used
system	140 day(s)	NA	NA		395.35 MB / -
config	140 day(s)	NA	NA		146.08 KB / -
userid	17 day(s)	NA	NA		760 Bytes / -
url	65 day(s)	NA	NA		3.16 MB / -
tunnel	1 day(s)	NA	NA		0 MB / -
traffic	87 day(s)	NA	NA		1.29 GB / -
threat	64 day(s)	NA	NA		130.53 KB / -
sctp	1 day(s)	NA	NA		0 MB / -
iptag	1 day(s)	NA	NA		0 MB / -
hipmatch	1 day(s)	NA	NA		0 MB / -
globalprotect	65 day(s)	NA	NA		869.22 MB / -
file_data	1 day(s)	NA	NA		0 MB / -
extpcap	1 day(s)	NA	NA		0 MB / -
dns_security	1 day(s)	NA	NA		0 MB / -
decryption	1 day(s)	NA	NA		0 MB / -
auth	1 day(s)	NA	NA		0 MB / -
ztna_agent	1 day(s)	NA	NA		0 MB / -

Figure 10.5 – Current log storage usage

From the previous screenshot, we can see that CDL estimates I can retain 87 days' worth of traffic logs using the current average influx of traffic logs. The threat logs are much smaller but indicate a smaller retention period, which, in this specific case, means the first threat log was only recorded 64 days ago. Since my Prisma Access tenant has only recently been deployed and I don't have much usage yet, I still have plenty of storage left, so the numbers will keep increasing until I add more users. The used storage here does give me an indication of how much storage is needed for each log type.

To guarantee adherence to the retention period, add a quota percentage to a log type. We can assign a quota to ensure the minimum retention period is achieved, but we can also set a maximum retention period if we are not allowed to retain logs longer than a certain number of days. Setting a log type to **0%** will prevent any of these logs from being stored.

For example, in the next screenshot, we have set up a maximum retention of one year for all logs; threat, traffic, and URL filtering logs have a volume assigned that should be enough to retain at least a year's worth of logs, and all other logs share the remaining storage:

Configuration

Configure granular storage and retention for every log type within Cortex Data Lake to meet your data retention requirements.

STORAGE USED
583.68 GB / 1 TB Total

● 583.68 GB Firewall logs | ● 0 MB Common logs | ● 0 MB Endpoint logs | ● 440.32 GB Unallocated

LOG TYPE	QUOTA (%)	ALLOCATED SIZE	MAX RETENTION DAYS	ACTUAL RETENTION DAYS
Endpoint		-		
ztna_agent	Empty or [0-100]	-	365	1
Firewall Logs		583.68 GB		
auth	Empty or [0-100]	-	365	1
decryption	Empty or [0-100]	-	365	1
dns_security	Empty or [0-100]	-	365	1
extpcap	Empty or [0-100]	-	365	1
file_data	Empty or [0-100]	-	365	1
globalprotect	Empty or [0-100]	-	365	65
hipmatch	Empty or [0-100]	-	365	1
iptag	Empty or [0-100]	-	365	1
sctp	Empty or [0-100]	-	365	1
threat	6 %	61.44 GB	365	64
traffic	36 %	368.64 GB	365	87
tunnel	Empty or [0-100]	-	365	1
url	15 %	153.6 GB	365	65
userid	Empty or [0-100]	-	365	17
Common Logs		-		
config	Empty or [0-100]	-	365	140
system	Empty or [0-100]	-	365	140

Cancel   Apply

Figure 10.6 – Log quotas

If you want to look at the logs that were collected, you can navigate to the **Explore** section, where you can select from all the available log types and use filters similar to how you would filter logs in Panorama or a firewall:

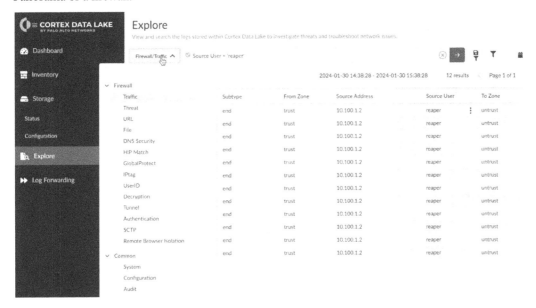

Figure 10.7 – Explore log viewer

Besides logs, **Insights** also contains a wealth of information.

Insights and ADEM

Regardless of whether your Prisma Access tenant is managed through Panorama or Strata Cloud Manager, Insights and ADEM can only be managed via Strata Cloud Manager.

Insights is a free dashboard available to all customers using Prisma Access; ADEM is an add-on license that needs to be activated before its features become available.

To access Insights, navigate to `https://apps.paloaltonetworks.com` and click the **Strata Cloud Manager** tile or go directly to `https://stratacloudmanager.com`. On the first page, you'll immediately see the **Insights** dashboard. You can enable additional dashboards by clicking the **More Dashboards** button in the top-right corner:

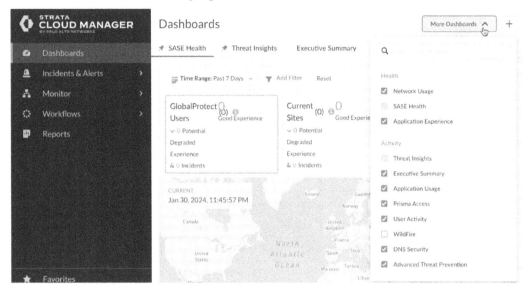

Figure 10.8 – More dashboards

The dashboard can provide a wealth of information regarding your deployment and what is happening in your environment. **SASE Health**, for example, displays your number of mobile users over the past number of days and which of your remote networks are connected:

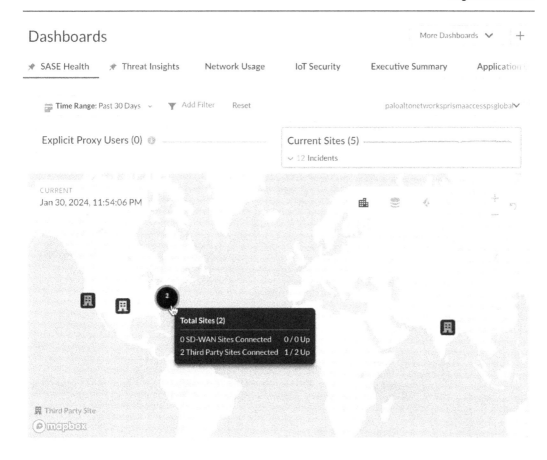

Dashboards

More Dashboards ∨   +

📌 SASE Health   📌 Threat Insights   Network Usage   IoT Security   Executive Summary   Application

📅 **Time Range:** Past 30 Days ∨   ▼ Add Filter   Reset   paloaltonetworksprismaaccesspsglobal∨

Explicit Proxy Users (0) ⊕ ──────────────   Current Sites (5) ──────────────
                                              ∨ 12 Incidents

CURRENT
Jan 30, 2024, 11:54:06 PM

Total Sites (2)

0 SD-WAN Sites Connected	0 / 0 Up
2 Third Party Sites Connected	1 / 2 Up

🏢 Third Party Site
ⓞ mapbox

Figure 10.9 – The SASE Health tab

Threat Insights gives you a quick glance at how many and which types of threats were detected, whether they were allowed or blocked, and a list of what was detected:

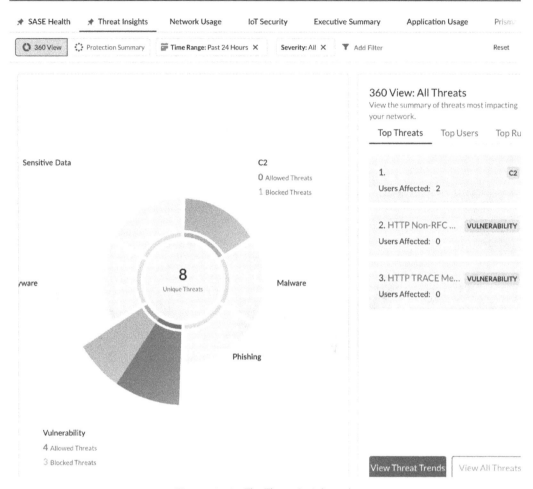

Figure 10.10 – The Threat Insights tab

Application Usage gives you a detailed overview of the types, risk categories, and data transferred by applications, plus the top 10 app IDs of each different application type:

Figure 10.11 – The Application Usage tab

With ADEM enabled, the wealth of information grows exponentially as we can gain deep-dive insight into all aspects of the user's connectivity, from their device's resource consumption, Wi-Fi connectivity, upstream ISP latency, and responsiveness of their connection to Prisma Access all the way to the SaaS application's responsiveness.

In the **Application Experience** tab, if the ADEM license is installed and endpoints loaded with the ADEM plugin, more details become available regarding the user experience:

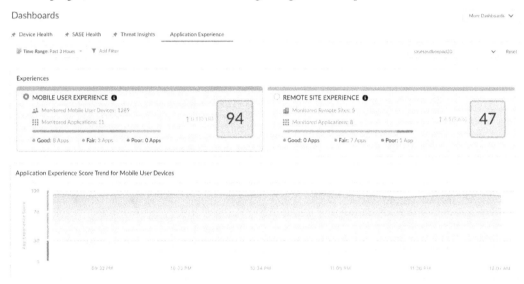

Figure 10.12 – The Application Experience tab

We get an easy-to-interpret overview of what could be the issue, if any, the user might be experiencing with color-coded segments. If an app were to go down or users experience connectivity issues with Prisma Access, the appropriate tile will indicate an issue is up and we can click deeper into that tile to investigate. The performance metrics also give us an indication of how applications are performing, such as if DNS responsiveness is slow, users might experience latency while their connectivity might be very good:

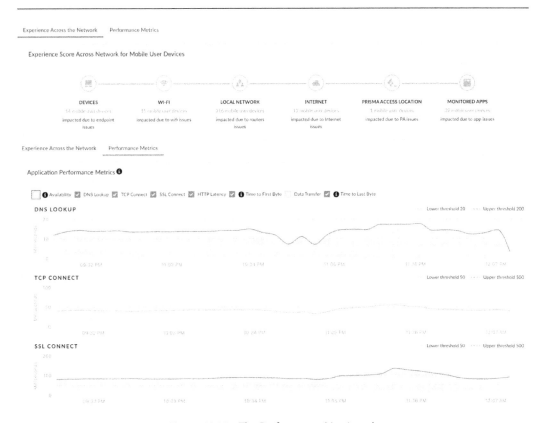

Figure 10.13 – The Performance Metrics tab

We can zoom into all kinds of details and see where latency or delays are introduced. In the following screenshot, you can see my local network is causing some latency:

Application Experience Trend

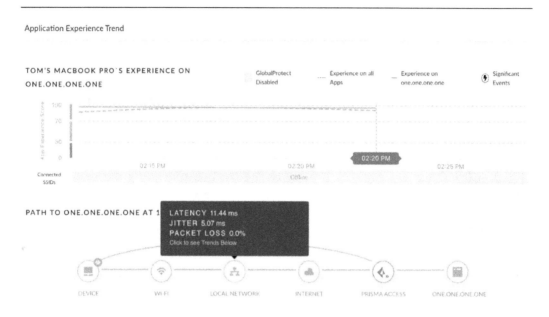

Figure 10.14 – Application experience trend

Adding ADEM to your Prisma Access deployment can help reduce your IT department's **mean time to resolve (MTTR)** by increasing visibility to such an extent that they can immediately focus on the real issue instead of spending time first trying to find where the problem exists.

Summary

In this chapter, we learned how we can configure Cortex Data Lake to ensure log retention is optimized toward our organization's needs. We learned about the three different licensing editions and their two flavors, and all the add-on licenses that can be added to tailor Prisma Access to your organization's needs. Lastly, we learned that Insights can be a valuable tool to gain a deeper understanding of networking and usage trends and that the ADEM add-on license deepens that insight to help the IT team troubleshoot user connectivity issues.

11

ZTNA Connector

The **Zero Trust Network Access** (**ZTNA**) connector provides an alternative to service connections so that enterprises can provide connectivity to privately hosted applications hosted on a cloud infrastructure. The ZTNA connector provides a reverse proxy connectivity mode over the network connectivity offered by the **Service Connection Corporate Access Node** (**SC-CAN**). This allows for a simplified and fast deployment into an app-driven environment.

In this chapter, we're going to cover the following main topics:

- Differences between the ZTNA connector and SC-CAN
- Preparing to deploy the ZTNA connector
- Setting up the ZTNA connector
- Setting up the connector VM
- Basic troubleshooting

Differences between the ZTNA connector and SC-CAN

While an SC-CAN provides a traditional connection to a data center or cloud environment via an IPSec tunnel, the ZTNA connector provides a simplified connection that is established automatically. There is no need for complex **Internet Key Exchange** (**IKE**) gateway and IPSec tunnel configuration, nor is there a need to set up routing.

The ZTNA connector is a VM that is deployed inside the intended environment and connects automatically to the nearest Prisma Access location. Each connector provides up to 1 Gbps of throughput, up to 10 Gbps per compute location. Access to resources behind the ZTNA connector is controlled via normal security policies.

Applications are made available by leveraging the built-in DNS proxy to attach custom internal **fully qualified domain names** (**FQDNs**) to applications (targets) behind each ZTNA connector using an internal **network address translation** (**NAT**) pool. This allows ZTNA connectors to be deployed in an environment that has overlapping IP subnets with the Prisma Access infrastructure without introducing routing issues, but it does require the use of FQDNs, and apps cannot be accessed by their IP.

Let's compare the ZTNA connector to SC-CAN.

The ZTNA connector has the following advantages:

- Access to applications in overlapped networks
- Automatic tunnel establishment to Prisma Access
- Automatic Prisma Access location discovery
- Automatic scaling of Prisma Access locations for up to 10 Gbps throughput

The advantages of SC-CAN include the following:

- Access to private apps using IP addresses and subnets
- Server-initiated traffic reaching out to a managed device (connection from remote to the user)
- Can be used with applications or services that require a unique client IP address
- Access to applications with dynamic ports
- Deployments with on-prem firewalls that apply user ID
- Can be used with apps that need to be reached via a clientless VPN

Preparing to deploy the ZTNA connector

When planning the ZTNA connector deployment, there are a few scaling considerations that apply globally and to individual compute node locations:

- A maximum of 2,000 applications can be made available across all connector groups
- A maximum of 64 applications per connector group
- A maximum of 100 connectors in total globally
- Up to 4 connectors per connector group
- Up to 10 connectors per compute node location
- 250,000 concurrent connections per connector group

The ZTNA connector VM should receive the following resources:

- 4 vCPUs
- 16 GB memory
- 4 GB disk

In the environment hosting the ZTNA connector, the VM must be allowed to create outbound UDP 4500 and UDP 500 (IPSec NAT traversal and IKE) and TCP 443 (SSL) connections from the WAN interface so that it can set up its connection to the nearest **ZTNA Tunnel Terminator (ZTT*)** in Prisma Access, and UDP 53 and 123 for DNS and NTP.

> **Note**
>
> A ZTT is really a **Mobile User Security Processing Node (MU-SPN)** functioning as a gateway for a ZTNA agent.

If outbound HTTPS connections from the WAN interface need to be restricted, a full list of FQDNs and IP addresses can be found here: `https://docs.paloaltonetworks.com/prisma-access/administration/ztna-connector-in-prisma-access/ztna-connector-requirements-and-guidelines`

On the internal interface, the ZTNA connector will need access to DNS and any ports used by the hosted applications. ICMP may be required for health checks.

Setting up the ZTNA connector

We can start setting up the ZTNA connector by first setting up the infrastructure subnets used by the ZTNA connector. Navigate to **Workflows | Prisma Access Setup | Prisma Access**:

Figure 11.1 – Prisma Access Setup

Click the little cogwheel icon to access the Prisma Access infrastructure configuration where you must configure two IP subnets. Both subnets should ideally be unique in your environment to prevent potential conflicts:

- **ZTNA Connector Application IP Blocks** is used inside Prisma Access to advertise applications. You can add multiple subnets and should make sure you have sufficient IP addresses available for the number of applications that will be advertised.

- **ZTNA Connectors Connector IP Blocks** will be used for internal routing between mobile users or remote networks and the connector VMs. Multiple subnets can be used:

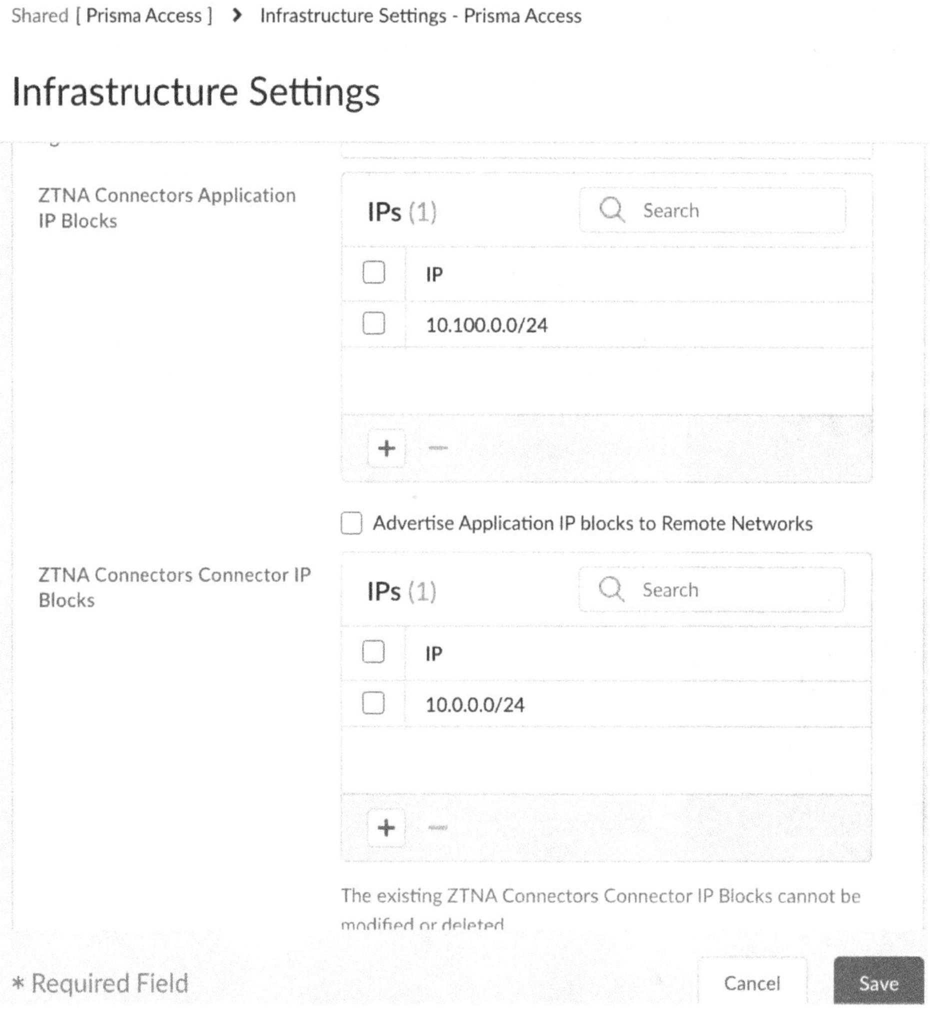

Shared [Prisma Access] ❯ Infrastructure Settings - Prisma Access

Infrastructure Settings

ZTNA Connectors Application IP Blocks	**IPs** (1)	Q Search
	☐ IP	
	☐ 10.100.0.0/24	
	+ —	

☐ Advertise Application IP blocks to Remote Networks

ZTNA Connectors Connector IP Blocks	**IPs** (1)	Q Search
	☐ IP	
	☐ 10.0.0.0/24	
	+ —	

The existing ZTNA Connectors Connector IP Blocks cannot be modified or deleted

* Required Field   Cancel   Save

Figure 11.2 – Infrastructure Settings

Click **Save** and then navigate to **Workflows** | **ZTNA Connector** | **Overview**. Click **Enable ZTNA Connector** to get started:

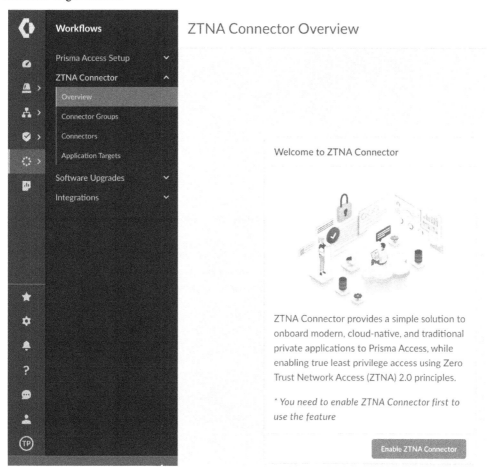

Figure 11.3 – ZTNA Connector Overview

In the next screen, we are guided through the initial setup process. On the bottom left, we see how many connectors we are allowed to set up and the number of applications we can enable (this depends on your license and any add-on licenses you may have).

We'll start by creating a connector group; this represents a connection to a remote environment. Click **Create a Connector Group**:

ZTNA Connector Overview

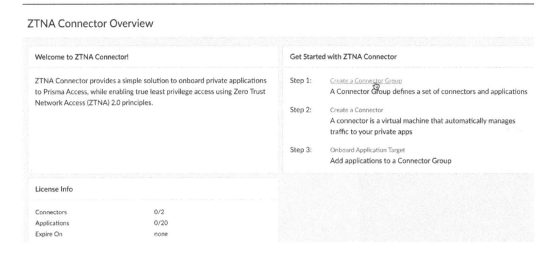

Figure 11.4 – Getting started with the ZTNA connector

You can provide a name and description for the new ZTNA connector group. If you're deploying the ZTNA connector to AWS or Azure, you can enable **Autoscale (Optional)** if you like. This setting will allow the spawning of additional ZTNA connectors automatically in the connector group:

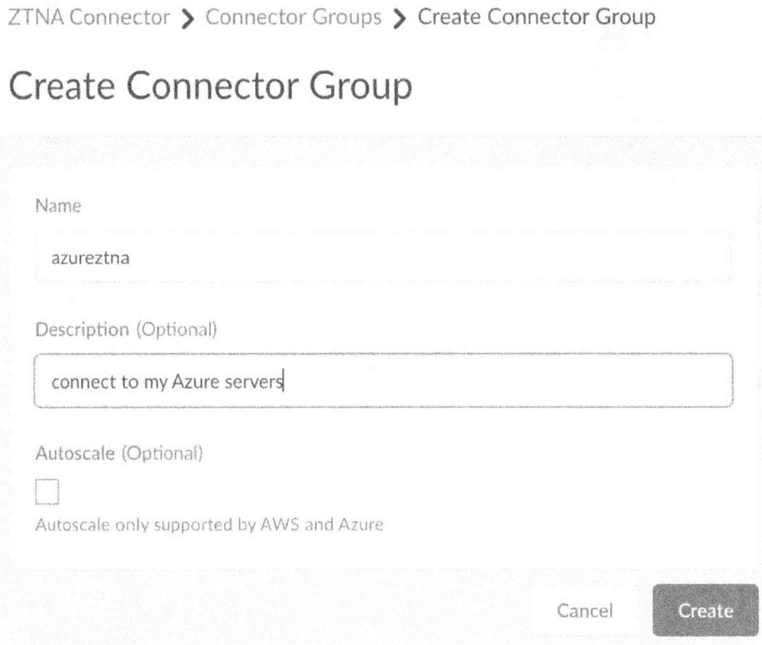

Figure 11.5 – Creating a connector group

With the connector group created, go back to the ZTNA connector setup page:

ZTNA Connector
Connector Groups
Connector Groups
Manage the ZTNA Connectors and applications associated with each Connector Group
Connector Groups (1)
Add Filter
Reset
Create Connector Group
Name
FQDN Targets
Wildcard Targets
IPSubnet Targets
Connectors
Type
Actions
azureztna
0
0
0
0
FQDN

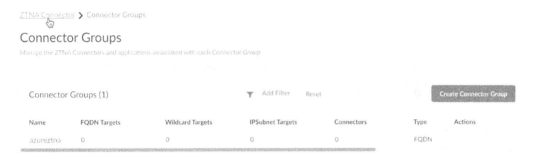

Figure 11.6 – First connector group

Click **Create a Connector**:

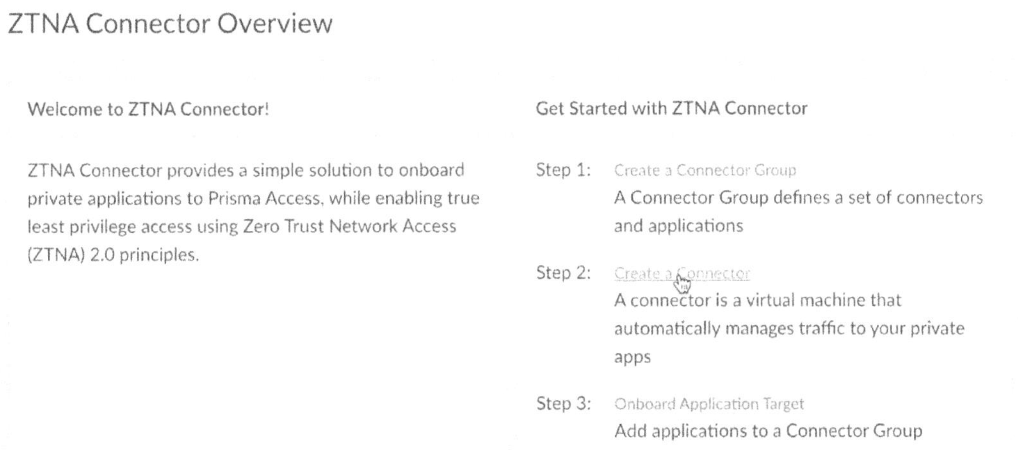

ZTNA Connector Overview
Welcome to ZTNA Connector!
ZTNA Connector provides a simple solution to onboard private applications to Prisma Access, while enabling true least privilege access using Zero Trust Network Access (ZTNA) 2.0 principles.
Get Started with ZTNA Connector
Step 1:
Create a Connector Group
A Connector Group defines a set of connectors and applications
Step 2:
Create a Connector
A connector is a virtual machine that automatically manages traffic to your private apps
Step 3:
Onboard Application Target
Add applications to a Connector Group

Figure 11.7 – Creating a connector

Provide a name, select the connector group you just created, and click **Create**:

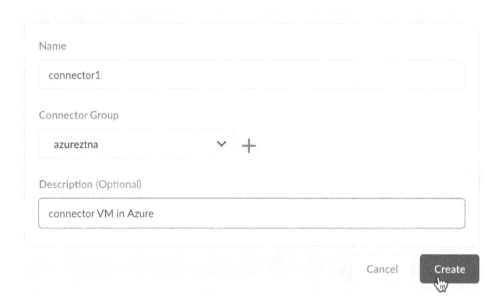

Figure 11.8 – Creating a connector

Once the connector is created, it will appear in the **Connectors** view. Keep in mind that the bar can be scrolled to the far right, containing all sorts of information such as tunnel status and control-plane status, and on the far right, the token key and secret if you click the little key icon, or some diagnostics if you click the tool icon. Go ahead and click the key icon, and copy the key and secret as these will be needed for the connector VM:

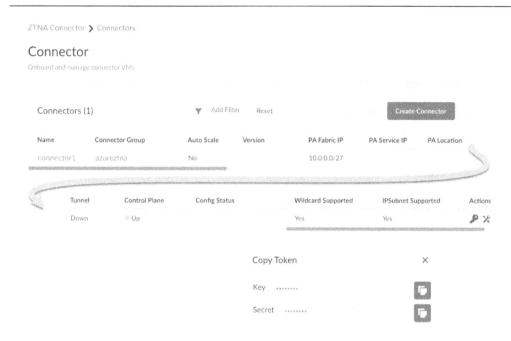

Figure 11.9 – New connector

In the navigation bar, click the blue **ZTNA Connector** link to go back to the main page where we can complete the onboarding of application targets:

ZTNA Connector Overview

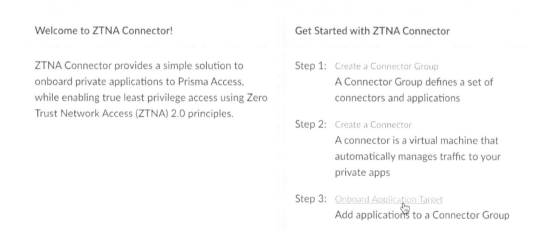

Welcome to ZTNA Connector!

ZTNA Connector provides a simple solution to onboard private applications to Prisma Access, while enabling true least privilege access using Zero Trust Network Access (ZTNA) 2.0 principles.

Get Started with ZTNA Connector

Step 1: Create a Connector Group
         A Connector Group defines a set of connectors and applications

Step 2: Create a Connector
         A connector is a virtual machine that automatically manages traffic to your private apps

Step 3: Onboard Application Target
         Add applications to a Connector Group

Figure 11.10 – Onboarding application targets

We can now create the first application target. The FQDN will be translated to a NAT address inside the Prisma Access infrastructure. The NAT address will be used to redirect traffic destined for the FQDN toward the ZTNA connector group instead of the regular DNS destination; that is public or internal DNS records may point toward an IP in the data center or on a public host, but in the Prisma Access infrastructure, the records will be changed to a **ZTNA connector application IP block IP** associated with the configured **ZTNA connector group**.

To create a new FQDN target, follow these steps:

1. Provide a name.
2. Assign the connector group we just created.
3. Set the appropriate FQDN.
4. Select TCP or UDP as the protocol.
5. Set a destination port. If needed, you can add multiple ports for applications that use different ports for each function.
6. **Probing Type** and **Probing Port** will automatically be set to the same protocol and port(s).
7. Add a description, if you like.
8. If needed, the FQDN target can be disabled by unchecking the **Enabled** box.
9. Click **Create**.

> **Note**
>
> Consider that the remote side where the connector VM will be installed will need to have a DNS record pointing to the final destination IP that hosts the application. Inside Prisma Access, the FQDN is used to redirect sessions toward the connector VM. The connector VM in turn will need to resolve the FQDN of the received connection to guide it to the correct server.

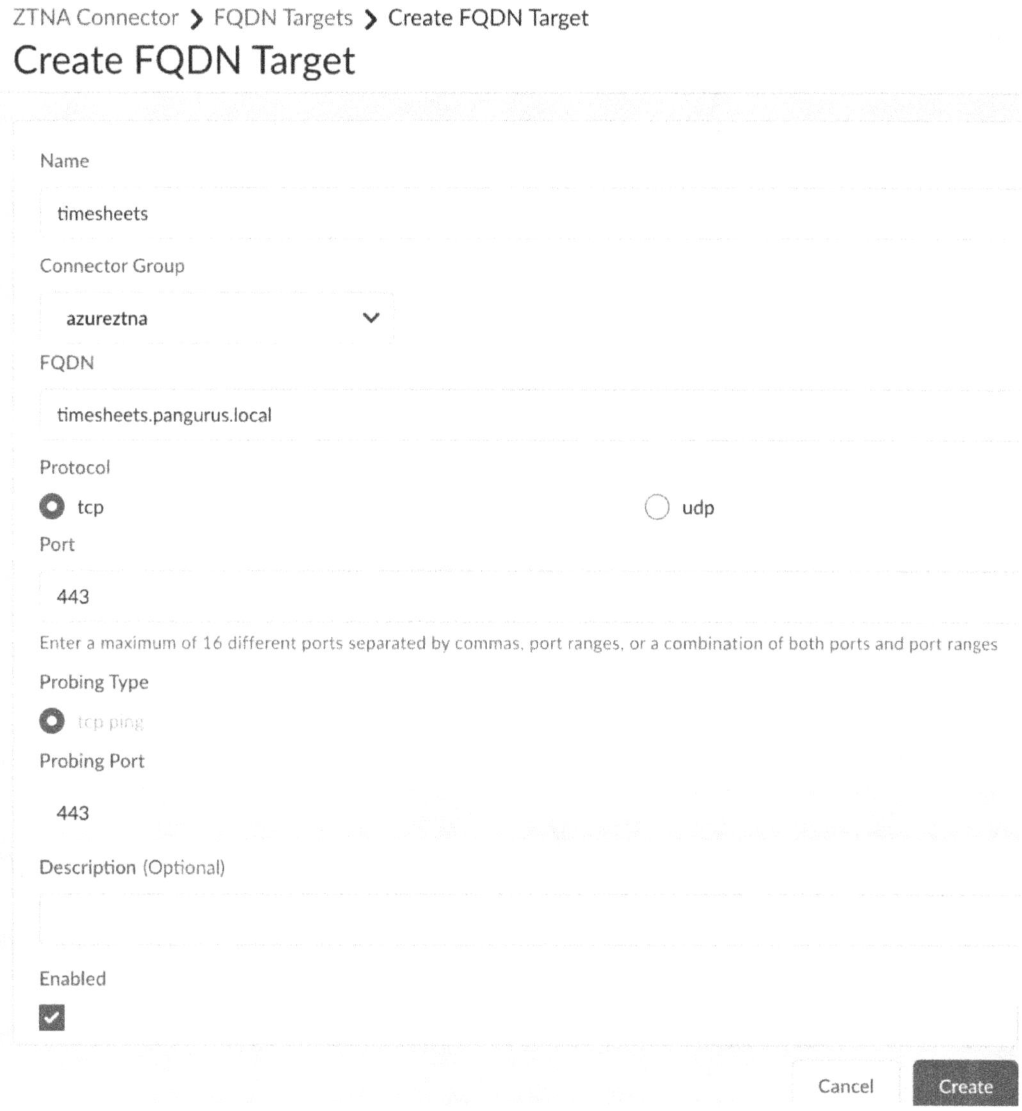

ZTNA Connector > FQDN Targets > Create FQDN Target

Create FQDN Target

Name

timesheets

Connector Group

azureztna ⌄

FQDN

timesheets.pangurus.local

Protocol

● tcp   ○ udp

Port

443

Enter a maximum of 16 different ports separated by commas, port ranges, or a combination of both ports and port ranges

Probing Type

● tcp ping

Probing Port

443

Description (Optional)

Enabled

☑

Cancel   Create

Figure 11.11 – Application FQDN target

Once your first FQDN target is created, it will appear in the **Targets** view. Here, you can also scroll to the right to view additional information about the FQDN target, such as the application status, which will turn green once the FQDN has been resolved by the connector VM:

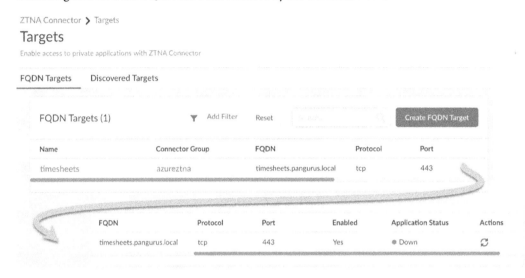

Figure 11.12 – Targets view

We can now proceed to set up the connector VM.

Setting up the connector VM

We can find the VM in the marketplace of our preferred cloud provider. There are a few flavors available:

- **1 Arm** has a single network interface for both ingress and egress connections
- **2 Arm** uses two interfaces: one to reach public resources such as Prisma Access, and an internal interface to reach internal resources

- **1 Arm Auto Scale** uses the **1 Arm** design but comes with the autoscaling feature:

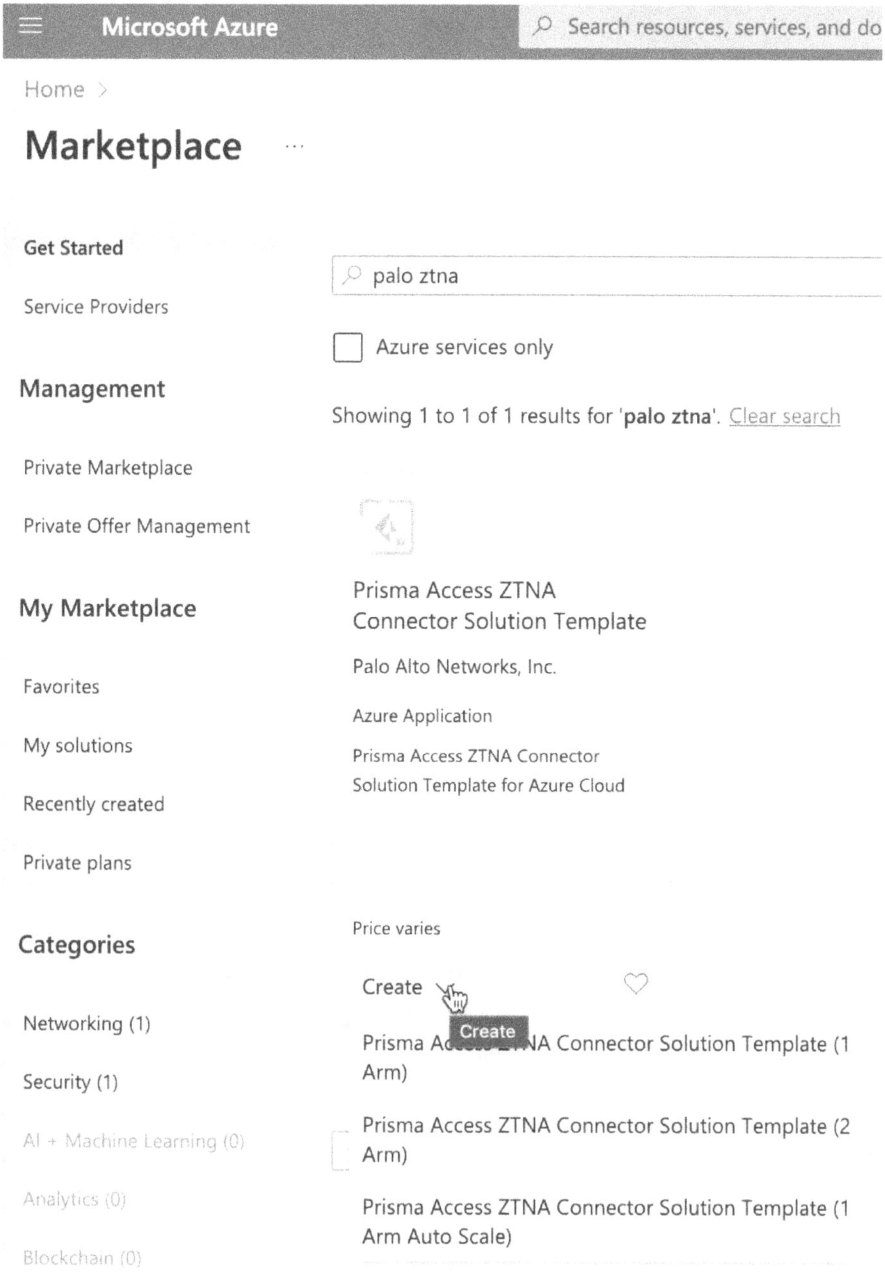

Figure 11.13 – ZTNA connector VM in the marketplace

Go ahead and place the connector in a resource group, and click **Next**:

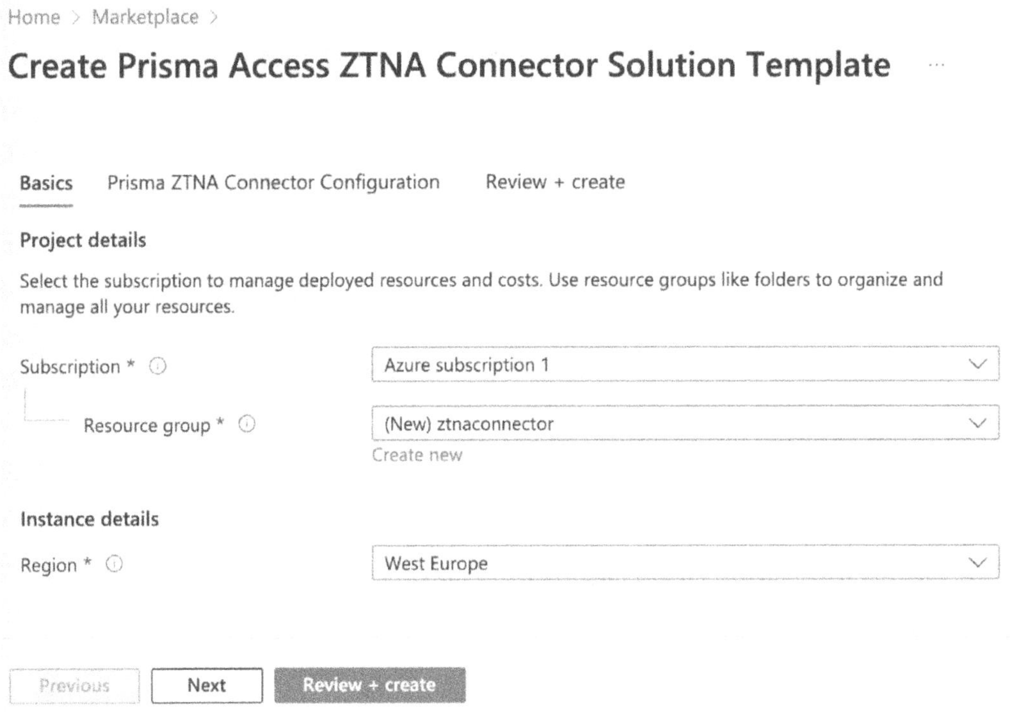

Home > Marketplace >

Create Prisma Access ZTNA Connector Solution Template   ...

Basics   Prisma ZTNA Connector Configuration   Review + create

Project details

Select the subscription to manage deployed resources and costs. Use resource groups like folders to organize and manage all your resources.

Subscription * ⓘ	Azure subscription 1 ⌄
Resource group * ⓘ	(New) ztnaconnector ⌄
	Create new

Instance details

Region * ⓘ	West Europe ⌄

Previous	Next	Review + create

Figure 11.14 – Creating a connector VM

In the **Prisma ZTNA Connector Configuration** tab, we need to assign a subnet to the connector and provide the key and secret we copied earlier in *Figure 11.9*. Once those are filled in, go ahead and click **Next** and **Create**:

Create Prisma Access ZTNA Connector Solution Template   ...

Basics   **Prisma ZTNA Connector Configuration**   Review + create

Virtual network ⓘ	(New) transitVNET (ztnaconnector) ⌄
	Edit virtual network

Data Center LAN Subnet *	(New) LAN ⌄
	Edit subnet 172.16.0.0 - 172.16.0.255 (256 addresses)

Prisma ZTNA Connector VM Name * ⓘ	connector1
Prisma ZTNA Connector License Key * ⓘ	1917
Prisma ZTNA Connector License Secret * ⓘ	8404

Previous   Next   **Review + create**

Figure 11.15 – Configuring subnet key and secret

Once the deployment is done, the connector will appear in Prisma Access. All the tabs will have new information with regard to the connector, and a new icon will appear in the far-right **Actions** column. The little hand icon will allow you to collect a tech support file in case you need assistance from Palo Alto's **Technical Assistance Center (TAC)**:

Figure 11.16 – Successfully setting up the connector

If the connector VM is able to resolve the FQDN to a local resource and is able to reach the app via the configured port (for example, TCP/443), the FQDN target will also show the status as **Up**:

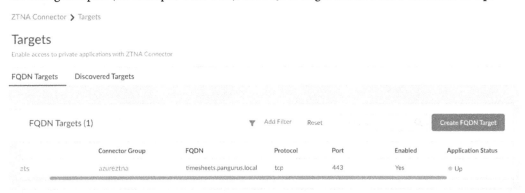

Figure 11.17 – Connected FQDN target

There's not a lot that can go wrong, but here are a few pointers in case something doesn't work as intended.

Basic troubleshooting

If the connector VM is not coming online, make sure the VNet has outbound connectivity allowed. This will most likely be due to an upstream firewall or **network security group** (**NSG**) where access needs to be allowed.

If the connector VM is online, but the FQDN target is not coming up, you can go to the connector (**Workflow | ZTNA Connector | Connectors**) and use the troubleshooting tool (the little tool icon at the far right, as seen in *Figure 11.16*) to run some rudimentary checks. For example, you can remotely test if the connector VM is capable of resolving the FQDN on its local DNS server. Try the FQDN, and also try a regular FQDN to see if the DNS server has the right record in its table and if it is able to resolve other domain names. In the following screenshot, you can see a DNS error where the DNS server in Azure does not have a record for pangurus.local:

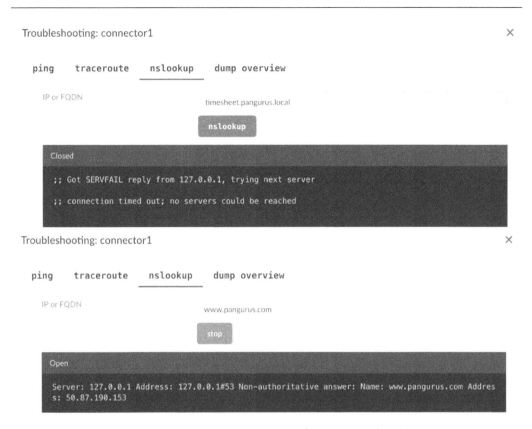

Figure 11.18 – FQDN target not configured on local DNS

With what you learned, you should now be able to add more connectors, groups, and FQDN targets as needed.

Summary

In this chapter, you learned how to plan for and set up a ZTNA connector. With what was learned, you should now be able to pick which choice is best for each of your available hosting environments.

Having managed to reach the end of the book, I'd like to thank you for your attention, and I hope you enjoyed the read. You should now fully understand all the building blocks that make up Prisma Access and be more than capable of designing and setting up Prisma Access from scratch.

If you are looking for your next big challenge, learning about BGP should probably be your next big project, if you haven't already mastered the subject. I would have loved to spend more time on this subject but quickly figured out that doing this properly would take up more space than the actual content of this book.

Stay curious!

Index

`packtpub.com`

Subscribe to our online digital library for full access to over 7,000 books and videos, as well as industry leading tools to help you plan your personal development and advance your career. For more information, please visit our website.

Why subscribe?

- Spend less time learning and more time coding with practical eBooks and Videos from over 4,000 industry professionals

- Improve your learning with Skill Plans built especially for you

- Get a free eBook or video every month

- Fully searchable for easy access to vital information

- Copy and paste, print, and bookmark content

Did you know that Packt offers eBook versions of every book published, with PDF and ePub files available? You can upgrade to the eBook version at `packtpub.com` and as a print book customer, you are entitled to a discount on the eBook copy. Get in touch with us at `customercare@packtpub.com` for more details.

At `www.packtpub.com`, you can also read a collection of free technical articles, sign up for a range of free newsletters, and receive exclusive discounts and offers on Packt books and eBooks.

Other Books You May Enjoy

If you enjoyed this book, you may be interested in these other books by Packt:

Windows APT Warfare

Sheng-Hao Ma

ISBN: 978-1-80461-811-0

- Explore various DLL injection techniques for setting API hooks
- Understand how to run an arbitrary program file in memory
- Become familiar with malware obfuscation techniques to evade antivirus detection
- Discover how malware circumvents current security measures and tools
- Use Microsoft Authenticode to sign your code to avoid tampering
- Explore various strategies to bypass UAC design for privilege escalation

Malware Science

Shane Molinari

ISBN: 978-1-80461-864-6

- Understand the science behind malware data and its management lifecycle
- Explore anomaly detection with signature and heuristics-based methods
- Analyze data to uncover relationships between data points and create a network graph
- Discover methods for reverse engineering and analyzing malware
- Use ML, advanced analytics, and data mining in malware data analysis and detection
- Explore practical insights and the future state of AI's use for malware data science
- Understand how NLP AI employs algorithms to analyze text for malware detection

Packt is searching for authors like you

If you're interested in becoming an author for Packt, please visit `authors.packtpub.com` and apply today. We have worked with thousands of developers and tech professionals, just like you, to help them share their insight with the global tech community. You can make a general application, apply for a specific hot topic that we are recruiting an author for, or submit your own idea.

Share Your Thoughts

Now you've finished *Implementing Palo Alto Networks Prisma® Access*, we'd love to hear your thoughts! Scan the QR code below to go straight to the Amazon review page for this book and share your feedback or leave a review on the site that you purchased it from.

`https://packt.link/r/1835081002`

Your review is important to us and the tech community and will help us make sure we're delivering excellent quality content.

Download a free PDF copy of this book

Thanks for purchasing this book!

Do you like to read on the go but are unable to carry your print books everywhere?

Is your eBook purchase not compatible with the device of your choice?

Don't worry, now with every Packt book you get a DRM-free PDF version of that book at no cost.

Read anywhere, any place, on any device. Search, copy, and paste code from your favorite technical books directly into your application.

The perks don't stop there, you can get exclusive access to discounts, newsletters, and great free content in your inbox daily

Follow these simple steps to get the benefits:

1. Scan the QR code or visit the link below

https://packt.link/free-ebook/978-1-83508-100-6

2. Submit your proof of purchase
3. That's it! We'll send your free PDF and other benefits to your email directly